Preventing workplace
substance abuse

Preventing Workplace Substance Abuse

Preventing Workplace Substance Abuse

Beyond Drug Testing to Wellness

Joel B. Bennett and Wayne E. K. Lehman, Editors

American Psychological Association
Washington, DC

Published by
American Psychological Association
750 First Street, NE
Washington, DC 20002
www.apa.org

To order   Tel: (800) 374-2721; Direct: (202) 336-5510
APA Order Department   Fax: (202) 336-5502; TDD/TTY: (202) 336-6123
P.O. Box 92984   Online: www.apa.org/books/
Washington, DC 20090-2984   Email: order@apa.org

In the U.K., Europe, Africa, and the Middle East, copies may be ordered from
American Psychological Association
3 Henrietta Street
Covent Garden, London
WC2E 8LU England

Typeset in Goudy by EPS Group Inc., Easton, MD

Printer: Sheridan Books, Ann Arbor, MI
Cover Designer: NiDesign, Baltimore, MD
Technical/Production Editor: Casey Ann Reever

The opinions and statements published are the responsibility of the authors, and such opinions and statements do not necessarily represent the policies of the American Psychological Association.

Library of Congress Cataloging-in-Publication Data
Preventing workplace substance abuse : beyond drug testing to wellness / edited by Joel B. Bennett and Wayne E. K. Lehman.
     p. cm.
   Includes bibliographical references and indexes.
   ISBN 1-55798-936-2 (hardcover : alk. paper)
     1. Drugs and employment—United States.   2. Substance abuse—United States—Prevention.   3. Drug testing—United States.   I. Bennett, Joel B.   II. Lehman, Wayne E. K.
   HF5549.5 D7 P74 2003
   658.3'822—dc21

                                                                              2002007306

British Library Cataloguing-in-Publication Data
A CIP record is available from the British Library.

Printed in the United States of America
First Edition

This book is dedicated to the loving memory of our mothers,
Jane Shapiro Bennett and Dorothy Lehman

CONTENTS

CONTRIBUTORS

Anita S. Back, MS, The ISA Group, Alexandria, VA

Joel B. Bennett, PhD, Institute of Behavioral Research, Organizational Wellness and Learning Systems, Fort Worth, TX

Royer F. Cook, PhD, President, The ISA Group, Alexandria, VA

Max Heirich, PhD, Worker Health Program, Institute of Labor and Industrial Relations, University of Michigan, Ann Arbor

Wayne E. K. Lehman, PhD, Institute of Behavioral Research, Texas Christian University, Fort Worth

Tracy McPherson, MS, The ISA Group, Alexandria, VA

G. Shawn Reynolds, MS, Institute of Behavioral Research, Texas Christian University, Fort Worth

Martin Shain, SJD, Centre for Addiction and Mental Health, Toronto, Ontario, Canada

Cynthia J. Sieck, PhD, Worker Health Program, Institute of Labor and Industrial Relations, University of Michigan, Ann Arbor

David L. Snow, PhD, School of Medicine, Department of Psychiatry, The Consultation Center and Division of Prevention and Community Research, Yale University, New Haven, CT

William J. Sonnenstuhl, PhD, School of Industrial and Labor Relations, Cornell University, Ithaca, NY

Helen Suurvali, BA, Centre for Addiction and Mental Health, Toronto, Ontario, Canada

Suzanne C. Swan, PhD, School of Medicine, Department of Psychiatry, The Consultation Center and Division of Prevention and Community Research, Yale University, New Haven, CT

James Trudeau, PhD, The ISA Group, Alexandria, VA

Leo Wilton, PhD, Department of Counseling and Clinical Psychology, Teachers College, Columbia University, New York

PREFACE

As trainers in adult substance abuse prevention, we have had the opportunity to talk directly with employees about their views of policy and substance abuse. Often, employees describe circumstances in which substance abuse policy and rudimentary training programs were not effective. We have heard stories of accidents, physical harm, exposure to toxic substances, and damaged equipment that were linked to one or more employees who did not monitor or control their drug or alcohol use. The incidents occurred in workplaces that had good policies in place, including drug testing and easily accessed employee assistance counselors. In our research, many employees tell us that they support drug testing, but they also convey a need for additional programs that somehow show a deeper appreciation of human potential. Two stories (modified to protect anonymity) illustrate the need for this new type of prevention program.

Sandy was a valued employee who had worked for the same company for more than 20 years. She pulled a trainer aside in the training room one day to tell him she would never had survived in her job if the current (and stricter) policy had been around even 10 years ago. "I would have been out of here if it weren't for people—the managers—who understand." She went on to describe her own recovery from alcoholism with the help of Alcoholics Anonymous (AA). She had been given, over a 10-year period, three separate chances to come back to work after struggling with recovery and relapse. The message Sandy wished to convey was that other employees could overcome addiction—if they had the right understanding and managerial support. She was concerned about a group of young employees who reminded her of her younger days. Sandy believed that with new, stricter policies, those "good people" would likely get fired. She believed that AA could help, but she did not know how to approach the situation.

Another time we listened as a group of senior supervisors were talking with a new supervisor, Fred, about a problem employee, Tom. Many of the supervisors had had previous dealings with Tom, who had a history of absences and safety concerns that they attributed to drug problems. They agreed that Tom had learned to beat the system and that it was too much trouble to do all the paperwork involved to implement drug testing for cause or reasonable suspicion. This discussion prompted another supervisor to describe a situation in which such testing of another employee had produced a positive test. The employee had executed his right to have a second (split) sample tested which, for unknown reasons, the testing lab had lost. This mishap resulted in no remedial action to this employee, and several supervisors agreed that they had lost faith in drug testing. Even though all the supervisors had been trained in employee assistance program (EAP) services and in informal referral skills, they did not see the EAP as helpful because of confidentiality concerns. As a result of this discussion, Fred grew anxious about doing anything to deal with Tom. Fred was caught between his desires to really help this troubled worker, to follow policy (i.e., to stay accountable), and to conform to the norms of passivity and tolerance that the older supervisors had learned and behaviorally modeled.

We believe that the above scenarios represent common situations in the workplace today. The situations involve substance abuse, but they also reflect or are symptomatic of general failures in organizational health and, in Fred's case, accountability. Workplace policies that deal with any sort of behavioral issue (e.g., substance abuse, sexual harassment, discrimination, or violence) often focus on compliance, legal liability, and safety issues and neglect the importance of fostering personal accountability and social interest. Such policies are necessary, but they require a healthy workplace to be effective. Various writers echo this call for a "healthy workplace" when writing about social health, a sense of shared responsibility, a vision of the common good, and a supportive organizational culture.

After hearing these and other stories, we explored the empirical and academic literature to see what kinds of research on workplace prevention existed. We discovered that most studies on employee substance abuse had focused on the problem rather than the solution. We reasoned that social scientists could play an important role by building on the research to develop and evaluate prevention programs. At the same time, we discovered a small group of studies on workplace educational programs that showed positive effects on employees, and we learned that other researchers—the authors of chapters in this volume—had or were conducting new studies.

It became increasingly clear that some venue was needed to showcase workplace programs and examine if, when, and how they work. This book was assembled because it is time to refocus our efforts—using scientific procedure and reason—on how the workplace can help employees. The ideas and findings in this volume represent a major, although early, step in this direction. We also believe that the best approaches to preventing employee substance abuse may eventually come from the research and ideas presented in this volume. Indeed, early evidence suggests that employers who enrich their policies with prevention programs will reap benefits far beyond what current approaches, including drug testing, can accomplish.

The term *beyond* in the title of this book has various meanings. It refers first to the need to enhance prevention as a necessary and critical complement to testing. The studies presented in this volume show that preventative interventions are key for addressing employee substance abuse. We are not suggesting that prevention programs replace testing. Rather, given the evidence in this book, employers should seriously consider *adding* or *enhancing* psychoeducational, training, or other prevention-oriented programs—regardless of what they might do with their testing programs.

In fact, rarely does a workplace program use only one component. In passing legislation to deal with the problem of employee substance abuse, the U.S. government requires that many workplaces have a multicomponent strategy that includes a written policy, employee education and training, drug testing, and access to counseling (in the form of EAPs). This critical point is overlooked in—and contributes to—much of the controversy about drug testing.

> Few topics generate as much debate and controversy as workplace drug testing. Opinions range from complete support to absolute rejection. Arguments concerning the safety of employees, the public and the environment are pitted against the perceived need to protect employee privacy. These strong opinions, however, may have been formed because drug testing is considered as a stand-alone programme, as opposed to one possible component of a comprehensive drug and alcohol policy.[1]

Thus, moving beyond drug testing also means moving beyond controversies about drug testing, conducting research on all aspects of policy, and determining and focusing on what works. In that sense, we believe that this book can have more practical or utilitarian value than continued debate about testing technologies. To be clear, none of the studies reviewed in subsequent chapters (nor any study of which we are aware) evaluate the relative effectiveness of different policy components. Our point is that whenever possible, multicomponent policies should become empirically driven and practical in focus.

Moving beyond drug testing also means that policies should take a holistic or humanistic view of the various risks for employee substance abuse. They should move beyond the view that problems only need to be authoritatively controlled. Instead, employers should proactively address factors that might lead to or aggravate the tendency to abuse alcohol or

---

[1] Campbell, D. J. (2001). The proactive employee: Managing workplace initiative. *Academy of Management Executive, 14(3),* 52–66.

drugs. In the scenarios described above, both Sandy and Fred, like most of their colleagues, actually supported drug testing. They also had received basic training and were aware of policy and their EAP. Apparently, that information was not enough for them. They were faced with circumstances requiring not only information but direct interpersonal, social, or cultural solutions. In short, they needed innovative programs similar to those presented in chapters 2 through 6. Of course, not all the solutions provided by researchers are likely to meet the needs of every organization. The areas covered herein, however—work–life balance, health, stress, teamwork, and employee involvement—show that substance abuse can be reduced by addressing the whole human being and the various contexts in which employees live and work. Moreover, those areas are of increasing interest to human resources personnel as well as to managers and policymakers.

This book is written for employers and their advisors who can shape policies and workplace training programs to support, help, and encourage employees who are at risk for or face problems related to substance abuse. The above two scenarios show employee concern about the effectiveness of current policies. Sandy, a recovering alcoholic, hoped that policies could be more lenient. Fred, a new supervisor, wanted to respond better to a troubled employee. Although the two scenarios reveal concerns, they also point to solutions. In both instances, the individual employee expressed a desire to do something to correct the situation. Sandy, partly because she herself was treated with respect as someone who could recover from alcoholism, wanted to help other employees in a similar way. Fred wanted to be responsible and "do the right thing" despite the fact that his colleagues had become cynical. Both Sandy and Fred had "higher level" motivations to do something for the common good. They were looking for both a method and a supportive environment for dealing with the problem. The methods described in this book help tap those motives of self-improvement and responsibility. Such methods should be useful in the changing workplace. Indeed, growing evidence indicates that employees are becoming proactive in handling problems and that programs encouraging worker initiative can be extremely helpful to managers.[2]

This book is also written for counselors and researchers in prevention, health promotion, and the various social sciences, including psychology. Each discipline can play a much more significant role than it currently does in addressing substance abuse within—and through—the employee population. The cross-disciplinary approach shown in the primary chapters speaks to the many opportunities and avenues for addressing problems. Researchers draw on a wide-ranging set of methodologies—from meta-analysis and multivariate statistics to narrative and discourse analysis. The

---

[2] Jardine-Tweedie, L., & Wright, P. C. (1988). Workplace drug testing: Avoiding the testing addiction. *Journal of Managerial Psychology, 13,* 534–543.

field of workplace substance abuse prevention is quite young, and we hope that the breadth represented will help spark the interest of practitioners from many backgrounds. We hope that the findings in this book will provide a foundation for researchers to explore new questions and lead to increasingly effective interventions. Finally, we hope that this book can be a resource for workplace trainers, counselors, and other practitioners in the helping professions. Readers who find something useful are encouraged to contact any of the authors for assistance in accessing and implementing the programs described herein.

This book was a 3-year collaboration during which the researchers and scholars interacted with the editors and with each other to help shape the volume.

Such collaboration was fostered through the support of the National Institute on Drug Abuse, which sponsored a forum at which several of us first met each other (Drugs and the Workplace: Planning the Research Agenda, May 1999, Bethesda, MD). Both the American Psychological Association and the National Institute of Occupational Health and Safety provided a venue for our collaborative efforts at the Third International Conference on Work, Stress, and Health (March 1999, Baltimore, MD). We also have benefited from the forum provided by the Center for Substance Abuse Prevention's Workplace Managed Care project on substance abuse (visit http://wmcare.samhsa.gov).

Finally, we extend our deepest appreciation to Linda Houser-Ferdinand for her patience, help, and clerical support through the many stages required to complete this book.

Preventing Workplace Substance Abuse

INTRODUCTION

JOEL B. BENNETT

Since Congress passed the Drug-Free Workplace Act in 1988, the percentage of working adults who use illicit drugs or who are heavy drinkers has remained at roughly 10%, without much change (Substance Abuse and Mental Health Services Administration [SAMHSA], 1999). This continuing trend is troublesome, given the clear link between alcohol and other drug (AOD) use and costs to employers, such as productivity loss (Normand, Lempert, & O'Brien, 1994) and medical problems (Center on Addiction and Substance Abuse, 2000). Those costs continue despite the efforts of businesses through drug testing and employee assistance programs (EAPs; Collins, 2001). In fact, the most recent U.S. national health agenda, *Healthy People 2010*, establishes a new objective: to "reduce the cost of lost productivity in the workplace due to alcohol and drug use" (U.S. Department of Health and Human Services, 2000, p. 26–21).

This book argues that prevention programs can play an important role in fulfilling the *Healthy People 2010* objective. In making this argument, it is also important to set realistic goals for prevention. We are just beginning to identify elements of effective programs, and significant barriers exist to implementing services. Moreover, substance abuse among employed adults—and forces that facilitate such abuse—cannot be solved through any single strategy. Subsequent chapters were chosen to show how a wide array of theoretical and methodological approaches can be applied to a complex problem. Our intent is to highlight innovation and provide a basis for replication and rigorous evaluations. For the most part, all the studies show positive and promising findings.

The studies are exploratory and preliminary and, as such, have a number of methodological shortcomings. We hope that readers from the field of prevention science will seek to replicate positive findings from both controlled and qualitative studies. Whether or not future research proves the effectiveness of prevention, a number of independent issues will need to be addressed before employers will invest in and implement programs with fidelity (McGinnis, 2001). Consequently, this chapter reviews arguments that support the "business case" for prevention. Employers may be reluctant to use a program, even when shown that it "works," unless their bottom line is positively affected.

This chapter also reviews some of the issues surrounding drug testing, because the misunderstandings generated by controversy often get in the way of a reasoned and analytic approach. The studies presented in this volume argue neither for nor against the abolition or strengthening of workplace testing. Our primary purpose is to stimulate research into and use of proactive, employee-centered prevention programs. Tremendous growth has occurred in the drug-testing industry, and although some research suggests that testing may be an effective deterrent (Hoffman & Larison, 1999; Macdonald & Wells, 1994; Shepard & Clifton, 1998), more studies are needed to demonstrate that testing helps reduce substance abuse. Also, drug testing is not sufficient because it generally ignores alcohol use and does not eliminate underlying causes of substance abuse.

We hope that the investment of financial and legal resources in testing technology, as well as energy previously spent on controversies about drug testing (see Harris & Heft, 1992), will be redirected toward prevention and its long-term benefits. Toward that end, this book presents employee-centered prevention programs that can complement or enhance testing regimens: strategies that emphasize health promotion as well as social, educative, and supportive services for employees at any stage of risk, rather than programs that emphasize surveillance of only problem users or any singular model of effectiveness (cf. "a pragmatic psychology"; Fishman, 2000).

Thus, we hope to inspire some readers to undertake focused research and application of the employee-centered technologies described in subsequent chapters. For other readers, we aim to provide a useful introduction to a young, promising, but complex area of prevention science. It is time to broaden our views of prevention and include the workplace as a viable context through which AOD abuse can be reduced. School-based prevention messages targeted at children and adolescents are necessary and helpful, but those messages may have limited or blunted impact when children return to households with adults who are under stress, who abuse alcohol or drugs, or who otherwise do not model healthy lifestyle behaviors (cf.

Crouter & Bumpus, 2001; Gutman & Clayton, 1999; Kung & Farrel, 2000).

Several of the interventions described in this book may provide workers with stress reduction and communication skills they can use at home. Increased conflict and stress within the family system place children at risk for drug use (Kolar, Brown, Haertzen, & Michaelson, 1994) as do other factors associated with substance abuse, such as physical abuse (Deren, 1986), antisocial behavior (Patterson, DeBaryshe, & Ramsey, 1989), and depression (Johnson, Boney, & Brown, 1990–1991). When adult employees are better able to balance work and life, they also are more apt to be psychologically available to their children and to monitor them for signs of substance abuse (cf. Chassin, Curran, Hussong, & Colder, 1996; Park et al., 2000; Rodgers-Farmer, 2000). Also, opportunities for prevention exist when adolescents or college students make the transition to work (see, e.g., Bachman, Johnston, O'Malley, & Schulenberg, 1996). Diverse groups of prevention scientists ought to know about, learn from, react to, extend, use, and advocate for the workplace interventions compiled in this volume.

The research in this volume also builds on studies showing that various types of interventions work. Those interventions reduce drinking, illicit drug use, smoking, prescription drug use, and stress; improve responsible attitudes toward drinking and social support for drinking reduction; and enhance help-seeking behaviors toward EAPs (Bennett & Lehman, 2001; Cook, Back, & Trudeau, 1996; Kishchuk et al., 1994; Shain, Suurvali, & Boutilier, 1986; Shore, 1994; Snow & Kline, 1991; Stoltzfus & Benson, 1994). Given that this evidence suggests consistently positive effects of prevention programs, it is curious that more companies are not using them.

The lack of workplace prevention programming stems from several factors. Employers simply do not know about the studies just cited, they do not feel they need programs, stigma still is attached to AOD abuse programs, cultural and political norms suggest a punitive orientation (e.g., the "Drug War"; see Sonnenstuhl, chapter 7, this volume), and the time it takes for prevention to show effects is much longer than the short time horizons within which businesses typically work. Alternatively, employers may believe that training is not worth the investment and view both drug testing and EAPs as sufficient. Regarding testing, some managers emphasize pre-employment and random screening more to comply with regulations than to understand substance abuse and get employees the help they need. Although EAPs enhance the likelihood that an organization will offer educational materials and training (Alles, 2000), their core function traditionally has been to identify and refer workers to treatment rather than offer prevention programs (Roman & Blum, 1999). When educational training is provided, it is often rudimentary and focuses on teaching policy, signs and symptoms of AOD abuse, and basic orientation to EAP services or mental health benefits (cf. Schreier, 1988).

THE BUSINESS CASE

For several reasons, business owners should consider prevention-training programs. First, as we explain below, prevention is a sound investment because of the costs of AOD abuse. Second, most employees (even those at risk for AOD problems) are motivated toward health and wellness and so stand to benefit from at least one of the prevention programs described in this book. Healthy employees are more productive than those in poor health. Third, each of the programs described here uses a different approach—whether stress management, health promotion, team development, or employee involvement. Businesses are likely to find something that fits with their objectives, work culture, or existing programs. Fourth, businesses have different levels of risk (in individuals as well as work groups) and, accordingly, take approaches to substance abuse that vary in their leniency or punitiveness. Prevention programs may be adapted to fit specific needs and risks. Fifth, companies that have problems with substance abuse often have difficulties in other areas. Each prevention program described in this book appeals to a wider, holistic sense of wellness in the individual or work environment.

Substance Abuse Prevention May Be a Sound Investment

Prevention programs may be a sound investment for businesses for at least four compelling reasons (cf. Cook & Schlenger, in press). First, substance abuse is relatively prevalent in the work force; more than 70% of illicit drug users or heavy drinkers are employed full-time, nearly 1 in 10 employees abuse drugs or alcohol, and many Americans do not even start using drugs or alcohol until after they join the work force (SAMHSA, 1997, 1999, 2001). Second, such abuse has significant costs to employers, including absenteeism, accidents, theft, performance problems, and medical expenditures as well as costs to public image and stakeholder trust. Third, because substance abuse is often associated with other behavioral problems (e.g., poor stress management, argumentativeness, hostility, withdrawal on the job, and illegal activities) and collateral costs to coworkers, prevention can enhance social health and safety within a company. Finally, because prevention programs can encourage employees to get help and receive the right form of treatment, employees are likely to recover their health. Scientific evidence has established the effectiveness of drug abuse treatment (National Institute on Drug Abuse, 1999), and the cost of treatment and rehabilitation is often less than the cost of firing and having to replace an employee (Collins, 1999; Sturm, Zhang, & Schoenbaum, 1999).

The case for prevention becomes particularly salient when considered against the background of positive findings described in chapters 2 through 6 of this book. When we couple knowledge that substance abuse is relatively prevalent and costly to employers with the knowledge that prevention training can reduce risks for substance abuse, it is fair to conclude that employers are likely to reduce costs at some point after implementing training programs.

Appeals to Higher Motives and Employee Mental Health

> The more evolved people get, the more psychologically healthy they get, the more will enlightened management policy be necessary in order to survive competition and the more handicapped will be an enterprise with an authoritarian policy. (Maslow, 1965/1998, p. 292)

All the chapters in this volume are based on a proactive, humanistic orientation toward dealing with substance abuse. The interventions described assume that employees desire to be healthy and safe and so are able to benefit from prevention strategies. The methods also assume that interactive, face-to-face, health promotion and psychoeducational programs appeal to the healthy strivings of employees in ways that control-oriented, impersonal, testing approaches may not. Indeed, growing evidence indicates that employees are becoming proactive in handling workplace problems and that, through programs that encourage worker initiative, the lines between employees and managers are blurring (Campbell, 2001).

We recognize that not all employers will share these assumptions. Despite increasing evidence that employee productivity is linked to wellness (e.g., Goetzel, 2001), many managers still take an authoritarian, command-and-control approach that tends to distrust employees (Heil, Bennis, & Stephens, 2000; Pfeffer & Veiga, 1999). Even after building the evidence base and making the financial case for prevention and wellness programs, some employers still may be reluctant to pull their employees away from work to attend intervention sessions or receive consultation.

A growing body of research indicates that managers and employees are interested in meaningful work and wish to be held accountable (Mitroff & Denton, 1999; Trott, 1996). Other signs show that employers are benefiting from policies that show increased concern for the whole person, including personal needs outside of work, and concerns for general wellness (cf. "health and productivity management"; Goetzel & Ozminkowski, 2000). One study of more than 300 companies found a clear positive relationship between organizational efforts to assist employees with managing their lives outside of work (work-family policies) and higher market performance and sales growth (Perry-Smith & Blum, 2000), perhaps because employees who perceive the availability of such benefits are also more likely to attend meetings, make suggestions, and be more helpful toward coworkers (Lambert, 2000). The studies in this volume show similar positive effects.

Adding to the Toolbox for Human Resources and Employee Assistance

For a number of reasons, executives and policymakers who rely on drug testing and who offer minimal training opportunities in health promotion may not be entirely at fault for their approach. Testing services are more widely available and advertised than prevention services. Furthermore, the people who can shape medical or training policy—EAP or benefits consultants, human resource managers, behavioral health care providers, and health promotion programmers—often have to meet financial goals. To them, it may seem that substance abuse is not as great a concern as other medical cost issues. Although the total costs associated with work force substance abuse are high, the medical claims for substance abuse are typically small relative to claims associated with other disorders, often because people with substance abuse problems tend to avoid the health care system until problems reach a critical stage. As a result, managed care may not give prevention the level of attention it deserves (Cook & Schlenger, in press). As mentioned earlier, the hidden and other behavioral costs associated with substance abuse (e.g., absenteeism, accidents, and work quality) have a cumulative effect on not only individual workers but also those who work with them.

It is partly for the above reasons that the researchers in this book have chosen to link substance abuse prevention with other areas that might be appealing to workers, employers, and policymakers, including stress management (chapter 2), general health promotion (chapter 3), cardiovascular wellness (chapter 4), team building and work group social health (chapter 5), and employee involvement and occupational health programming (chapter 6). Something from this menu also should appeal to business owners, employee benefits managers, and behavioral health care providers. For example, interventions may be incorporated into population-based health or risk management programs (Chapman, 1999; Rosse, 2000) or absence management strategies (Ritter, 2000).

Moreover, those links should give EAP representatives tools for influencing policy and incorporating prevention strategies. Behavioral health or EAP consultants can describe programmatic options when they meet with human resource and employee benefits managers. Particularly because the programs in this book are grounded in scientific evidence, consultants might use them to challenge unexamined assumptions and values implicit in company policy.

Corporate policies and procedures embody the values and strongly held beliefs of corporate executives. Excessive drinking and the use of illicit substances are emotional issues for many people, including those who hold senior management positions in corporate America. . . . Some line managers view substance abusers as social deviants, who have no business in the workforce. Company attorneys are paid to focus on minimizing corporate legal exposure. Human resource managers today typically feel compelled to find expedient solutions to complex problems.

The best approach is to ground one's recommendations in available research, knowledge of industry practices, and a clear understanding of company objectives. The challenge is to demonstrate how human policies are also the best approach to ensuring a safe and sane work environment. . . . *Providing employee education about substance abuse and the company's rehabilitation program acts as a preventative measure in discouraging the occasional user who can be influenced by an educational program and in encouraging the frequent user to get help sooner rather than later* [italics added]. (Collins, 1999, p. 390)

As Collins makes clear, an important goal of policy is to encourage employees to self-refer for treatment. Highly punitive (i.e., first-strike, zero tolerance) policies that randomly test and then fire employees "drive the problem underground." Indeed, in the Chevron Corporation, about which Collins writes, substantial differences in self-referral rates were found between oil refineries with lenient policies and those with punitive policies.

Beyond a One-Size-Fits-All Approach

Substance abusers and people at risk for abuse are a heterogeneous group. Some at-risk workers may be motivated to moderate their use of alcohol or illicit drugs because of health concerns, others because they care about social health (e.g., of their family or work team), and others because they learn that drinking is not the best way to handle stress. In those instances, programs directed at individual employees may be most appropriate (e.g., chapter 4). Some users find ingenious ways to avoid detection; they are more likely than others to float from job to job, can subvert policies, and can form coalitions with other employees to protect each other. In those instances, programs that target work groups (chapter 5) or the entire workplace (chapter 6) may be particularly effective.

This heterogeneity suggests that a one-size-fits-all approach is not likely to be as effective as a customized strategy that considers the unique occupational portrait of a company, its work culture, and its particular goals and objectives. As discussed above, managers hold different assumptions and views of policy, and different types of training appeal to the various motives of employees. Just as companies may be relatively punitive or lenient once they discover or identify substance abuse, they also may be relatively proactive or laissez-faire in their general approach to substance abuse.

> Each workplace has its own personality and its own view of drug use. Some are militantly antidrug, with mandatory urine testing policies, active EAP programs, and employee outreach services. Others are relatively laissez-faire, where "soft" drug use and drinking are openly tolerated. (Rosecan, 1993, p. 353)

Taken together, the various prevention programs described in this book can be used to strategically address the distinctions just referred to —that is, differences in policy orientation, employee motivation, and company personality or occupational culture (cf. Roman, 1990). For prevention to be transportable and effective, programs should be sensitive to workplace differences. At the same time, they should be comprehensive enough to be able to reach a wide range of employees—regardless of level of intelligence, health, or sociability—and find ways to help them improve their situation.

TRANSCENDING THE DRUG-TESTING CONTROVERSY

We recognize the potential for drug testing to deter employees from abusing drugs when it functions as one component of substance abuse policy. Indeed, if testing had no positive effects, it is unlikely that it would have gained so much popularity among businesses within the past 10 years. Testing, however, is not sufficient to encourage people either to get help for problems or to modify lifestyle factors that put them at risk for developing drug dependence. Also, despite more than 10 years of employer drug testing, substance abuse among employed workers remains a problem for many, if not most, businesses.

We list some drawbacks not to argue against drug testing as a prevention strategy but to show that a broad approach is needed. First, testing appears to detect primarily recreational use of less harmful drugs that may or may not affect performance. Companies often do not test for alcohol, which can be more costly than other drug use. U.S. Department of Transportation regulations also require more frequent testing for drugs than alcohol. Random and pre-employment testing may deter workers from using in ways that can be detected, but those control measures do not necessarily prevent use altogether. People with an AOD habit may get complacent, may try to beat the system, or may be in denial about problems. Moreover, for employees using drugs in response to chronic work stress or workplace culture pressures, testing functions as a Band-Aid rather than as a systematic solution to the underlying problem. Finally, some zero-tolerance policies may result in the firing of employees who could have been successfully rehabilitated through treatment.

In developing this book's title, we wished to convey our intent to transcend the following issues, among others, that prevail in the field of workplace drug testing:

- Civil, legal, or scientific debates about the effectiveness or fairness of drug testing (e.g., American Civil Liberties Union [ACLU], 1999; Comer, 1995; Dorancy-Williams, 1998; Shepard & Clifton, 1998)
- Management science concerns about how best to design testing to enhance its perceived fairness (see Konovsky & Cropanzano, 1991, 1993)
- Arguments about the symbolic value that testing has for organizations (e.g., restoring an organization's image of control and legitimacy; Cavanaugh & Prasad, 1994; Trice & Steele, 1995)
- Employee or managerial acceptance of testing (e.g., Blum, Fields, Milne, & Spell, 1992)
- The relative effectiveness of different testing techniques (e.g., hair vs. urine; Cook, Hersch, & McPherson, 1999; Overman, 1999)
- Concerns that most testing seems to detect casual marijuana users, who may not be a large problem for the workplace (e.g., ACLU, 1999)
- Arguments about the relative benefits of medical testing versus noninvasive fitness-for-duty, integrity, or impairment tests (Beck, 2001; Comer, 1995; Ones & Viswesvaran, 1998)
- Related psychometric concerns about test validity (McDaniel, 1988; Winfred & Doverspike, 1997)
- Concerns—supported by empirical evidence (Macdonald, 1997)—that testing should focus more on alcohol than on drugs.

We encourage readers who are interested in these topics to consult the cited references, the debate between Harris (1993) and Crow and Hartman (1992; see also Hartman & Crow, 1993), and Macdonald and Roman (1994).

Implicit in many of these discussions and in the research on drug testing is the idea that politically guided technology might be used to control social problems (cf. Gilliom, 1994; Irwin, 1991). As a result of the emphasis on control, research has tended to underemphasize the field of prevention and the importance of preventive factors such as education, health, social health, and employee assistance programming. The axiom "when all you have is a hammer, everything else looks like a nail" is perhaps a crude way of expressing this dilemma.

For example, most workplace testing assesses the presence of illicit drugs (primarily marijuana and cocaine) rather than alcohol (Hartwell, Steele, & Rodman, 1998). This approach seems out of kilter with evidence pointing to the greater negative effects of alcohol problems and alcohol dependence on productivity (e.g., Harwood, Fountain, & Livermore, 1998; Lennox, Steele, Zarkin, & Bray, 1998). In one study, this misplaced emphasis was actually seen as a barrier to effective management of alcohol problems (Bell, Mangione, Howland, Levine, & Amick, 1996). In a survey of more than 7,000 supervisors and managers, 58% reported that their company was tough on illicit drugs but soft on alcohol. Moreover, marijuana is the predominant drug seen in testing results, yet a recent review of the literature shows "no clear causal relationship between marijuana use and job performance" (Schwenk, 1998).

Another issue pertains to the social or cultural aspects of employee drinking, as discussed by Sonnenstuhl (1990, 1996; Trice & Sonnenstuhl, 1990) and others. A growing body of literature implicates workplace culture and local employee social networks (known as *drinking networks*) as playing a critical role in influencing misuse of alcohol (and, to some extent, illicit drug use; Ames & Janes, 1992; Howland et al., 1996; Macdonald, Wells, & Wild, 1999; Martin, Roman, & Blum, 1996; Walsh, Rudd, & Mangione, 1993). No studies show the effects of alcohol testing in settings in which long-standing drinking cultures promote social use of alcohol. Alcohol testing may lead to some regulation of use within such settings (and in ways that do not show up at work) but have no real impact on heavy drinkers. More research on alcohol testing across different work cultures is needed to understand its impact.

A final issue pertains to the tendency in modern culture to address problems with packaged or expedient technologies. Employers are focused on getting the job done and on the bottom line. Businesses concentrate on showing that they comply with regulations, or they settle for solutions that are more attractive than approaches that may take longer but ultimately may be more effective. The expedient and technological solution suggested by drug testing is compelling to many Americans, especially employers of larger companies, who face an increasingly unstable and mobile work force (Borg, 2000). As a result, employers tend to ignore the conditions that contribute to employee substance use and its related problems. The technological solution that drug testing appears to provide distracts policymakers from comprehensive and employee-centered attempts at prevention:

> American companies look to science and technology for a quick fix, and most tests, particularly drug tests, have the intoxicating illusion of science. By nature, Americans are impatient managers and look to technology to bypass human input at almost any cost. As managers, we want to avoid headaches associated with dealing one-on-one with employees. (Crow & Hartman, 1992, p. 934)

The Drug-Testing Economy

The need to find evidence for the effectiveness of drug testing is driven, in part, by a growing and profitable industry of drug-testing businesses. The relatively high profile of this industry may have led some employers to place undue emphasis on testing, perhaps to the detriment of prevention. A survey of the training industry shows that workplaces may be more likely to use testing procedures than employee educational training and that the amount of employee training for substance abuse education declined from 1991 to 1996 (Hequet & Lee, 1996). Having implemented testing, some employers may become overconfident about their ability to control the problem or feel that their investment in technology is sufficient. Drug testing, however, does not fully prevent all employees from using drugs. A 1999 survey of about 900 small businesses in the Chicago area showed that more than three-fourths conducted drug testing (78.7%). Nevertheless, a substantial number (40.6%) reported that they still had to discipline, refer for assistance, or terminate employees who came to work under the influence of drugs or alcohol (Chicagoland Chamber of Commerce, 2000).

Moreover, written policies—as they should—often emphasize legal and technological requirements of drug-testing procedures (e.g., chain of custody, medical director requirements, and specimen analyses; see Thompson, 1990). As mentioned, an entire industry assists with those requirements (Harrison, Backenheimer, & Inciardi, 1995; Zwerling, 1995). An informal search over the Internet revealed nearly 1,000 separate testing services within the United States and other major professional organizations involved in testing (e.g., the Drug & Alcohol Testing Industry Association, the Substance Abuse Program Administrators Association, and the American Association of Medical Review Officers). No parallel associations are devoted to broad workplace prevention.

Of course, these organizations and the government have made considerable efforts to promote prevention. Here, too, several organizations have been established to give readily accessible information (including manuals and kits) that emphasize prevention and help businesses establish a drug-free workplace (Working Partners for an Alcohol- and Drug-Free Workplace, 2000; the Workplace Managed Care Project, and the National Clearinghouse for Alcohol and Drug Information). The economic activity surrounding drug testing (Kolasky, 1999), however, appears to outweigh similar activity geared toward proactive, educational prevention. The growth of this industry continues even at the time of this writing. Recently, a company that develops drugs-of-abuse diagnostic kits announced the patent for a rapid drug screen that tests nine drugs (American Bio Medica, 2000), and interest is growing in technologies that test urine immediately after collection (Sagall, 2000). This unabated growth in the testing industry continues despite the lack of evidence for effectiveness and continuing debate over the issues listed above. Other observers have commented that the major reason for this growth is economic:

> A large industry of drug testers has arisen with a financial stake in expanding the market for workplace drug tests. The industry includes the companies that manufacture the equipment and chemicals used in drug testing, the laboratories that carry out the test, the companies that collect the urine specimens, the medical review officers (MROs) who review the test results, and the consultants who advise companies on drug testing. (Zwerling, 1995, p. 1468)

Economic exigencies, political climate, and compliance concerns, more so than scientific knowledge, often dictate policy. One wonders if this state of affairs would be different if government regulations required rigorous standards for prevention training in the workplace. Would a parallel boom in business occur if regulations required educational or prevention programs that were monitored with the same stringency as that required in testing?

Positive Aspects of Drug Testing

The above sections are meant to convey the need to move beyond drug testing, rather than to criticize testing per se. In fact, detection and deterrence provided by testing might itself be a form of prevention, at least in combination with other policy components. First, testing may keep employees from using in worksites that test (SAMHSA, 1999; see Bennett, Chapter 1, this volume). One study suggested that testing correlates with diminished use within working populations (Hoffman & Larison, 1999). Compared with people who had never used marijuana, employees who reported weekly marijuana use were significantly less likely to work for companies that had at-hiring, random, or a combination of drug-testing programs. Moreover, weekly marijuana users were about 20 times as likely as those who had never used marijuana to report aversion to working for a company with an at-hiring drug-testing program. Similar, although less striking, results were found for cocaine use.

The military, which has the strictest policies of random testing and zero tolerance, shows relatively greater reductions in use than the civilian population (Mehay & Pacula, 1999), and rates of illicit drug use in the military have decreased since testing began (Bray, Marsden, Herbold, & Peterson, 1992). A study by the Louisiana Workers' Compensation Corporation suggested fewer accidents in businesses that include testing compared with those without testing (Daniels, 1997). Moreover, testing seems effective as a way of getting employees into treatment (Lawental, McLellan, Grissom, Brill, & O'Brien, 1996).

A recent study of the construction industry also suggested the positive impact of drug testing on workplace safety. Gerber and Yacoubian (2001) surveyed 69 different companies about their annual number of workers' compensation losses, injury-related incidents, and perception of impact of drug testing. Results, which were based on all measures, indicated that drug testing had a positive impact on safety in the work environment. For example, the study found that the average company that used drug testing reduced its injury rate by 51% within 2 years of implementation; such rates were significantly lower compared with companies that did not test employees for drugs. A drawback of this study is its extremely low response rate (17%) and lack of analysis of other factors that could account for lowered injury rates.

In reviewing research that points to the positive impact of testing, it should be emphasized that testing does not occur in a vacuum. Caveats are required about the lack of appropriate controls and alternative explanations, such as societal trends, that could explain testing's positive effects. Those trends include stricter workplace policies, growth in EAP and behavioral health programs, and general declines in drug use. Along with testing, effective workplace antidrug programs include employee education, supervisor training, and written policies as well as EAPs and access to counseling and rehabilitation. Studies of testing effectiveness cannot rule out the combined or synergistic effects of other components, and few studies have attempted to tease out the different effects of those components (see the review by Dusenbury, 1999). As a result, it is not clear what specific role testing plays. Companies that combine testing with education and treatment have reported positive test rates that are one third to one half lower than those that rely on testing alone (American Management Association, 2000; also see Dillon-Riley, 2000).

Additional positive aspects of testing include the fact that, despite popular claims that testing violates privacy rights, independent studies show that most employees and managers support different types of testing; random testing is often less preferred than pre-employment or postaccident testing (Bennett & Lehman, 1997; Gilliom, 1994; SAMHSA, 1999). In Gerber and Yacoubian's (2001) survey, managers and executives of construction companies felt strongly that testing promoted the safety of workers, that it contributed positively to the company image, and that it was an effective deterrent. Also, the threat of testing may motivate some users to seek help or counseling before they get caught, thereby reducing medical expenditures for problems that go untreated. Finally, companies that test employees for drugs foster stakeholder trust by offering assurances that they take drug abuse seriously.

PREVIEW OF CHAPTERS

The following chapter summaries introduce readers to the approaches taken by researchers to prevent substance abuse among employed workers. As noted earlier, most of the approaches are relatively humanistic and are proactive, employee-centered, and interpersonal.

- *Humanistic* refers to the fact that each program appeals to employees' desires to secure health and well-being for themselves and others (including coworkers), but does not interfere with employees' rights and freedoms as human beings. "Whenever possible, we should adopt those methods for preventing and controlling harm to self and others that are the least likely to interfere with the enjoyment of personal rights and freedoms" (Shain, 1994, p. 257).

- *Proactive* approaches in the field of substance abuse prevention are typical because such programs try to target youths before they use alcohol and other drugs (e.g., Pentz, 1999) and because they focus on providing skills and alternatives to drug abuse before a problem surfaces or too many risk factors accumulate. The proactive approach also applies to adults, as was first seen in the 1970s (e.g., DuPont & Basen, 1980) with the growth of *early detection* and *constructive confrontation* strategies. Those strategies provided supervisors with skills to focus on deteriorations in employee performance and to suggest EAP counseling as a possible source of help (Trice & Beyer, 1982). Recent evidence suggests that supervisors with easy and on-site access to the EAP are significantly more likely to identify and refer employees with substance abuse problems (Collins, 2001). This proactive early intervention approach extends to the current set of prevention programs which, to various degrees, teach "about the dangers of substance use, positive alternatives to substance use, stress and coping skills, refusal skills, how to manage alcohol consumption, and (promote) social support" (Dusenbury, 1999, p. 153).

- *Employee-centered* refers to the fact that many of the programs take a bottom-up organizational strategy—that is, they view and directly empower employees as the key to policy effectiveness—rather than a top-down administrative stance, which places primary emphasis on policy compliance. "Effective policy requires active support (from employees), communication about how substance use is a social problem that affects everyone, and sensitivity to employee relationships" (Bennett & Lehman, 1997, p. 97).

- *Interpersonal* indicates that each program uses interpersonal interaction between employees and the program agent (e.g., trainers, nurses, and consultants) and focuses on employee social relations at home, the workplace culture, and the social context of substance abuse. That is, programs seek not only to prevent isolated employees from substance abuse but also to build interpersonal supports and coping strategies that can buffer against risks for substance abuse. For example, employees might experience stress at home that can lead to substance abuse, or coworkers who drink together away from the worksite can significantly influence each other to sustain bad habits. Moreover, sometimes an employee needs information that will help family members or other dependents who are at risk for substance abuse.

Chapter 1, by Joel Bennett, Shawn Reynolds, and Wayne Lehman, describes the need to consider a multilevel approach that addresses substance use in individuals as well as in work groups, organizations, and occupations as a whole. This multilevel theme is echoed throughout the book. For example, Heirich and Sieck (chapter 4) developed a health promotion counseling program targeted at individual employees, yet many coworkers not involved in the study saw or heard about the counseling and sought help. In some ways, the individual-level prevention program evolved into social health promotion for the work culture. Chapter 1 showcases a preliminary meta-analysis of existing research in the field of workplace substance abuse prevention.

In chapter 2, David Snow, Suzanne Swan, and Leo Wilton introduce a model of risk and protective factors that serves as a general heuristic for subsequent chapters. This model postulates that work and family stressors and the use of avoidance coping are risk factors for substance abuse and other negative health outcomes, whereas active coping strategies and social support from work and nonwork sources operate as protective factors. The workplace coping-skills intervention is derived directly from this risk factor–protective factor model. The intervention teaches employees how to modify or eliminate the sources of stress, rethink problems, and use specific stress management approaches as alternatives to substance use when confronted with stressful situations. Chapter 2 describes two studies, both of which found that employees improved on a number of factors compared with control groups. Both studies showed reductions in stressors and ineffective coping strategies (i.e., avoidance coping), increased use of active coping, and reduced alcohol consumption. The authors also found positive effects for an "at-risk" group of heavy alcohol users. Similar analyses of at-risk employees, as echoed in chapters 4 and 5, provide an important window into the populations for whom the interventions may be most effective. The authors also found some worksite effects (i.e., times when various effects emerged in certain worksites and not in others). This variation across worksites is echoed in chapter 5 and again points to the importance of a multilevel perspective.

Royer Cook, Anita Back, James Trudeau, and Tracy McPherson have been developing and testing a variety of substance abuse prevention programs for more than a decade. Each program (*SAY YES!*, *Working People: Decisions About Drinking, and Connections*) links workplace health promotion programs with substance abuse prevention and uses a social learning conceptual model ("healthful alternatives") first developed by Cook in 1985. The chapter extends and elaborates on this model. Like chapter 2, the new model views healthy coping skills (e.g., not using alcohol to reduce tension) as important to the success of prevention programs. Cook and colleagues build on this basic model and suggest that both attitudes and beliefs about alcohol and other drugs, as well as workplace culture (e.g., norms about alcohol use), mediate the effects of programs. The chapter describes research studies that show positive effects of training and focuses on the *Connections* program, which combines messages about substance abuse reduction with information on healthy eating, exercise, and stress reduction. Results show that substance abuse prevention can be inserted or "piggy-backed" onto other health promotion programs without diluting a program's impact.

Chapter 4, by Max Heirich and Cynthia Sieck, describes The Wellness Outreach at Work model developed by Jack Erfurt and Andrea Foote to promote cardiovascular health and implemented in more than 100 worksites since the 1970s. The chapter describes how the model effectively incorporated messages for alcohol reduction into cardiovascular wellness programs in three separate studies with different samples (i.e., a public utility, a manufacturing plant, and a university). Unlike approaches in other chapters, the outreach model steps outside the training or classroom environment: Health counselors provide workers with cardiovascular screening, individualized and proactive counseling, and follow up. Counselors call attention to any potential alcohol risks in the context of general wellness counseling. The studies show that outreach can attract employees with alcohol risks, improve recidivism rates for EAP clients, and reduce alcohol and risks for cardiovascular disease.

The Workplace Project at The Institute of Behavioral Research (Texas Christian University) has conducted more than 10 years of survey research on factors associated with employee substance abuse. Much of this work has focused on the diverse occupations represented by municipal employees, on work environments, and on group processes associated with substance abuse. In chapter 5, Lehman, Reynolds, and Bennett describe how they developed a risk factor–protective factor model by applying results from their past research and then used that model to develop two training programs. The team-oriented prevention training (*Team Awareness*) focuses on improving social health among employees and encouraging help-seeking behaviors, and the informational training is an enhanced version of the typical orientations that many workplaces provide to their employees. The chapter describes the results of a study in which work groups from two samples were randomly assigned to either the team or the informational training. Results suggested that the team training may be more effective in settings with high levels of risk (e.g., safety-sensitive jobs or exposure to coworker substance abuse) and that the informational training had positive effects over and above standard trainings provided to control groups.

Unlike the quantitative approach of other chapters, chapter 6 provides Martin Shain and Helen Suurvali's narrative analysis of the development of a workplace prevention program within a large Canadian forest products company. The narrative recalls events over a 5-year period and documents the relationship between the authors (acting as prevention and health promotion consultants) and the employee family assistance program and occupational health and safety departments of the company. The focus of the chapter is on how an idea or innovation—in this case, a method for preventing injuries and accidents—can be developed, diffused within an organization, and ultimately adopted. Thus, unlike previous approaches, in which the initial goal was to scientifically develop and test a prevention program, Shain and Suurvali were more interested in getting a program accepted and institutionalized than in determining whether it was effective. Their approach was not unscientific, however. Rather, the *Courage to Care* program that ultimately was created was the result of the company's adapting and assimilating ideas that were developed and researched by Shain and Suurvali, who have been working in the area of workplace substance abuse prevention for 15 years (see Shain et al., 1986). This chapter is important because, too often, the programs that are developed through scientific research (like those described in chapters 2–5) never get used beyond initial efficacy trials. The authors' narrative account provides a template for how prevention scientists—acting as consultants—can facilitate the adoption of such programs in companies that need them.

In chapter 7, William Sonnenstuhl places the current set of interventions within the cultural context of temperance reform in American history. Specifically, he suggests that workplace substance abuse prevention programs may be paving the way for a new cycle of temperance reform that dates back to colonial times (cf. Blocker, 1989). The cycles vacillate between attempts that appeal through persuasion and those that emphasize coercion. Currently, the persuasive approach is seen in the EAP movement, whereas coercion is symbolized in the U.S. Drug War and drug-testing technologies. Workplace AOD prevention programs indicate a new, evidence-based or scientific approach, whereas previous persuasive approaches were steeped in symbolic moral arguments. Sonnenstuhl implies that companies will be more likely to adopt evidence-based interventions if the cultural ethos tends more to the persuasive than to the coercive points of the temperance reform cycle, regardless of other arguments (e.g., cost-effectiveness and humanistic concerns). To be clear, the programs assessed here will not drive the persuasive cycle of reform. However, Sonnenstuhl concludes on an optimistic note by suggesting that the authors of the current volume are part of a vanguard whose underlying purpose is to extend this persuasive approach into the culture through employee education.

The final chapter, by Bennett, Reynolds, and Lehman, provides recommendations to businesses, providers of prevention programs, and prevention scientists. It also appeals to researchers in psychology—who typically may not study the problem of employee substance abuse—to apply knowledge from diverse areas of the field. Those areas include group processes (i.e., conformity and social influence), clinical and counseling psychology (i.e., work dysfunction), prosocial behavior (i.e., help-giving and -seeking behavior), and stigma.

A Note About Workplace Smoking Cessation Programs

This volume focuses on preventing AOD abuse and does not address workplace programs that help employees with smoking cessation. The significant advances in workplace prevention models present an untapped opportunity to explore ways in which all types of prevention—alcohol, drug, and tobacco—may be coordinated to the benefit of a broad employee population. Describing the extensive literature on workplace tobacco prevention and intervention would take an entire volume in and of itself. Interested readers should consult Borland et al. (1999); Eriksen and Gottlieb (1998); Farkas, Gilpin, Diatefan, and Pierce (1999); Gottlieb (2001); Jason, Salina, McMahon, Hedeker, and Stockton (1997); Koffman, Lee, Hopp, and Emont (1998); Longo et al. (1996); and Sorenson et al. (1998).

REFERENCES

Alles, P. (2000). *Substance abuse services for multiemployer fund participants.* Retrieved May 6, 2002 from http://www.ifebp.org/knowledge/resubab.asp.

American Bio Medica. (2000). *American Bio Medica receives patent for its 9 panel Rapid Drug Screen.* Retrieved May 6, 2002, from http://www.americanbiomedica.com/investor/pressreleases/pr000906.html.

American Civil Liberties Union. (1999). *Drug testing: A bad investment.* Retrieved April 11, 2002, from http://www.aclu.org/issues/worker/drugtesting1999.pdf

American Management Association. (2000). *Workplace testing: Medical testing (2000 AMA Survey and previous surveys)*. Retrieved April 11, 2002, from http://www.amanet.org/research/pdfs/medic12.0.pdf

Ames, G. M., & Janes, C. (1992). A cultural approach to conceptualizing alcohol and the workplace. *Alcohol Health and Research World, 16,* 112–119.

Bachman, J. G., Johnston, L. D., O'Malley, P. M., & Schulenberg, J. (1996). Transitions in drug use during late adolescence and young adulthood. In J. A. Graber & J. Brooks-Gunn (Eds.), *Transitions through adolescence: Interpersonal domains and context* (pp. 111–140). Hillsdale, NJ: Erlbaum.

Beck, E. (2001, February). Is the time right for impairment testing? *Workforce, 80,* 69–71.

Bell, S. N., Mangione, T. W., Howland, J., Levine, S., & Amick, B., III. (1996). Worksite barriers to the effective management of alcohol problems. *Journal of Occupational and Environmental Medicine, 38,* 1213–1219.

Bennett, J. B., & Lehman, W. E. K. (1997). Workplace drinking climate, stress, and problem indicators: Assessing the influence of teamwork (group cohesion). *Journal of Studies on Alcohol, 59,* 608–618.

Bennett, J. B., & Lehman, W. E. K. (2001). Workplace substance abuse prevention and help-seeking: Comparing a team-oriented and informational training. *Journal of Occupational Health Psychology, 6,* 243–254.

Blocker, J. (1989). *American temperance movements: Cycles of reform.* Boston: Twayne.

Blum, T. C., Fields D. L., Milne S. H., & Spell, C. S. (1992). Workplace drug testing programs: A review of research and a survey of work sites. *Journal of Employee Assistance Research, 1,* 315–349.

Borg, M. J. (2000). Drug testing in organizations: Applying Horwitz's theory of the effectiveness of social control. *Deviant Behavior: An Interdisciplinary Journal, 21,* 123–154.

Borland, R., Owen, N., Tooley, G., Treijs, G., Robert, L., & Hill, D. (1999). Promoting reduced smoking rates in the context of workplace smoking bans. *American Journal of Health Promotion, 14,* 1–3.

Bray, R. M., Marsden, M. E., Herbold, J. R., & Peterson, M. R. (1992). Progress toward eliminating drug and alcohol use among US military personnel. *Armed Forces and Society, 18,* 476–496.

Campbell, D. J. (2001). The proactive employee: Managing workplace initiative. *Academy of Management Executive, 14*(3), 52–66.

Cavanaugh, J. M., & Prasad, P. (1994). Drug testing as symbolic managerial action: In response to "a case against workplace drug testing." *Organization Science, 5*(2), 190–198.

Center on Addiction and Substance Abuse. (2000). *Missed opportunity: National survey of primary care physicians and patients on substance abuse.* New York: Columbia University, Author.

Chapman, L. S. (1999). Population health management. *Art of Health Promotion*, 3(2), 1–10.

Chassin, L., Curran, P. J., Hussong, A. M., & Colder, C. R. (1996). The relation of parent alcoholism to adolescent substance use: A longitudinal follow-up study. *Journal of Abnormal Psychology, 105,* 70–80.

Chicagoland Chamber of Commerce. (2000). *Drug-free workplace survey results for 1998 and 1999.* Unpublished report.

Collins, K. R. (1999). Workplace safety, drug testing, and the role of the EAP professional. In J. M. Oher (Ed.), *The employee assistance handbook* (pp. 387–404). New York: Wiley.

Collins, K. (2001). Why U.S. companies are not winning the war on drugs. *HR News, 20*(4), 11, 16.

Comer, D. R. (1995, August). An evaluation of fitness-for-duty testing. Paper presented at the 103rd Annual Convention of the American Psychological Association, New York. Retrieved April 11, 2002, from http://www.soros.org/lindesmith/library/tlccomer.html

Cook, R. F., Back, A. S., & Trudeau, J. (1996). Preventing alcohol use problems among blue-collar workers: A field test of the working people program. *Substance Use and Misuse, 31,* 255–275.

Cook, R. F., Hersch, R. K., & McPherson, T. L. (1999). Drug assessment methods in the workplace. In T. Mieczkowski (Ed.), *Drug testing technology: Assessment of field applications* (pp. 255–282). Boca Raton, FL: CRC Press.

Cook, R., & Schlenger, W. (in press). Prevention of substance abuse in the workplace: Review of research on the delivery of services. *Journal of Primary Prevention.*

Crouter, A. C., & Bumpus, M. F. (2001). Linking parents' work stress to children's and adolescents' psychological adjustment. *Current Directions in Psychological Science, 10,* 156–159.

Crow, S. M., & Hartman, S. J. (1992). Drugs in the workplace: Overstating the problems and the cures. *Journal of Drug Issues, 22,* 923–937.

Daniels, S. (1997, June 23). Drug-testing cuts accidents, costs: Study. *National Underwriter (Property & Casualty/Risk & Benefits Management Edition), 101,* 19.

Deren, S. (1986). Children of substance abusers: A review of the literature. *Journal of Substance Abuse Treatment, 3,* 77–94.

Dillon-Riley, J. (2000). Elements of a drug/alcohol free workplace. In Center for Substance Abuse Prevention (Producer). (1999). *Towards a healthier workplace: A search for better practices in the management of workplace substance abuse prevention in a managed care environment* (Knowledge Exchange Workshop II) [Videotape]. Rockville, MD: Substance Abuse and Mental Health Services Administration.

Dorancy-Williams, J. (1998, Summer). The difference between mine and thine: The constitutionality of public employee drug testing. *New Mexico Law Review, 28,* 451–485.

DuPont, R. L., & Basen, M. M. (1980). Control of alcohol and drug abuse in industry—A literature review. *Public Health Reports, 95,* 137–148.

Dusenbury, L. (1999). Workplace drug abuse prevention initiatives: A review. *Journal of Primary Prevention, 20,* 145–156.

Eriksen, M. P., & Gottlieb, N. H. (1998). A review of the health impact of smoking control at the workplace. *American Journal of Health Promotion, 13,* 83–104.

Farkas, A., Gilpin, E., Diatefan, J., & Pierce, J. (1999). The effects of household and workplace smoking restrictions on quitting behaviours. *Tobacco Control, 8,* 261–265.

Fishman, D. B. (2000, May 3). Transcending the efficacy versus effectiveness research debate: Proposal for a new, electronic "Journal of Pragmatic Case Studies." *Prevention & Treatment, 3,* Article 8. Retrieved April 11, 2002, from http://journals.apa.org/prevention/volume3/pre0030008a.html

Gerber, J. K., & Yacoubian, G. S., Jr. (2001). Evaluation of drug testing in the workplace: a Study of the construction industry. *Journal of Construction Engineering and Management, 127,* 438–444.

Gilliom, J. (Ed.). (1994). *Surveillance, privacy, and the law.* Ann Arbor: University of Michigan Press.

Goetzel, R. (2001). Special issue: The financial impact of health promotion. *American Journal of Health Promotion, 15*(5).

Goetzel, R. Z., & Ozminkowski, R. J. (2000). Health and productivity management: Emerging opportunities for health promotion professionals for the 21st century. *American Journal of Health Promotion, 14,* 211–214.

Gottlieb, N. H. (2001). Tobacco control and cessation. In M. P. O'Donnell (Ed.), *Health promotion in the workplace* (3rd ed.). Albany, NY: Delmar.

Gutman, M., & Clayton, R. (1999). Treatment and prevention of use and abuse of illegal drugs: Progress on interventions and future directions. *American Journal of Health Promotion, 14,* 92–97.

Harris, M. M. (1993). Drugs in the workplace: Setting the record straight. *Journal of Drug Issues, 23,* 727–732.

Harris, M. M., & Heft, L. L. (1992). Alcohol and drug use in the workplace: Issues, controversies, and directions for future research. *Journal of Management, 18,* 239–266.

Harrison, L. D., Backenheimer, M., & Inciardi, J. A. (1995). Cannabis use in the United States: Implications for policy. In P. Cohen & A. Sas (Eds.), *Cannabisbeleid in Duitsland, Frankrijk en de Verenigde Staten [Cannabis Policy in Germany, France, and the United States]* (pp. 179–276). Amsterdam, Centrum voor Drugsonderzoek, University of Amsterdam.

Hartman, S. J., & Crow, S. M. (1993). Setting Harris straight. *Journal of Drug Issues, 23,* 733–738.

Hartwell, T. D., Steele, P. D., & Rodman, N. F. (1998, June). Workplace alcohol-testing programs: Prevalence and trends. *Monthly Labor Review,* 27–34.

Harwood H., Fountain D., & Livermore G. (1998). *The economic costs of alcohol and drug abuse in the United States, 1992* (NIH Publication No. 98-4327). Retrieved April 11, 2002, from http://www.nida.nih.gov/EconomicCosts/Intro.html

Heil, G., Bennis, W., & Stephens, D. C. (2000). *Douglas McGregor, revisited: Managing the human side of the enterprise*. New York: Wiley.

Hequet, M. & Lee, C. (1996, December). Drug-test positives drop as testing rises, training falls. *Training (Minneapolis, Minn.)*, *33*, 14–15.

Hoffman, J., & Larison, C. (1999). Worker drug use and workplace drug-testing programs: Results from the 1994 national household survey on drug abuse. *Contemporary Drug Problems*, *26*, 331–354.

Howland, J., Mangione, T. W., Kuhlthau, K., Bell, N., Heeren, T., Lee. M., & Levine, S. (1996). Work-site variation in managerial drinking. *Addiction*, *91*, 1007–1017.

Irwin, D. D. (1991). *Deviance in the workplace: Case studies of drug testing in large organizations*. San Francisco, CA: Mellen Research University Press.

Jason, L. A., Salina, D., McMahon, S. D., Hedeker, D., & Stockton, M. (1997). A worksite smoking intervention: A 2 year assessment of groups, incentives and self-help. *Health Education Research: Theory and Practice*, *12*, 129–138.

Johnson, J. L., Boney, T. Y., & Brown, B. S. (1990–1991). Evidence of depressive symptoms in children of substance abusers. *International Journal of the Addictions*, *25*(4A), 465–479.

Kishchuk, N., Peters, C., Towers, A. M., Sylvestre, M., Bourgault, C., & Richard, L. (1994). Formative and effectiveness evaluation of a worksite program promoting healthy alcohol consumption. *American Journal of Health Promotion*, *8*, 353–362.

Koffman, D. M., Lee, J. W., Hopp, J. W., & Emont, S. L. (1998). The impact of including incentives and competition in a workplace smoking cessation program on quit rates. *American Journal of Health Promotion*, *13*, 105–111.

Kolar, A. F., Brown, B. S., Haertzen, C. A., & Michaelson, B. S. (1994). Children of substance abusers: The life experiences of children of opiate addicts in methadone maintenance. *American Journal of Drug and Alcohol Abuse*, *20*, 159–171.

Kolasky, B. (1999). *Issue of the week: Business is good*. Retrieved May 6, 2002, from http://speakout.com/activism/opinions/4352-1.html

Konovsky, M. A., & Cropanzano, R. (1991). Perceived fairness of employee drug testing as a predictor of employee attitudes and job performance. *Journal of Applied Psychology*, *76*, 698–707.

Konovsky, M. A., & Cropanzano, R. (1993). Justice considerations in employee drug testing. In R. Cropanzano (Ed.), *Justice in the workplace: Approaching fairness in human resource management* (pp. 171–192). Hillsdale, NJ: Erlbaum.

Kung, E. M., & Farrell, A. D. (2000). The role of parents and peers in early adolescent substance use: An examination of mediating and moderating effects. *Journal of Child and Family Studies*, *9*, 509–528.

Lambert, S. J. (2000). Added benefits: The link between work-life benefits and organizational citizenship behavior. *Academy of Management Journal, 43*, 801–815.

Lawental, E., McLellan, A. T., Grissom, G. R., Brill, P., & O'Brien, C. (1996). Coerced treatment for substance abuse problems detected through workplace urine surveillance: Is it effective? *Journal of Substance Abuse, 8*, 115–128.

Lennox, R. D., Steele, P. D., Zarkin, G. A., & Bray, J. W. (1998). The differential effects of alcohol consumption and dependence on adverse alcohol-related consequences: Implications for the workforce. *Drug and Alcohol Dependence, 50*, 211–220.

Longo, D. R., Brownson, R. C., Johnson, J. C., Hewett, J. E., Kruse, R. L., Novotny, T. E., & Logan, R. A. (1996). Hospital smoking bans and employee smoking behavior: Results of a national survey. *Journal of the American Medical Association, 275*, 1252–1257.

Macdonald, S. (1997). Work-place alcohol and other drug testing: Review of the scientific evidence. *Drug and Alcohol Review, 16*, 251–259.

Macdonald, S., & Roman, P. M. (1994). *Drug testing in the workplace: Research advances in alcohol and drug problems* (Vol. 11). New York: Plenum Press.

Macdonald, S., & Wells, S. (1994). The impact and effectiveness of drug testing programs in the workplace. In S. Macdonald, & P. M. Roman (Eds.), *Drug testing in the workplace: Research advances in alcohol and drug problems* (Vol. 11, pp. 121–142). New York: Plenum Press.

Macdonald, S., Wells, S., & Wild, T. C. (1999). Occupational risk factors associated with alcohol and drug problems. *American Journal of Drug and Alcohol Abuse, 25*, 351–369.

Martin, J. K., Roman, P. M., & Blum, T. C. (1996). Job stress, drinking networks, and social support at work: A comprehensive model of employees' problem drinking behaviors. *Sociological Quarterly, 37*, 579–599.

Maslow, A. H. (1965/1998). Eupsychian management. (reprinted as "Maslow on Management"). Eupsychian management; a journal, by Abraham H. Maslow. Homewood, IL, R. D. Irwin, 1965. Maslow on management, Abraham H. Maslow with Deobrah C. Stephens and Gary Heil. New York: John Wiley, 1998.

McDaniel, M. A. (1988). Does pre-employment drug use predict on-the-job suitability? *Personnel Psychology, 41*, 717–729.

McGinnis, J. M. (2001). Does proof matter? Why strong evidence sometimes yields weak action. *American Journal of Health Promotion, 15*, 391–396.

Mehay, S. L., & Pacula, R. L. (1999). *The effectiveness of workplace drug prevention policies: Does 'Zero Tolerance' work?* (NBER Working Paper No. w7383). Retrieved April 11, 2002, from http://www.nber.org/papers/w7383

Mitroff, I., & Denton, E. (1999). A spiritual audit of corporate America: A hard look at spirituality, religion, and values in the workplace. San Francisco, CA: Jossey-Bass.

National Institute on Drug Abuse. (1999). *Principles of drug addiction treatment: A research-based guide* (NIH Publication No. 00-4180). Retrieved April 11, 2002, from http://www.nida.nih.gov/PODAT/PODATIndex.html

Normand, J., Lempert, R. O., & O'Brien, C. P. (1994). *Under the influence? Drugs and the American work force.* Washington, DC: National Academy Press.

Ones, D. S., & Viswesvaran, C. (1998). Integrity testing in organizations. In R. W. Griffin, A. O'Leary-Kelly, & J. M. Collins (Eds.), *Dysfunctional behavior in organizations: Violent and deviant behavior. Monographs in organizational behavior and industrial relations,* (Vol. 23, Parts A & B, pp. 243–276). Stamford, CT: JAI Press.

Overman, S. (1999). Splitting hairs. *HRMagazine, 44*(8), 42–44.

Park, J., Kosterman, R., Hawkins, J. D., Haggerty, K. P., Ducan, T. E., Duncan, S. C., & Spoth, R. (2000). Effects of the "Preparing for the Drug Free Years" curriculum on growth in alcohol use and risk for alcohol use in early adolescence. *Prevention Science, 1,* 125–138.

Patterson, G. R., DeBaryshe, B. D., & Ramsey, E. (1989). A developmental perspective on antisocial behavior. *American Psychologist, 44,* 329–335.

Pentz, M. A. (1999). Prevention aimed at individuals: An integrative transactional approach. In B. S. McCrady & E. E. Epstein (Eds.), *Addictions: A Comprehensive Guidebook* (pp. 555–572). New York: Oxford University Press.

Perry-Smith, J. E., & Blum, T. C. (2000). Work-family human resource bundles and perceived organizational performance. *Academy of Management Journal, 43,* 1107–1117.

Pfeffer, J., & Veiga, J. F. (1999). Putting people first for organizational success. *Academy of Management Executive, 13*(2), 37–48.

Ritter, A. (2000). Total absence management: Practical solutions to prevent and minimize employee absence. *Employee Benefits Journal, 25*(4), 3–7.

Rodgers-Farmer, A. Y. (2000). Parental monitoring and peer group association: Their influence on adolescent substance use. *Journal of Social Service Research, 27*(2), 1–18.

Roman, P. M. (1990). Strategic considerations in designing interventions to deal with alcohol problems in the workplace. In P. M. Roman (Ed.), *Alcohol problem intervention in the workplace: Employee assistance programs and strategic alternatives* (pp. 371–406). New York: Quorum Books.

Roman, P. M., & Blum, T. C. (1999). Prevention in the workplace. In R. T. Ammerman, P. J. Ott, & R. E. Tarter (Eds.), *Prevention and societal impact of drug and alcohol abuse* (pp. 307–325). Mahwah, NJ: Erlbaum.

Rosecan, J. S. (1993). Drug abuse and dependence. In J. P. Kahn (Ed.), *Mental health in the workplace: A practical psychiatric guide* (pp. 346–365). New York: Van Nostrand.

Rosse, C. (2000). Disease management: The broader, the better. *Behavioral Health Management, 20*(6), 46–47.

Sagall, R. (2000, December 17). Issues and problems of drug testing. *Workforce.* Retrieved May 6, 2002, from http://www.workforce.com/archive/feature/22/25/60/223633.php

Schreier, J. W. (1988). Combating drugs at work. *Training and Development Journal*, *42*(10), 56–60.

Schwenk, C. R. (1998). Marijuana and job performance: Comparing the major streams of research. *Journal of Drug Issues, 28*, 941–970.

Shain, M. (1994). Alternatives to drug testing programs: Employee assistance and health promotion programs. In S. Macdonald & P. Roman (Eds.), *Drug testing in the workplace: Research advances in alcohol and drug problems* (Vol. 11, pp. 257–278). New York: Plenum Press.

Shain, M., Suurvali, H., & Boutilier, M. (1986). *Healthier workers: Health promotion and employee assistance programs.* Lexington, MA: Lexington Books.

Shepard, E., & Clifton, C. (1998, September). *Drug testing and labor productivity: Estimates applying a production function model* (Le Moyne College Institute of Industrial Relations Research Paper 18, pp. 1–30). Retrieved April 11, 2002, from http://www.lindesmith.org/library/shepard2.html

Shore, E. R. (1994). Outcomes of a primary prevention project for business and professional women. *Journal of Studies on Alcohol, 55*, 657–659.

Snow, D. L., & Kline, M. L. (1991). A worksite coping skills intervention: Effects on women's psychological symptomatology & substance use. *Community Psychologist, 24*, 14–17.

Sonnenstuhl, W. J. (1990). Help-seeking and helping processes within the workplace: Assisting alcoholic and other troubled employees. In P. M. Roman (Ed.), *Alcohol problem intervention in the workplace: Employee assistance programs and strategic alternatives* (pp. 237–259). New York: Quorum Books.

Sonnenstuhl, W. J. (1996). *Working sober: The transformation of an occupational drinking culture.* Ithaca, NY: ILR Press/Cornell University Press.

Sorenson, G., Thompson, B., Basen-Enquist, K., Abrams, D., Kuniyuki, A., DiClemente, C., & Biener, L. (1998). Durability, dissemination, and institutionalization of worksite tobacco control programs: Results from the working well trial. *International Journal of Behavioral Medicine, 5*, 335–351.

Stoltzfus, J. A., & Benson, P. L. (1994). The 3M Alcohol and Other Drug Prevention Program: Description and evaluation. *Journal of Primary Prevention, 15*, 147–159.

Sturm, R., Zhang, W., & Schoenbaum, M. (1999). How expensive are unlimited substance abuse benefits under managed care? *Journal of Behavioral Health Services and Research, 26*, 203–210.

Substance Abuse and Mental Health Services Administration. (2001). *Summary of findings from the 2000 National Household Survey on Drug Abuse.* (Office of Applied Studies, NHSDA Series H-13, DHHS Publication No. SMA 01-3549). Rockville, MD: Center for Substance Abuse Prevention. Retrieved May 3, 2002, from http://www.samhsa.gov/oas/NHSDA/2kNHSDA/2kNHSDA.htm

Substance Abuse and Mental Health Services Administration. (1999). *Worker drug use and workplace policies and programs: Results from the National Household Survey on Drug Abuse (NHSDA).* Retrieved May 3, 2002, from http://www.samhsa.gov/oas/NHSDA/A-11/TOC.htm

Substance Abuse and Mental Health Services Administration. (1997). *Guidelines and Benchmarks for Prevention Programming: Implementation Guide*. DHHS Publication No. (SMA) 95-3033. Rockville, MD.

Thompson, R., Jr. (1990). *Substance abuse and employee rehabilitation*. Washington, DC: Bureau of National Affairs.

Trice, H. M., & Beyer, J. M. (1982). Social control in work settings: Using the constructive confrontation strategy with problem drinking employees. *Journal of Drug Issues, 12*, 21–49.

Trice, H. M., & Sonnenstuhl, W. J. (1990). On the construction of drinking norms in work organizations. *Journal of Studies on Alcohol, 51*, 201–220.

Trice, H. M., & Steele, P. D. (1995). Impairment testing: Issues and convergence with employee assistance programs. *Journal of Drug Issues, 25*, 471–503.

Trott, D. C. (1996). *Spiritual well-being of workers: An exploratory study of spirituality in the workplace*. Austin: University of Texas.

U.S. Department of Health and Human Services. (2000). *Healthy people 2010*. Retrieved May 6, 2002, from http://web.health.gov/healthypeople/document/pdf/Volume2/26Substance.pdf

Walsh, D. C., Rudd, R. E., & Mangione, T. (1993). Researching and preventing alcohol problems at work: Toward an integrative model. *American Journal of Health Promotion, 7*, 289–295.

Winfred, A., & Doverspike, D. (1997, Spring). Employment-related drug testing: Idiosyncratic characteristics and issues. *Public Personnel Management, 26*, 77–88.

Working Partners for an Alcohol- and Drug-Free Workplace. (2000). *Facts and figures about drugs and alcohol in the workplace*. Retrieved May 3, 2002, from http://www.dol.gov/asp/programs/drugs/workingpartners/Screen15.htm

Zwerling, C. (1995). *Under the influence? Drugs and the American Workforce* [Book review]. *Journal of the American Medical Association, 272*, 1467–1468.

1

UNDERSTANDING EMPLOYEE ALCOHOL AND OTHER DRUG USE: TOWARD A MULTILEVEL APPROACH

JOEL B. BENNETT, G. SHAWN REYNOLDS, AND WAYNE E. K. LEHMAN

The introduction of this book outlined several claims, which we restate here: Employee alcohol and other drug (AOD) abuse remains a problem for workplaces; drug testing alone is not sufficient to address the problem because it generally ignores alcohol use, does not address underlying causes of AOD abuse, and ignores contextual workplace factors; and prevention programs can be effective in reducing AOD use.

This chapter reinforces those claims in several ways. First, it reviews national trends in employee AOD abuse as well as evidence for the negative consequences of employee AOD abuse. Second, it reviews evidence showing the importance of work environment and organizational- and occupational-level factors as potential risks for AOD abuse. Because organizational and occupational factors (e.g., work climate) can influence employee AOD use, prevention programmers and evaluators should be aware of contextual influences when designing, implementing, and evaluating their interventions. Third, the chapter offers a preliminary quantitative meta-analysis of research on workplace prevention programs.

The three sections together define three areas on a map for the scientific study of workplace AOD abuse prevention. The first area covers the different approaches and types of prevention, including those examined in this book. The goal of this area of inquiry is to understand what approaches work and how they work. The preliminary meta-analysis reviewed below is a first step toward answering those questions.

The second area consists of the different contextual and multilevel factors that can either facilitate or constrain the effects of prevention programs. Those factors include individual, work group, departmental, and organizational variables. They also include variance in AOD abuse due to occupation, worksite, and the overlap between occupation and worksite. As explained below, within a single organization, great variation in AOD abuse can exist from worksite (i.e., business unit) to worksite. In addition, evidence indicates that some occupations contain more risks for AOD abuse than others. Through research on contextual factors, prevention scientists can increase sensitivity to environmental features that moderate effective prevention programs, and program designers can customize programs to increase effectiveness.

The third area pertains to the different types of outcomes that prevention programs should target. Ultimately, researchers seek two primary outcomes: (1) evidence indicating that the prevention program led to a reduction of AOD use and abuse (i.e., lowered levels of drinking and illicit drug use) and (2) evidence indicating that at-risk employees who participated in the program did not develop or increase levels of use compared with control groups (i.e., workers who did not participate in the program). In prevention science, the primary outcomes are often *distal* to the intervention; that is, they either take time to develop or are otherwise difficult to detect as a result of low base rates in the population.

In addition to primary or distal outcomes, researchers should also target *intermediary* or *proximal* outcomes, which are often observable, emerge soon after the intervention, and—most important—correlate with the primary goal of prevention of AOD abuse. In addition, the meta-analysis distinguishes different types of proximal outcomes: beliefs and attitudes associated with drug use and workplace policies, stress and coping, psychological symptomatology, and knowledge about AOD use (e.g., signs and symptoms).

Clearly, the three areas of prevention science are related, and knowledge will be advanced through continued understanding of those relationships. For example, understanding whether a specific type of prevention technology works requires some knowledge of the conditions (i.e., contextual factors) that enhance or diminish a program's effectiveness as well as knowledge of the type of outcomes that are affected. As knowledge of conditions and outcomes grows, program designers will increase their sensitivity to the unique environment of particular worksites and adapt programs accordingly. In addition, through iterative and cumulative feedback about effectiveness, designers can eventually learn which parts of their programs need to be enhanced, modified, or ultimately abandoned.

AOD ABUSE IN THE WORKPLACE: A BRIEF OVERVIEW

It is often thought that alcohol and other drug use by the work force has a significant impact on society. This perception appears corroborated by the extant research, for virtually all of it, including the best-designed studies, report some associations between alcohol or other drug use and distressing, dangerous, or other dysfunctional behaviors. However, it is difficult, given the current research base, to make definitive statements regarding the magnitude of the impact of alcohol or other drug use at work. (Normand, Lempert, & O'Brien, 1994, p. 160)

The above conclusion comes from a report by the Institute of Medicine (IOM) on drugs and alcohol in the American workplace. A fair amount of research about employee substance abuse, which demonstrates associations between employee substance use and problems, has accumulated since that report. Moreover, studies have identified workplace factors (e.g., stress and work group culture) associated with AOD use and potential avenues for prevention. Despite the connection between AOD abuse and problems, some claim that prevalence rates are relatively low and thus do not support what is described as an irrational hysteria about the problem (Crow & Hartman, 1992; Newcomb, 1994). In addition, many fact sheets that disseminate research information to the general public often focus on prevalence rates and ignore the surrounding context as well as possible solutions. A 1999 report by the American Civil Liberties Union claims that such broad problem statements result in the dissemination of misleading information.

Despite these issues, a substantial amount of research suggests that significant individual and social costs are associated with employee AOD use. Numerous case studies and clinical reports demonstrate that one employee with drug or alcohol dependence or one employee who deals drugs can have a significant impact not only on his or her own productivity and medical or legal costs but also on those of others—both specific coworkers and business operations. Research studies describe relationships between illicit drug use and productivity concerns such as absenteeism, tardiness, absenteeism due to injuries, and accidents (Bass et al., 1996; Bross, Pace, & Cronin, 1992; Hoffman & Larison, 1999; Holcom, Lehman, & Simpson, 1993). Although some of those studies are based on self-report, others use objective measures, such as urinalysis tests. Several studies found that positive drug-test results predicted absenteeism, especially unexcused absences (Crouch, Webb, & Peterson, 1989; Normand, Salyards, & Mahony, 1990;

Sheridan & Winkler, 1989). A recent longitudinal study found that poly-drug use was both a predictor and a consequence of work adjustment (Galaif, Newcomb, & Carmona, 2001).

Across independent studies, problem alcohol use or heavy drinking has been shown to correlate with different types of self-reported performance measures, such as poor-quality work, (Mangione et al., 1999), losing or almost losing a job (Lennox, Steele, Zarkin, & Bray, 1998), working below normal performance levels (Fisher, Hoffman, Austin-Lane, & Kao, 2000), psychological withdrawal from work (e.g., laziness or loafing), and work-related antagonism (Bennett & Lehman, 1995; Lehman & Simpson, 1992). Other studies point to relationships between AOD use and turnover (e.g., Kandel & Yamaguchi, 1987). Moreover, heavy drinking, if left unchecked, can lead to catastrophic illness and high medical costs to companies (Anderson et al., 2000), and even former drinkers may affect costs (Polen, Green, Freeborn, Mullooly, & Lynch, 2001).

All the studies cited above make assumptions about the relationship between AOD use and outcomes. First, they assume a monotonic or linear relationship between employee drinking and costs. As Moore, Grunberg, and Greenberg (2000) recently showed, however, that assumption is not always warranted; a "threshold" effect may exist for some outcomes. For example, in their study, only the most problematic drinkers had high levels of job stress and increased intentions to quit work. Second, employee AOD use may serve as a precipitator, trigger, mediator, or marker variable for other employee characteristics, such as risk taking and deviance; those latter characteristics may be the most important or robust predictors of problems (see Brief & Folger, 1992; Mensch & Kandel, 1988). Moreover, the work environment—as discussed below—may provide salient conditions that interact with employee characteristics that serve to increase risk. Lehman and Bennett (2002) showed that employees with a greater number of indicators of deviance (i.e., low religious attendance, arrest history, risk taking, and tolerance of AOD use) were particularly susceptible to drug use and problem drinking when they worked with coworkers who also drank alcohol.

The relationship between AOD abuse and performance problems also appears to vary according to job environment or job type. As discussed later in this chapter, the causes or precipitators of problems vary across occupations and require different approaches to prevention programming. For example, within occupations that are safety sensitive (e.g., operation of heavy equipment or truck driving) or expose workers to hazards (e.g., injury risk), employees are more likely to engage in binge drinking and drinking and driving (Conrad, Furner, & Qian, 1999), drug users are more likely to report accidents (Holcom et al., 1993), and their coworkers are more apt to report problems (Bennett & Lehman, 1999). The importance of the work environment as a contributor to drinking problems or illicit drug use is also seen in studies showing that job climate factors contribute variance to AOD use at work (Lehman, Farabee, Holcom, & Simpson, 1995; Ames, Grube, & Moore, 2000). Moreover, heavy alcohol consumption is associated with different dimensions of occupational stress in various occupations, including time pressure among male white-collar workers (Hagihara, Tarumi, Miller, Nebeshima, & Nobutomo, 1999), severity of various stressors for transit operators (e.g., problems with supervisors; Ragland, Greiner, Yen, & Fisher, 2000), increased workload for military men (Bray, Fairbank, & Marsden, 1999), and shift work for nurses (Trinkoff & Storr, 1998). The relationships between stress and AOD abuse extend to illicit drugs, such as cocaine and marijuana (Bray et al., 1999; Storr, Trinkoff, & Anthony, 1999).

Despite the apparent levels and correlates of AOD abuse, many employees with problems do not seek help (Cook & Schlenger, in press; Kaskutas, Weisner, & Caetano, 1996). Heavy alcohol users are generally less willing to seek help than nonusers or light alcohol users (Reynolds & Lehman, 2001). When help is sought, it often occurs after significant negative consequences have accumulated (Shapiro et al., 1984). Although denial and resistance are major barriers to help seeking, studies show that coworker encouragement to get help or abstain from use can influence employees to seek treatment or other forms of help (e.g., Alcoholics Anonymous; George & Tucker, 1996; Rice, Longabaugh, & Stout, 1997).

TOWARD A NATIONAL PREVENTION AGENDA: BEYOND "ONE SIZE FITS ALL"

Drug testing and other policy mechanisms are rarely implemented in a one-size-fits-all fashion. Differences in parameters such as company size, occupation, health care, and human resource practices reveal that those factors influence company approaches to drug testing and rehabilitative practices (Blum, Fields, Milne, & Spell, 1994; Milne & Blum, 1998). That variety is important to the motif of this book; namely, that prevention programming should refrain from broad generalizations about effectiveness and instead advocate sensitivity to differences across occupations and companies and, most important, sensitivity to the particular needs of individual employees. Prevention programs can be implemented more effectively when AOD abuse problems are examined across different levels of analysis: national, occupational, company or corporate, and individual. The following sections, which integrate data from national surveys and cross-site studies, describe changes in the 10 years since the advent of drug testing. The data point to significant variation in policies and AOD use across occupations and companies; those differences suggest the need for a strategic approach to addressing workplace AOD abuse problems.

National Trends

Table 1.1 integrates information from various sources to show rates of AOD use and drug testing for the years 1990 to 2000. The table provides national data on full-time employees reporting AOD abuse and the percentage of positive workplace drug tests. The table also provides data on the proportion of business firms that report using drug tests. Because the data shown in the table come from different sources (i.e., employees, managers, and chemical tests) and represent different sampling techniques, the table provides no basis for drawing inferences about causal relationships between variables. The table shows that since 1990, rates of drug use among full-time workers have remained fairly stable, ranging from 7.9% to 8.9% for illicit drug use and 6.8% to 8.3% for heavy alcohol use. Those rates at least double for different subgroups: workers age 18 to 29, certain safety-sensitive occupations (e.g., transportation and construction), and workers in small businesses (SAMHSA, 1999, 2001). Although self-reported rates of illicit drug use did not decline from 1990 to 1997, the rate of positive drug tests shows a steady decline from 1988 (13.6%; not shown) to 1999 (4.6%). One explanation for that discrepancy may be that AOD users have adapted to drug testing by seeking out jobs where testing is less likely. In fact, survey data from the Substance Abuse and Mental Health Services Administration (SAMHSA, 1999) showed that compared with nonusers, current illicit drug users are significantly less likely to work for employers who test for drugs at hiring, on a random basis, or under suspicion. A second explanation is that illicit drug users have learned to dupe the urine-screening process (e.g., through the use of adulterants). Employees also may find out when random testing is going to occur. A report from Quest Diagnostics (2000) showed an increase in "test cheating" in 1999, whereby "more than 5,400 test results were reported as positive for the use of adulterants. In addition, 2,400 other samples were identified as having been 'substituted' for valid test specimens." Still, those numbers are quite small compared with the approximately 6 million tests conducted and the 4.6% positivity rate. A third explanation for the decline in positive drug tests is that the mixture of industries in the sample has changed over time.

Table 1.1 shows that the percentage of firms that test employees for illicit drugs steadily decreased from 1996 (70%) to 2000 (47%). A report from the American Management Association (Greenberg, Canzoneri, & Joe, 2000) suggested that the decline "may reflect alterations in hiring policies by companies caught in the skill shortages that affect recruitment and retention nationwide" (p. 2). In other words, the risk of discovering and having to address employee AOD use appears to be outweighed by the costs associated with not having enough employees to maintain a business. Companies may also reason that despite the potential costs of illicit drug

TABLE 1.1

Trends in Substance Use and Drug Testing: A Comparison Across Different Data Sources

	Year											
	1990	1991	1992	1993	1994	1995	1996	1997	1998	1999	2000	2001
	Percent											
Drug testing positivity rate	11.0	8.8	8.8	8.4	7.5	6.7	5.8	5.0	4.8	4.6	4.7	—
Heavy alcohol use	8.6	8.5	7.8	8.5	8.4	7.8	8.2	7.6	5.6	5.4	—[a]	—
Illicit drug use	8.6	7.9	7.4	7.7	7.6	6.8	7.7	7.7	8.9	9.3	—[a]	—
Firms that test current employees	—	52	62	66	65	68	70	62	62	54	47	50
Firms that test applicants[c]	—	48	57	65	61	63	68	64	62	63	61	61

Notes. Data on drug testing are from Quest Diagnostics (2000) and are based on all tests performed by the company (estimated at more than 6 million tests annually for 2000). Quest Diagnostics is the leading provider of drug-testing services in the United States; according to the company, "the Drug Testing Index is released every six months as a service for government, media and industry, and is considered a benchmark for national trends" (Quest Diagnostics, 2000). Data on alcohol and illicit drug use are from the National Household Survey of Drug Abuse (NHSDA: Substance Abuse and Mental Health Services Administration [SAMHSA], 1999). Data are based on full-time workers ages 18 to 49. Data representing heavy alcohol use and illicit drug use trends for 1998 and 1999 have been computed using SAMHSA's online analysis utility [http://www.icpsr.umich.edu:8080/SERIES/00064.xml?format=SAMHDA#das], and added to the table. Data on the proportion of firms that test employees or applicants are from Greenberg, Canzoneri, & Joe (2000), which summarizes the American Management Association's annual survey of medical testing in the workplace. [a]The 2000 NHSDA (SAMHSA, 2001) did not provide information for the age grouping 18 to 49; the following breakdowns are provided for full-time employees. For ages 18 to 25, heavy drinking was 14.9% (2000); illicit drug use was 4.9% (2000). For ages 26 or older, heavy drinking was 6.1% (2000); illicit drug use was 13.4% (2000).

use, the probability of detecting AOD abuse is low enough to warrant relaxing surveillance in the name of economic solvency.

Occupational Differences

Just as economic or national factors may shape policies, so too do factors that are distinct within occupations. Twice within the past decade (1994 and 1997), SAMHSA has included a special module within the National Household Survey on Drug Abuse (NHSDA) that asks respondents about their personal AOD use. A recent publication (SAMHSA, 1999) tabulates data across 14 occupational categories.

Across occupations, SAMHSA (1999) reported a tendency for illicit drug or heavy alcohol users to be less likely than nonusers to indicate access to the employee assistance program (EAP) or other counseling services. Illicit drug users also were more likely than nonusers to report that their workplace did not test as part of hiring. Other highlights showed higher AOD use in the absence of written policies and, among users, less willingness to work in companies that test for drugs at hiring, on a random basis, or under suspicion. Importantly, this resistance to testing varied according to size of organization and occupation. This finding is consistent with a recent study showing that AOD dependence varies across occupations (Kessler & Frank, 1997).

Figure 1.1 tabulates the 1997 NHSDA information in order to explore variations across occupations. The bar portion of the chart displays occupations, ordered from left to right by prevalence of heavy alcohol use (5 or more drinks on the same occasion on each of at least five days in the past 30 days). The frequency of illicit drug use is also reported (striped bars). Figure 1.1 also displays the percentage of full-time workers (in the 18–49 age group) that reported their workplace provided access to any type of employee assistance program (EAP) or other type of counseling program for alcohol or drug-related problems (dark circle/line chart). Figure 1.1 shows occupational variation in AOD use. To illustrate, compare occupations with the lowest and highest rates of illicit drug use. Protective services, with the lowest levels of self-reported drug use (3%), report the highest levels of EAP access (80%) and also highest levels of drug testing (e.g., 60% random testing; not shown in Figure). These trends are likely because protective services often have strong safety regulations and a culture of risk control. In contrast, restaurant and hospitality occupations (e.g., bartending) report both the highest levels of alcohol (15%) and drug (18.7%) use and also among the lowest degree of EAP access and drug testing (e.g., 16.7% random testing). These occupations are more mobile, less regulated, and, moreover, have ready access to alcohol as part of the job. It is not possible—using these two examples alone—to deduce that more EAP access or drug testing is associated with less drug use. For ex-

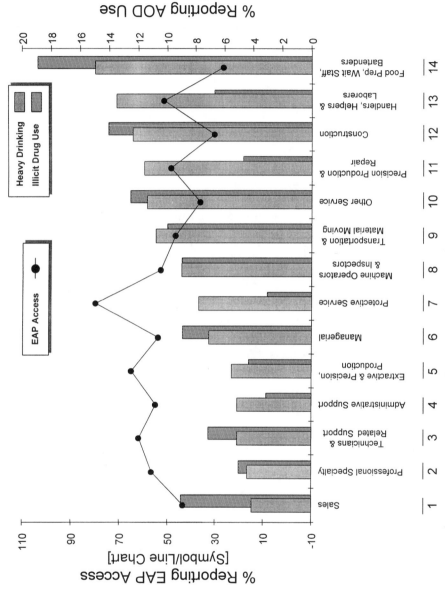

Figure 1.1. Heavy drinking, illicit drug use, and EAP access (Substance Abuse and Mental Health Services Administration, 1997).

ample, transportation workers—one of the most heavily tested occupations (at 53%)—report relatively high use of illicit drugs (10%).

Despite occupational differences, the NHSDA data show some relationships between policy components and self-reported AOD abuse. In fact, the correlation—calculated across 14 occupations—between EAP access and heavy drinking is statistically significant, $r = -.60$; $p = .01$. Of all policy components, occupations with greater access to an EAP were also those occupations with less heavy drinking. Interestingly, occupations with greater EAP access also reported less illicit drug use ($r = -.85$, $p < .0001$). Among the testing variables, reasonable suspicion was negatively related to illicit drug use ($r = -.56$, $p = .017$). Overall, access to an EAP showed the strongest relationship to levels of use and was more related to illicit drug use than were the testing variables. These findings suggest that EAPs represent a preventative or rehabilitative mechanism within occupations.

It is not clear whether higher levels of EAP access would reduce heavy drinking or illicit drug use. The data, however, suggest that prevention scientists should pay attention to variability in occupational cultures, consider differences in the risk profile of employees within occupations, and customize prevention services accordingly. Other studies support the relevance of occupational risk for the prevention of work group climates that might support drinking or drug use. Case studies and ethnographic analyses suggest that climates of use and tolerance exist in a variety of occupations, including train operators (Mannello, 1979), nurses (Hood & Duphorne, 1995), airline flight attendants (Bamberger & Sonnenstuhl, 1995), municipal employees (Bennett & Lehman, 1997), tunnel workers (Sonnenstuhl, 1996), assembly-line workers (Ames & Janes, 1990), restaurant cooks (Kjaerheim, Mykletun, Aasland, & Haldorsen, 1995), and the military (Cosper 1979). Although the incidence of illicit drug use among military personnel declined from 1980 (28%) to 1995 (3%), corresponding decreases in heavy drinking have been minimal (from 21% to 17%; Bray & Marsden, 2000). Using data from the 1984 U.S. General Population Survey, Fillmore (1990) found that within each of five occupations (i.e., technicians, sales representatives, clerks, protective services, and food handlers), more than 40% of workers almost always drank when socializing with coworkers.

Variation Across Organizations and the Importance of Workplace Culture

Recent studies have examined differences in AOD abuse across different organizations (Ames et al., 2000; French, Zarkin, Hartwell, & Bray, 1995; Greenburg & Grunberg, 1995). Each study suggests that beyond occupational variation, different organizational social environments may influence levels of AOD abuse. Greenburg and Grunberg (1995) surveyed production workers in 15 mills in the wood products industry. The mills varied in their participatory environments from producer cooperatives, where employees were involved in decision making, to conventional union and nonunion environments. Results showed that work setting had an indirect relationship with heavy drinking. Employees in mills with high worker participation had more job satisfaction than workers in other mills; satisfaction, in turn, was associated with less drinking to cope with stress. Worksites with the most employee involvement, however, had the highest level of heavy drinking, but this finding appeared to be a result of job dissatisfaction produced by cuts or stagnation in wages and benefits. Worksites with the most employee involvement also appeared to be worksites with the most cuts or stagnation in wages and benefits.

Ames et al. (2000) found that work team disapproval of drinking was significantly greater in manufacturing plants that used Japanese (i.e., team-oriented) versus U.S. (i.e., hierarchical) management principles. Their study comparing two plants showed that the team-oriented plant exercised greater social control over coworker use of alcohol and that alcohol was less easily available than in the traditional, hierarchical plant. For example, among workers in the team-oriented plant, 94% indicated that their work team disapproved of drinking at work, compared with 49% of workers in the traditional setting. The authors' statistical model showed that the strongest predictors of drinking at work were work-related drinking by one's closest friend at work and one's own drinking patterns.

French et al. (1995) discovered differences in AOD use across five different types of worksites. For example, the proportion of employees who drank alcohol daily differed for a financial services business (15%), a manufacturer (14%), a municipal government (11%), a service organization (7%), and health care services (5%). The authors also found differences in the misuse of prescription drugs (i.e., use for nonmedical reasons or taking higher doses than prescribed), ranging from 23% in the finance business to 12% in the municipality.

Howland and colleagues (1996) asked managers at 114 different worksites about their drinking habits. Regression analyses showed an independent worksite effect on daily and heavy drinking, controlling for respondent demographics (e.g., age, sex, education, and marital status) and type of work (e.g., job level and function, such as customer service, sales, or technical assistance). The authors concluded that "knowing where one works provides, on average, some information about what an individual drinks and that this explanatory power is substantial relative to that of demographics, functional area of job, and region of the country" (p. 1014).

Taken together, the studies suggest that occupations and workplaces vary in the prevalence of AOD use and that such variation may be due, in part, to differences in work environment. This finding is consistent with theory suggesting that workplace cultures have a role in controlling or condoning the use of alcohol for purposes of coworker socializing, joint leisure, and coping with stress (Ames & Janes, 1990, 1992; Trice & Sonnenstuhl, 1990; Walsh, Rudd, & Mangione, 1993). A recent multivariate study of more than 3,000 union employees from diverse worksites showed that compared with other risk factors (i.e., stress, alienation, and lack of policy enforcement), coworker drinking norms were the strongest direct predictor of employee problem drinking (Bacharach, Bamberger, & Sonnenstuhl, in press). This study is significant not only because it supports the importance of work culture as a risk factor but also because it shows that drinking norms may mediate and moderate how worker stress and alienation affect employee drinking. Work environments also may influence drug use. Research shows that job factors (e.g., working alone) and perceptions of job climate contribute variance to the prediction of past-year drug use beyond that explained by personal demographic or background factors (Lehman et al., 1995).

Moreover, the above set of findings offers support for the idea, developed by Roman (1990), that alcohol intervention strategies should pay close attention to three different frames of reference along an "occupational-organizational continuum": occupational subcultures, occupational drinking cultures, and dominant organizational cultures. In some cases, occupational groups or subcultures within an organization have norms that significantly influence drinking and other AOD use. In other cases, a particular occupation (across organizations) may promote heavy drinking as part of the occupational identity (see, e.g., Sonnenstuhl's analysis of the Tunnel Workers Union in New York City, 1996). Finally, an entire organization may have a considerable mixture of occupations and—as a single culture—contain uniform social norms that influence AOD use-related behaviors. Following this analysis, Roman concludes,

> When considering the design or mix of intervention and alcohol control efforts in the workplace, it is critical to examine the placement of a given workplace on this occupational–organizational continuum, adding to this consideration of the effects of union presence. This derivation of the need for such "customized" program design is a crucial example of where the possibility of a single "recipe" for workplace efforts to address employee alcohol problems is fallacious. One key difference may be that in settings where occupational structures dominate, there are norms in place that must be considered if new norms are to be imposed or superimposed on existing structures. (Roman, 1990, p. 383)

Summary and Implications for Prevention

The preceding review suggests that workplace AOD use and related policies may be shaped by socioeconomic, occupational, and organizational factors and that employee AOD use and its regulation are highly contextualized. This contextual, or multilevel, aspect of employee AOD use parallels models of prevention research in the field of drug education in public schools (Boddington, Perry, Clements, Wetton, & McWhiter, 1999). Recognition is growing that to be effective, school-based interventions must involve entire communities or multiple agencies and train not only key adults within a community but also parents, teachers, staff, principals, and students. Although workplace prevention programs may not follow this multilevel, contextual approach, programmers should be aware of contextual influences when designing and implementing their interventions (SAMHSA, 1997).

Variation in levels of AOD use across industry, occupation, and work culture (and the occupational–organizational continuum) also suggest that prevention efforts may be best geared to the specific level of need or risk within a given workplace. The IOM developed a classification system for prevention programming that could be applied here (Mrazek & Haggerty, 1994). The system distinguishes between three types of interventions—universal, selective, or indicated:

- *Universal* preventive interventions are targeted to the general public or a whole population group that has not been identified on the basis of individual risk.
- *Selective* preventive interventions are targeted to individuals or a subgroup of the population whose risk of developing a disorder is significantly higher than average.
- *Indicated* preventive interventions are targeted to people at high risk who are identified as having minimal but detectable signs or symptoms foreshadowing disorder, or biological markers indicating predisposition for disorder, but who do not meet diagnostic levels at the current time.

As a first step in developing prevention strategy, this broad framework might be applied along with the occupational information presented earlier. Generally speaking, universal approaches may resemble standard informational and employee orientation programs already in place in many organizations. Those organizations—with no known or identifiable risks—may be satisfied with such programs. Alternatively, a selective intervention may be more appropriate for organizations that include occupations with higher prevalence rates and where risk is also presumably higher (e.g., food handlers). The programs described in subsequent chapters may be seen as examples of selective interventions. Prevention programmers should use the IOM scheme as a first step in strategy because it is likely that AOD use varies across businesses within any occupational category. Moreover, many businesses involve a mixture of occupations and may sometimes need a combination of universal, selective, and indicated strategies.

PREVIOUS QUANTITATIVE RESEARCH IN WORKPLACE AOD PREVENTION TRAINING: AN INITIAL META-ANALYTIC REVIEW

The preceding sections reviewed several factors that should be considered in designing workplace prevention programs, including the various problem types associated with workplace AOD abuse, how drug testing has attempted (to a certain extent, successfully) to deal with the problem, and how workplaces are complex multilevel environments. Currently, published research in workplace AOD prevention has been conducted without much attention to those background factors. This research may best be described as "developmental" (Holder et al., 1999); extant studies provide preliminary tests of the likely effectiveness of a new intervention. Further research is needed to demonstrate whether those interventions will work across various settings and when background factors, such as occupation, are taken into consideration. Nonetheless, results from existing preliminary studies are promising.

This section reviews a number of workplace AOD prevention programs that have been evaluated. Many of the programs (and their assessments) were developed by the authors of subsequent chapters in the volume (in fact, we have included results from chapter 3, by Cook and colleagues). A quantitative review of the studies is in progress (Reynolds & Bennett, 2000); this section offers an initial report of that review.

A Meta-Analytic Approach

We wished to determine the general level of efficacy of previous AOD prevention programs and used meta-analysis for this purpose. Meta-analysis is a procedure for examining the statistical results of previous research using quantitative methods. It relies on the actual statistical effects of those studies, rather than a subjective perception of study results. For example, instead of subjectively reporting that a program appeared "minimally" versus "strongly" effective, a meta-analysis provides an aggregate statistic that indicates the magnitude of effectiveness. In the case of workplace AOD prevention, a number of studies have examined the effects of programs that have directly sought to prevent employee AOD use or enhance an employee's use of services related to prevention of or early intervention in AOD abuse. The meta-analysis requires several steps, including: (a) a comprehensive search of the literature for relevant studies, (b) specifying criteria for including a study in the meta-analysis, (c) identifying whether the studies can be distinguished according to the types of outcomes that were examined, and (d) calculating "effect sizes," which are statistics that indicate the magnitude of any relationship between two variables. In this meta-analysis, those two variables are (a) whether someone received the prevention program and (b) any number of outcomes associated with receiving that program.

Methods and Results

A full description of methods and results is provided in the appendix to this chapter. A total of 22 studies were identified, all of which measured one or more of five different types of outcomes: levels of AOD abuse (alcohol, drugs, or both), beliefs and attitudes associated with AOD use and workplace policies, stress and coping, psychological symptomatology, and knowledge about AOD use (e.g., signs and symptoms). Many of the studies measured variables both before and after the prevention program and included a control group (see Appendix). Researchers offered interventions to samples of employees from diverse occupational settings, including municipal employees and manufacturing and clerical workers.

The results from the meta-analysis suggest that workplace AOD abuse prevention programs hold some promise for reducing AOD use as well as for having positive effects on stress and mental health. The average effect size was .299 for 12 studies that measured results at 1 to 4 months following training and .334 for the 4 studies that measured results 6 to 10 months posttraining. An effect size of .299 is interpreted to mean that an employee who received a training program (compared with one who did not) would be likely to change his or her score on some measured outcome (e.g., coping skills) by .299 of a standard deviation of that measured outcome. Effect sizes in this range ($\sim$.20) are considered to be relatively small. The average effect size was significantly different from zero, however, and every combined effect size for each study was significantly greater than zero. This result indicates that all the programs evaluated in the meta-analysis were relatively effective, even though the effects were weak. The effect of training on AOD use outcomes was lower than on other types of outcomes (i.e., behavior/attitudes, stress, and mental health), but both classes of outcomes showed significant positive results.

Discussion

Results from this preliminary meta-analysis suggest that prevention can enhance other aspects of employee well-being (e.g., stress) while improving AOD abuse levels. The results echo the conclusion Dusenbury

TABLE 1.2
Characteristics of Worksite Substance Abuse Prevention Effectiveness Studies and Weighted Mean Effect Sizes

Study	Program	Focus of Intervention	Pretest–Posttest Interval (months)	N Intervention Group	N Control Group	N Training Effects	Effect Types*	g	g_{su}
Bennett & Lehman, 2001a	Team Prevention	Group Climate	1.5–2	101	86	10	K, B/A, Stress	0.314	
Bennett & Lehman, 2001a	Informational Prevention	Knowledge	1.5–2	73	86	10	K, B/A, Stress	0.420	
Bennett & Lehman, 2002	Team Prevention for Supervisors	Group Climate	1.5–2	29	17	4	B/A	0.578	
Cook, Back, MacPherson, & Trudeau, this vol.	Integrated Health Promotion	Substance Use	2	99	72	16	K, B/A, SU, Stress	0.163	0.160
			11	50	118	6	SU	0.229	0.229
Cook, Back, & Trudeau, 1996a	Working People	Alcohol	1	38	26	10	SU, B/A	0.493	0.515
Cook, Back, & Trudeau, 1996b	Say Yes	Substance Use	.75	159	130	8	SU, B/A	0.226	0.146

Study	Program	Domain		N	n		Effect Types		
Heirich & Sieck, 2000	CVD risk screening	Physical Health	36	483	424	2	SU	0.165	0.165
Kishchuk et al., 1994	EAP Enhanced Program	Alcohol	2	122	100	9	K, B/A, SU	0.246	0.200
Kline & Snow, 1994	Coping Skills Intervention	Coping w/Stress	4	81	47	12	SU, B/A, Stress, MH	0.269	0.407
			10	72	43	12	SU, B/A, Stress, MH	0.285	0.178
Snow & Kline, 1995	Work and Family Stress Project	Coping w/Stress	4	125	80	11	SU, B/A, Stress, MH	0.213	0.300
			10	110	75	11	SU, B/A, Stress, MH	0.262	0.288
			26	90	68	11	SU, B/A, Stress, MH	0.193	0.287
Snow & Kline, 1991	Coping Skills Intervention	Coping w/Stress	4	101	103	6	SU, B/A, Stress, MH	0.333	0.314
Snow, 1996	Coping Skills Intervention	Coping w/Stress	4	126	111	4	SU, Stress	0.401	0.300
			10	99	96	4	SU, Stress	0.510	0.360
		TOTAL		2030	1756	146	AVERAGE Time 1	0.299	0.215
							Time 2	0.334	0.241
							Time 3	0.193	0.287

Notes. For Effect Types—SU = Substance Use; B/A = Beliefs/Attitudes; K = Knowledge; MH = Mental Health (e.g., depression).

(1999) reached in her qualitative review of the field: "The consistency of results across different studies and different research groups suggests that research is well on its way to identifying likely ingredients of effective programs" (p. 154). Although this quantitative review supports Dusenbury's claim, readers should treat our meta-analytic results with some caution. The reported effect sizes may be inflated for the simple reasons that not many worksites use these programs, research in this area is relatively sparse, and negative results may be underrepresented in the literature.

Aside from this cautionary note, the results should—at a minimum—lead to further research in the area. All 12 studies that reported statistical tests of outcomes between some intervention and a control group also reported decreased risk of abuse. The application of these results into work settings or the increased use of programs will require strategies that address many barriers to prevention. That is, despite the extent of the AOD problem and evidence that prevention programs are helpful, such programs are not likely to be used. A recent survey asked more than 7,000 supervisors across 114 worksites about barriers to the effective management of alcohol problems (Bell, Mangione, Howland, Levine, & Amick, 1996). Lack of training was the most frequently cited barrier (80% of those surveyed). Other barriers were management being "tough on drugs, soft on alcohol"; beliefs that treatment is not effective; failure of senior management to take a stand; and an emphasis on efficiency and productivity that gets in the way of program implementation. Roman and Blum (1999) also described major barriers to the development of workplace prevention programming:

1. Compared to other workplace factors, substance abuse is not an ongoing or salient concern that has gained sufficient attention among managers and human resources.
2. Because of its legal status, alcohol use tends to be normalized such that when problems do occur employees are reluctant to take action.
3. Tremendous societal attention has been drawn to dealing with illicit drug use, resulting in remarkably large investments in drug-testing programs. Despite the limited efficacy of these programs (Macdonald & Roman, 1995), this attention to drugs and the sense of "doing something" tends to mute attention to alcohol use and other prevention strategies.

We highlight these barriers because a program may have demonstrated effectiveness in one setting but, because of barriers, fail to be useful in another setting. Organizations vary in their readiness for prevention programs and in how much they would actively implement programs (Holder et al., 1999). Such readiness for prevention is an important contextual factor that varies across occupations and worksites.

One finding among the current results should interest employers and possibly help overcome some barriers to prevention training: Most of the effects on AOD abuse reported in the studies (see Table 1.2) pertain to alcohol use (rather than drug use), and it is interesting that the effects of training on alcohol reduction increased over time. This finding can be interpreted in several ways. For example, the intervention could have had a "sleeper" effect (i.e., take time to have an impact), or perhaps participants who remained in the study and reported reductions were more receptive to begin with. Either way, the delayed effects suggest that it is important to measure results at least 6 months following an intervention. Most important, any reduction in alcohol use represents potential savings in medical and health care costs. A growing body of literature suggests that heavy drinkers are resistant to getting medical help for their problems. Anderson and colleagues (2000) found a negative relationship between alcohol use and health care costs. As they point out:

> This finding has been reported by others (Anderson, Brink, & Courtney, 1995; Brink, 1987), who speculated that alcoholics or those consuming high levels of alcohol may avoid the health care system. This avoidance behavior would result in lower costs being associated with alcohol use over short-term periods, followed later by serious or catastrophic health problems that require costly treatment. (p. 51)

The delayed effects of programs on alcohol reduction seem important, given evidence suggesting that heavy alcohol use is associated with avoidance of health care. When seen in the context of potentially "serious or catastrophic" health problems, the positive effects of such programs should be of interest to organizations that are concerned about reducing health and medical claims.

APPENDIX: A PRELIMINARY META-ANALYSIS
OF EXISTING RESEARCH

Methods

Identification of Evaluations

We attempted to locate all evaluations of worksite AOD prevention programs by searching for relevant terms using computerized databases such as PsychLit, PsychInfo, and Medline. Additional references surfaced by examining several reviews of the relevant literature (Dusenbury, 1999; Mieczkowski, 1999; Roman & Blum, 1996). Unpublished manuscripts and conference presentations were acquired through informal contacts within the field.

Selection Criteria

To be selected for the meta-analysis, an evaluation must have met the following criteria: (a) an intention of the program to "modify" AOD abuse, (b) use of a control or comparison group, (c) use of reliably operationalized outcome measures, and (d) availability of significance tests or group means and standard deviations. In addition, attention was focused on studies using pretest–posttest designs.

Data Analysis

For each study, an effect size (g) was calculated to quantify the magnitude of the program's effectiveness across as many as five types of outcomes that reflected the purposes of the prevention programs. An effect size is defined as the difference between the intervention and the control group means for each outcome measure, standardized by dividing by the pooled standard deviation ($g = M_I - M_C/SD$; Rosenthal, 1991). If means and standard deviations were not available, effect sizes were calculated using formulas developed to convert other test statistics to effect sizes (Perry & Tobler, 1992). In all cases, statistics that were converted into our effect size measures reflected covariance-adjusted means, with pretest values as covariates, so that any differences between the comparison groups on any variable measured at pretest would not be reflected in the effect sizes.

Outcomes were classified into five categories: knowledge of AOD abuse, beliefs and attitudes, stress and coping, psychological symptomatology, and AOD use. Some studies did not include all five types, and some types were measured by more than one indicator. When multiple indicators were used, we calculated separate effect sizes and then averaged them (Tobler, 1992). This procedure yielded one effect size per study for each outcome type. Effect sizes also were calculated across outcome types, yielding one effect size per study. After calculating one effect size per outcome type per study and the combined effect size per study, the weighted mean effect size and 95% confidence interval were calculated for each outcome type and combined across studies. The weighted mean was computed by weighting each effect size by the inverse of its variance, which is a reflection of the sample size (variance of $g = N/N_I * N_C + ES^2/2(N - 2)$; Rosenthal, 1991). Effect size estimates that are based on larger sample sizes are generally more precise.

One manuscript reported results from three pretest–posttest intervals, and three manuscripts reported results from two pretest–posttest occurrences. Effect sizes were calculated for each time interval separately. Results from studies whose findings were based on only one posttest occurrence were combined with the results from the first test–retest interval from the four studies with multiple testing intervals.

Results

Characteristics of the Evaluations

Of the 22 studies originally uncovered for the meta-analysis, 12 met the criteria for inclusion. Characteristics and effect sizes from each study are shown in Table 1.2. Five programs focused primarily on increasing knowledge and influencing beliefs and attitudes about AOD abuse, four programs focused on stress and coping, two programs highlighted group dynamics and team support as protective factors, and one program focused only on risk of cardiovascular disease.

Each study reported results that were based on 2 to 12 effects. Each study's sample size varied: N's ranged from about 50 to about 1,000. The meta-analysis used a total of 102 effects, which were based on responses from 2,965 employees.

Program Effect Sizes

For the 12 studies combined, the weighted mean effect size for the first (or only) test–retest interval was .299 (95% CI = .297–.301). For four studies with a second test-retest interval, the total effect size was .334 (95% CI = .328–.340). One study included a third test interval (g = .193; 95% CI = .167–.219).

For the first test interval, the weighted mean effect size of the worksite program on self-reported AOD use was .215 (95% CI = .213–.217). The AOD use effect size was .241 at time 2 (95% CI = .235–.247) and .287 at time 3 (95% CI = .261–.313).

Comparison of Effect Sizes

The average effect sizes (particularly the effect sizes for AOD use outcomes) are reasonably larger than effects of other types of substance use prevention programs. A meta-analysis of eight evaluations of DARE (Drug and Alcohol Resistance Education) reported a weighted mean effect size of .06 for substance use (Ennett, Tobler, Ringwalt, & Flewelling, 1994). Also, in a meta-analysis of all school-based substance use prevention programs, a substance use effect size of .18 was reported for programs categorized as interactive. Noninteractive programs yielded a weighted mean effect size of .08 (Tobler, 1992).

REFERENCES

References marked with an asterisk indicate studies included in the meta-analysis.

Ames, G. M., Grube, J. W., & Moore, R. S. (2000). Social control and workplace drinking norms: A comparison of two organizational cultures. *Journal of Studies on Alcohol, 61,* 203–219.

Ames, G. M., & Janes, C. (1990). Drinking, social networks, and the workplace: Results of an environmentally focused study. In P. M. Roman (Ed.), *Alcohol problem intervention in the workplace: Employee assistance programs and strategic alternatives* (pp. 95–111). New York: Quorum Books.

Ames, G. M., & Janes, C. (1992). A cultural approach to conceptualizing alcohol and the workplace. *Alcohol Health and Research World, 16,* 112–119.

Anderson, D., Brink, S., & Courtney, T. (1995). *Risks and their impact on medical costs.* Milwaukee, WI: Milliman & Robertson.

Anderson, D., Whitmer, W., Goetzel, R., Ozminkowski, R. J., Wasserman, J., & Serxner, S. (2000). The relationship between modifiable health risks and group-level health care expenditures. *American Journal of Health Promotion, 15,* 45–52.

Bacharach, S. B., Bamberger, P., & Sonnenstuhl, W. J. (in press). Driven to drink: Managerial control, work-related risk factors and employee drinking behavior. *Academy of Management Journal.*

Bamberger, P., & Sonnenstuhl, W. J. (1995). Peer referral networks and utilization of a union-based EAP. *Journal of Drug Issues, 25,* 291–312.

Bass, A. R., Rodabe, B., Delaplane-Harris, K., Schork, M. A., Kaufmann, R., McCann, D., Foxman, B., Fraser, W., & Cook, S. (1996). Employee drug use, demographic characteristics, work reactions, and absenteeism. *Journal of Occupational Health Psychology, 1,* 92–99.

Bell, S. N., Mangione, T. W., Howland, J., Levine, S., & Amick, B., III. (1996). Worksite barriers to the effective management of alcohol problems. *Journal of Occupational and Environmental Medicine, 38,* 1213–1219.

Bennett, J. B., & Lehman, W. E. K. (1995, September). *Job stress, teamwork, and drinking climates: Distinguishing cohesiveness from socializing.* Paper presented at Work, Stress and Health '95: Creating Healthier Workplaces, Washington, DC.

Bennett, J. B., & Lehman, W. E. K. (1997). Workplace drinking climate, stress, and problem indicators: Assessing the influence of teamwork (group cohesion). *Journal of Studies on Alcohol, 59,* 608–618.

Bennett, J. B., & Lehman, W. E. K. (1999). Exposure to problem coworkers and quality work practices: A case study of employee violence, sexual harassment, and substance abuse. *Work and Stress: An International Journal, 13,* 299–311.

*Bennett, J. B., & Lehman, W. E. K. (2001). Workplace substance abuse prevention and help seeking: Comparing a team-oriented and informational training. *Journal of Occupational Health Psychology, 6,* 243–254.

*Bennett, J. B., & Lehman, W. E. K. (2002). Supervisor tolerance-responsiveness to substance abuse and workplace prevention training: Use of a cognitive mapping tool. *Health Education Research, 17,* 27–42.

Blum, T., Fields, D. L., Milne, S. H., & Spell, C. S. (1994). The interrelations of drug testing with other human resource management practices and organizational characteristics. In S. Macdonald & P. M. Roman (Eds.), *Drug testing in the workplace: Research advances in alcohol and drug problems* (Vol. 11, pp. 279–302). New York: Plenum Press.

Boddington, N., Perry, D., Clements, I., Wetton, N., & McWhiter, J. (1999). A multi-level approach to community-focused training in drug education: Part 1—Working with parents, governors and school staff. *Health Education, 6,* 244–252.

Bray, R. M., Fairbank, J. A., & Marsden, M. E. (1999). Stress and substance use among military women and men. *American Journal of Drug and Alcohol Abuse, 25,* 239–256.

Bray, R. M., & Marsden, M. E. (2000). Trends in substance use among US military personnel: The impact of changing demographic composition. *Substance Use and Misuse, 25,* 949–969.

Brief, A. P., & Folger, R. G. (1992). The workplace as seen by two novices. *Alcoholism: Clinical and Experimental Research, 16,* 190–198.

Brink, S. (1987). *Health risks and behavior: The impact on medical costs.* Milwaukee, WI: Milliman & Robertson.

Bross, M. H., Pace, S. K., & Cronin, I. H. (1992). Chemical dependence: Analysis of work absenteeism and associated medical illnesses. *Journal of Occupational Medicine, 34,* 16–19.

Conrad, K., Furner, S., & Qian, Y. (1999). Occupational hazard exposure and at risk drinking. *Journal of the American Association of Occupational Health Nurses, 47,* 9–16.

*Cook, R. F., Back, A. S., & Trudeau, J. (1996a). Preventing alcohol use problems among blue-collar workers: A field test of the working people program. *Substance Use and Misuse, 31,* 255–275.

*Cook, R. F., Back, A., & Trudeau, J. (1996b). Substance abuse prevention in the workplace: Recent findings and an expanded conceptual model. *Journal of Primary Prevention, 16,* 319–339.

Cook, R., & Schlenger, W. (in press). Prevention of substance abuse in the workplace: Review of research on the delivery of services. *Journal of Primary Prevention.*

Cosper, R. (1979). Drinking as conformity: A critique of sociological literature on occupational differences in drinking. *Journal of Studies on Alcohol, 40,* 868–891.

Crouch, D. J., Webb, D. O., & Peterson, L. V. (1989). A critical evaluation of the Utah Power and Light Company's substance abuse management program: Absenteeism, accidents and costs. In S. W. Gust & J. M. Walsh (Eds.), *Drugs in the workplace: Research and evaluation data* (NIDA Research Monograph No. 91, DHHS Pub. No. ADM 89–1612). Rockville, MD: National Institute on Drug Abuse.

Crow, S. M., & Hartman, S. J. (1992). Drugs in the workplace: Overstating the problems and the cures. *Journal of Drug Issues, 22,* 923–937.

Dusenbury, L. (1999). Workplace drug abuse prevention initiatives: A review. *Journal of Primary Prevention, 20,* 145–156.

Ennet, S. T., Tobler, N. S., Ringwalt, C. L., & Flewelling, R. L. (1994). How effective is drug abuse resistance education? A meta-analysis of project DARE outcome evaluations. *American Journal of Public Health, 84,* 1394–1401.

Fillmore, K. M. (1990). Occupational drinking subcultures: An exploratory epidemiological study. In P. M. Roman (Ed.), *Alcohol problem intervention in the workplace: Employee assistance programs and strategic alternatives* (pp. 77–94). New York: Quorum Books.

Fisher, C. A., Hoffman, K. J., Austin-Lane, J., & Kao, T. (2000). The relationship between heavy alcohol use and work productivity loss in active duty military personnel: A secondary analysis of the 1995 Department of Defense Worldwide Survey. *Military Medicine, 165,* 355–361.

French, M. T., Zarkin, G. A., Hartwell T. D., &. Bray, J. W. (1995). Prevalence and consequences of smoking, alcohol use, and illicit drug use at five worksites. *Public Health Reports, 110,* 593–599.

Galaif, E. R., Newcomb, M. D., & Carmona, J. V. (2001). Prospective relationships between drug problems and work adjustment in a community sample of adults. *Journal of Applied Psychology, 86,* 337–350.

George, A. A., & Tucker, J. A. (1996). Help-seeking for alcohol-related problems: Social contexts surrounding entry into alcoholism treatment or alcoholics anonymous. *Journal of Studies on Alcohol, 57,* 449–457.

Goetzel, R. (Ed.). (2001). The financial impact of health promotion [Special issue]. *American Journal of Health Promotion, 15*(5).

Greenberg, E. R., Canzoneri, C., & Joe, A. (2000). *Workplace testing: Medical testing.* Retrieved April 2, 2002, from the American Management Association Web site: http://www.amanet.org/research/pdfs/medicl2.0.pdf

Greenberg, E. S., & Grunberg, L. (1995). Work alienation and problem alcohol behavior. *Journal of Health and Social Behavior, 36,* 83–102.

Hagihara, A., Tarumi, K., Miller, A. S., Nebeshima, F., & Nobutomo, K. (1999). Work stressors and alcohol consumption among white-collar workers: A signal detection approach. *Journal of Studies on Alcohol, 61,* 462–465.

*Heirich, M., & Sieck, C. J. (2000). Worksite cardiovascular wellness programs as a route to substance abuse prevention. *Journal of Occupational and Environmental Management, 42,* 47–56.

Hoffman, J., & Larison, C. (1999). Drug use, workplace accidents and employee turnover. *Journal of Drug Issues, 29,* 341–364.

Holcom, M. L., Lehman, W. E. K., & Simpson D. D. (1993). Employee accidents: Influences of personal characteristics, job characteristics, and substance use in jobs differing in accident potential. *Journal of Safety Research, 24,* 205–221.

Holder, H., Flay, B., Howard, J., Boyd, G., Voas, R., & Grossman, M. (1999). Phases of alcohol problem prevention research. *Alcoholism: Clinical and Experimental Research, 23,* 183–194.

Hood, J. C., & Duphorne, P. L. (1995). To report or not to report: Nurses' attitudes toward reporting co-workers suspected of substance abuse. *Journal of Drug Issues, 25,* 313–340.

Howland, J., Mangione, T. W., Kuhlthau, K., Bell, N., Heeren, T., Lee. M., & Levine, S. (1996). Work-site variation in managerial drinking. *Addiction, 91,* 1007–1017.

Kandel, D. B., & Yamaguchi, K. (1987). Job mobility and drug use: An event history analysis. *American Journal of Sociology, 92,* 836–878.

Kaskutas, L., Weisner, C., & Caetano, R. (1996). Predictors of help seeking among a longitudinal sample of the general population, 1984–1992. *Journal of Studies on Alcohol, 58,* 155–161.

Kessler, R. C., & Frank, R. G. (1997). The impact of psychiatric disorders on work loss days. *Psychological Medicine, 27,* 861–873.

*Kishchuk, N., Peters, C., Towers, A. M., Sylvestre, M., Bourgault, C., & Richard, L. (1994). Formative and effectiveness evaluation of a worksite program promoting healthy alcohol consumption. *American Journal of Health Promotion, 8,* 353–362.

Kjaerheim, K., Mykletun, R., Aasland, O. G., & Haldorsen, T. (1995). Heavy drinking in the restaurant business: The role of social modeling and structural factors of the work-place. *Addiction, 90,* 1487–1495.

*Kline, M. L., & Snow, D. L. (1994). Effects of a worksite coping skills intervention on the stress, social support, and health outcomes of working mothers. *Journal of Primary Prevention, 15,* 105–121.

Lehman, W. E. K., & Bennett, J. B. (2002). Job risk and employee substance use: The influence of personal background and work environment factors. *American Journal of Alcohol and Drug Abuse, 28,* 263–286.

Lehman, W. E. K., Farabee, D. J., Holcom, M. L., & Simpson, D. D. (1995). Prediction of substance use in the workplace: Unique contributions of personal background and work environment variables. *Journal of Drug Issues, 25,* 253–274.

Lehman, W. E. K., & Simpson, D. D. (1992). Employee substance use and on-the-job behaviors. *Journal of Applied Psychology, 77,* 309–321.

Lennox, R. D., Steele, P. D., Zarkin, G. A., & Bray, J. W. (1998). The differential effects of alcohol consumption and dependence on adverse alcohol-related consequences: Implications for the workforce. *Drug and Alcohol Dependence, 50,* 211–220.

Macdonald, S., & Roman, P. M. (Eds.). (1995). *Drug testing in the workplace.* New York: Plenum Press.

Mangione, T. W., Howland, J., Amick, B., Cote, J., Lee, M., Bell, N., & Levine, S. (1999). Employee drinking practices and work performance. *Journal of Studies on Alcohol, 60,* 261–270.

Mannello, T. A. (1979). *Problem drinking among railroad workers: Extent, impact, and solutions* (Monograph Series No. 4). Washington, DC: University Research Corporation.

Mensch, B. S., & Kandel, D. B. (1988). Do job conditions influence the use of drugs? *Journal of Health and Social Behavior, 29,* 169–184.

Mieczkowski, T. (1999). *Drug testing technology: Assessment of field applications.* Boca Raton, FL: CRC Press.

Milne, S. H., & Blum, T. C. (1998). Organizational characteristics of employer responses to employee substance abuse. *Journal of Management, 24,* 693–715.

Moore, S., Grunberg, L., & Greenberg, E. (2000). The relationship between alcohol problems and well-being, work attitudes, and performance: Are they monotonic? *Journal of Substance Abuse, 11,* 183–204.

Mrazek, P. J., & Haggerty, R. J. (Eds.). (1994). *Reducing risk for mental disorders: Frontiers for preventive intervention research.* Washington, DC: National Academy Press.

Newcomb, M. D. (1994). Prevalence of alcohol and other drug use on the job: Cause for concern or irrational hysteria? *Journal of Drug Issues, 24,* 403–417.

Normand, J., Lempert, R. O., & O'Brien, C. P. (1994). *Under the influence? Drugs and the American work force.* Washington, DC: National Academy Press.

Normand, J., Salyards, S. D., & Mahony, J. J. (1990). An evaluation of preemployment drug testing. *Journal of Applied Psychology, 75,* 629–639.

Perry, P. D., & Tobler, N. S. (1992). Meta-analysis of drug prevention programs: Final report. *Manual for effect size calculation: Formula used in the Meta-Analysis of adolescent drug prevention programs.* Rockville, MD: National Institute on Drug Abuse.

Polen, M. R., Green, C. A., Freeborn, D. K., Mullooly, J. P., & Lynch, F. (2001). Drinking patterns, health care utilization, and costs among HMO primary care patients. *Journal of Behavioral Health Services & Research, 28,* 378–399.

Quest Diagnostics (2000). Positive drug test results in 1999 decline to record low in Quest Diagnostics workplace drug testing index. Retrieved May 2, 2002, from http://www.questdiagnostics.com/brand/company/news/b_comp_news_0620b00.html

Ragland, D. R., Greiner, B. A., Yen, I. H., & Fisher, J. M. (2000). Occupational stress factors and alcohol-related behavior in urban transit operators. *Alcoholism: Clinical and Experimental Research, 24,* 1011–1019.

Reynolds, G. S., & Bennett, J. B. (2000). *Workplace training for prevention of substance abuse: A meta-analytic review.* Unpublished manuscript, Texas Christian University.

Reynolds, G. S., & Lehman, W. E. K. (2001). *Levels of substance use and employee willingness to use the EAP.* Manuscript submitted for publication.

Rice, C., Longabaugh, R., & Stout, R. L. (1997). A comparison sample validation of "Your Workplace": An instrument to measure perceived alcohol support and consequences from the work environment. *Addictive Behaviors, 22,* 711–722.

Roman, P. M. (1990). Strategic considerations in designing interventions to deal with alcohol problems in the workplace. In P. M. Roman (Ed.), *Alcohol problem intervention in the workplace: Employee assistance programs and strategic alternatives* (pp. 371–406). New York: Quorum Books.

Roman, P. M., & Blum, T. C. (1996). Alcohol: A review of the impact of worksite interventions on health and behavioral outcomes. *American Journal of Health Promotion, 11,* 136–149.

Roman, P. M., & Blum, T. C. (1999). Prevention in the workplace. In R. T. Ammerman, P. J. Ott, & R. E. Tarter (Eds.), *Prevention and societal impact of drug and alcohol abuse* (pp. 307–325). Mahwah, NJ: Erlbaum.

Rosenthal, R. N. (1991). *Meta-analytic procedures for social research. Applied social research methods series* (Vol. 6). Newbury Park, CA: Sage.

Shapiro, S., Skinner, E. A., Kessler, L. G., Von Korff, M., German, P. S., Tischler, G. L., et al. (1984). Utilization of health and mental health services: Three epidemiologic catchment area sites. *Archives of General Psychiatry, 41,* 971–978.

Sheridan, J. R., & Winkler, H. (1989). An evaluation of drug testing in the workplace. In S. W. Gust & J. M. Walsh (Eds.). *Drugs in the workplace: Research and evaluation data* (NIDA Research Monograph No. 91, DHHS Publication No. ADM 89-1612, pp. 195–218). Rockville, MD: National Institute on Drug Abuse.

*Snow, D. L. (1996). *A workplace intervention to address work and family stressors: Effects on coping and alcohol use.* Paper presented at the Conference on Research on Alcohol Problems in the Worksite: Moving toward Prevention Research. Washington, DC: National Institute on Alcohol Abuse and Alcoholism.

*Snow, D. L., & Kline, M. L. (1991). A worksite coping skills intervention : Effects on women's psychological symptomatology & substance use. *Community Psychologist, 24,* 14–17.

*Snow, D. L., & Kline, M. L. (1995). Preventive interventions in the workplace to reduce negative psychiatric consequences of work and family stress. In C. M. Mazure (Ed.), *Does stress cause psychiatric illness?* (pp. 221–270). Washington, DC: American Psychiatric Press.

Sonnenstuhl, W. J. (1996). *Working sober: The transformation of an occupational drinking culture.* Ithaca, NY: ILR Press/Cornell University Press.

Storr, C. L., Trinkoff, A. M., & Anthony, J. C. (1999). Job strain and non-medical drug use. *Drug and Alcohol Dependence, 55,* 45–51.

Substance Abuse and Mental Health Services Administration. (1997). *Guidelines and benchmarks for prevention programming* (DHHS Pub. No. SMA 95-3033). Rockville, MD: Center for Substance Abuse Prevention.

Substance Abuse and Mental Health Services Administration. (1999). *Worker drug use and workplace policies and programs: Results from the National Household Survey on Drug Abuse* (NHSDA). Retrieved May 3, 2002, from http://www.samhsa.gov/oas/NHSDA/A-11/TOC.htm

Substance Abuse and Mental Health Services Administration. (2001). *Summary of findings from the 2000 National Household Survey on Drug Abuse.* (Office of Applied Studies, NHSDA Series H-13, DHHS Pub. No. SMA 01-3549). Rockville, MD: Center for Substance Abuse Prevention. Retrieved May 3, 2002, from http://www.samhsa.gov/oas/NHSDA/2kNHSDA/2kNHSDA.htm

Tobler, N. S. (1992). *Meta-analysis of adolescent drug prevention programs: Final report.* Rockville, MD: National Institute on Drug Abuse.

Trice, H. M., & Sonnenstuhl, W. J. (1990). On the construction of drinking norms in work organizations. *Journal of Studies on Alcohol, 51,* 201–220.

Trinkoff, A. M., & Storr, C. L. (1998). Work schedule characteristics and substance use in nurses. *American Journal of Industrial Medicine, 34,* 266–271.

Walsh, D.C., Rudd, R. E., & Mangione, T. (1993). Researching and preventing alcohol problems at work: Toward an integrative model. *American Journal of Health Promotion, 7,* 289–295.

2

A WORKPLACE COPING-SKILLS INTERVENTION TO PREVENT ALCOHOL ABUSE

DAVID L. SNOW, SUZANNE C. SWAN, AND LEO WILTON

Nearly 8 million Americans experience alcohol abuse or dependence in any given 6-month period (Regier et al., 1984). In a study of alcohol consumption and dependence within the United States, 13.2% of working men and 5.9% of working women were classified as alcohol dependent (Harford, Parker, Grant, & Dawson, 1992). Daily drinking (more than 20 days in the past month) or heavy drinking occurs among at least 15% of full-time employees (Voss, 1989) and can be as high as 25% among some occupational groups (Taggart, 1989). Although men abuse alcohol to a greater extent than women do (Grant, 1997; Hanna & Grant, 1997), rates of lifetime use by men versus women are less discrepant among young adults than among older cohorts (Grant, 1997; Voss, 1989), a finding suggesting that differences in alcohol consumption between men and women may be narrowing.

The prevalence and severity of alcohol problems result in substantial direct and indirect social and economic costs in the workplace (Harford et al., 1992; Harwood, Napolitano, Kristiansen, & Collins, 1984). Yet, only 10% of people with a diagnosis of alcohol abuse or dependence in the previous 6 months seek treatment during that period (Shapiro et al., 1984). Given the enormous costs of alcohol abuse to organizations, on the one hand, and the reluctance of most people with alcohol problems to seek treatment, on the other, the development of alternative strategies to reach this population has gained some momentum. Locating such innovative programs in work settings makes it possible to reach large numbers of working adults, not only those who already abuse alcohol but also those at risk of developing problematic drinking behavior. The workplace offers the potential for implementing broad-based preventive interventions, and employers are increasingly motivated to offer such programs to their employees to address issues of decreased productivity, increased health care costs, and maintenance of an able work force in a tight labor market.

In this chapter we first present a model, central to prevention research and intervention, that focuses on the identification and modification of key risk and protective factors that influence such health-related behaviors and outcomes as alcohol use and abuse. We then summarize research linking selected risk and protective factors to alcohol use, namely work and work–family stressors, social support, and individual coping strategies. We then describe a workplace coping-skills intervention that is based on that model and present findings from two studies that examined the effects of the intervention on employee alcohol use. We conclude by discussing lessons learned and suggesting possible directions for future workplace research and intervention strategies.

RISK AND PROTECTIVE FACTORS

In the emerging field of prevention science, a core theoretical element is the notion of modifiable risk and protective factors (Coie et al., 1993; Reiss & Price, 1996). *Risk factors* are characteristics of both individuals and their environments that contribute to increased levels of psychological symptomatology and problem behaviors, such as alcohol and other drug (AOD) abuse. Risk-focused approaches to prevention aim to determine the factors that play an important role in the formation of a given problem and the processes through which they influence that problem. Those processes most likely involve interactions of individual and environmental characteristics that have various levels of influence, depending on the developmental, situational, and cultural contexts in which they occur (Hawkins, Catalano, & Miller, 1992; Reiss & Price, 1996). It is increasingly clear, however, that exposure to multiple risk factors increases total risk for serious psychological disorder or problem behavior and that the deleterious effects of risk factors are cumulative (Coie et al., 1993; Hawkins et al., 1992; Heller, 1996).

Protective factors are "those factors that modify, ameliorate, or alter a person's response to some environmental hazard that predisposes to a maladaptive outcome" (Rutter, 1985, p. 600). Exposure to risk can be mitigated by a variety of individual characteristics (e.g., active coping strategies, sense of self-efficacy and personal control) and social features (e.g., availability of social support; Coie et al., 1993). Protective factors operate to moderate or mediate the relationship between risk factors and outcomes and lead to reductions in risk. The focus on protective factors is particularly important in situations in which it is not possible to alter risk factors directly. For example, in the work setting, it may not be possible to reduce the level of job stressors affecting employees. If workers have a strong network of co-worker and supervisor support, however, the stressors may be less likely to lead to negative outcomes, such as increased alcohol use in an effort to reduce work-related tension. In such cases, protective factors have enhanced the employees' resilient responses to risk exposure (i.e., have increased their ability to withstand risk; Rutter, 1985).

Preventive interventions that are based on the knowledge derived from research on risk and protective factors are designed to eliminate or reduce risk factors and/or enhance protective factors, thereby mediating or moderating the effects of risk (Hawkins et al., 1992). Methods may involve individual, group, organizational, or community interventions and may be *universal* (i.e., directed at either all people within a given setting or community) or *targeted* (i.e., directed toward a high-risk subgroup). The effectiveness of the intervention is determined by the extent to which it results in modifications of designated risk and protective factors and leads to corresponding changes in maladaptive behavior.

RISK AND PROTECTIVE FACTORS RELATED TO ALCOHOL USE

Research on risk and protective factors in the workplace has focused considerable attention on determining the extent to which stressors, coping, and social support increase or mitigate the risk for alcohol use or abuse. Using a basic stress–social support–coping paradigm, this research is guided by the assumption that work and family stressors and avoidance coping strategies serve to increase risk, whereas social support and the use of active coping strategies operate as protective factors. This model is illustrated in Figure 2.1.

As depicted in the model, higher levels of work and family stressors predict greater alcohol use. In addition, higher stressor levels also lead to increased use of avoidance coping, which in turn predicts increased use of alcohol. By contrast, greater levels of social support both directly and indirectly reduce the likelihood of alcohol use by enhancing the use of active coping strategies and by decreasing the perception or experience of work

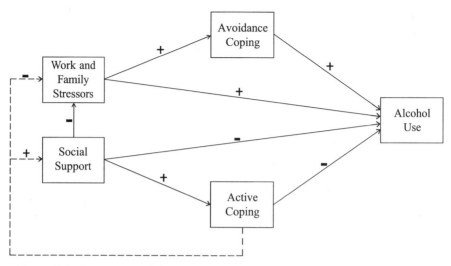

Figure 2.1. A stress–social support–coping model for predicting alcohol use.

and family stressors. Similarly, although increased use of active coping predicts reduced alcohol consumption, the use of active coping strategies is also instrumental over time in building and using social networks and in modifying stress-inducing conditions in work and family environments. The following sections summarize empirical evidence regarding the relationship of each major component of the model to alcohol use.

Work Stressors

Considerable research has been conducted on the impact of work-related stressors, such as workload, role conflict and ambiguity, time pressures, and role and organizational change, on alcohol use and abuse. This research has encompassed a wide range of occupational groups, work settings, and demographic characteristics (Ferguson, 1974; Kunda, 1992; Ragland, Greiner, Krause, Holman, & Fisher, 1995; Snow & Kline, 1995; Trice, 1992; Trice & Roman, 1971). A number of early studies in this area suggested a significant relationship between work stressors and the development of problem drinking (Parker & Farmer, 1988; Trice & Sonnenstuhl, 1988). Watts and Short (1990) found a relationship between job overload and alcohol use among a mostly female sample of teachers, and Mensch and Kandel (1988) reported that work pressure was associated with increased alcohol use, a relationship that held for men but not for women. Furthermore, higher work role conflict emerged as a significant correlate of increased alcohol use among both male and female managers (Havlovic & Keenan, 1991), and chronic strain from ongoing work circumstances and intermittent life events, coupled with high powerlessness, typified a sample of men most vulnerable to high drinking quantity and drinking problems such as drinking alone, missing work because of drinking, and morning drinking (Seeman & Seeman, 1992).

A number of recent studies have provided further evidence that people who experience increased levels of work-related stressors are at increased risk for engaging in alcohol use and abuse (Frone, Russell, & Cooper, 1995, 1997; Jasinski, Asdigian, & Kantor, 1998; Kjerheim, Haldorsen, Anderson, Mykletun, & Aasland, 1997; Steptoe et al., 1998). Role ambiguity and work pressure were associated with heavy alcohol use in a community sample of employed adults especially when the job role was important for self-identity (Frone et al., 1995). Work stressors emerged as a strong predictor of alcohol use among urban transit workers (Ragland et al., 1995). Further, participants believed both that alcohol use had a significant role in reducing stress and that increased levels of stress were directly related to AOD problems. Finally, a large study of employed men and women (Crum, Muntaner, Eaton, & Anthony, 1995) found that men in high-strain jobs were 27.5 times more likely to develop alcohol abuse or dependence and were at 3.4 times greater risk for an alcohol disorder than men in low-strain jobs. No increased risk was found for women in high-strain job categories.

Work–Family Stressors

Although research on the contribution of work stressors to alcohol use and abuse underscores the important role those risk factors play, the research evidence reflects a certain degree of inconsistency (e.g., in some studies, gender differences emerge), suggesting that a more complex set of factors needs to be taken into account. In this regard, models have been advanced to include stressors from family as well as work domains. As Snow and Kline (1995) wrote, "multiple-role occupancy increases the chances of experiencing higher levels of demand and of being exposed to a broader range of stressful conditions, as well as the potential for conflict between work and family domains" (p. 225). One such model (Greenhaus & Parasuraman, 1986) identifies three categories of stressors: job stressors, stressors related to conditions within nonwork domains, and stressors involving the interface of work and nonwork domains. All three types of stressors are viewed as having the potential to make unique contributions to well-being.

Given those models, therefore, much of what influences employees' drinking may be a result of factors outside the workplace or of the complex interplay of factors between work and nonwork domains (Hollinger, 1988; Parker & Brody, 1982). Drawing on those models, a growing body of literature suggests that factors in nonwork domains that involve the interface of work and family stressors contribute to alcohol use and abuse (Frone,

Russell, & Barnes, 1996; Frone, Russell, & Cooper, 1993; Frone et al., 1997; Moos, Fenn, Billings, & Moos, 1989). In a study of employed parents from two community samples (Frone et al., 1996), work–family conflict was significantly and positively related to increased levels of alcohol consumption, depression, and poor physical health. Work–family conflict also was positively related to heavy alcohol use at follow up in a 4-year longitudinal study of employed parents (Frone et al., 1997). Parker and Harford (1992) analyzed data on men and women from a national longitudinal survey and found interactions of job pressure and gender role attitudes related to increased alcohol consumption. Greater alcohol consumption was found with employed traditional women and egalitarian men who believe they have substantial obligations at home and who have high job competition. Other research supports the contention that the combination of work and family stressors contributes to increased alcohol use for both women (Cohen, Schwartz, Bromet, & Parkinson, 1991; Ehrensaft, 1980) and men (Bray, Fairbank, & Marsden, 1999).

Frone et al. (1993) examined the relationship between work–family conflict and alcohol abuse in relation to gender and tension reduction expectancies. They found that work–family conflict was associated with alcohol abuse among employees who believed that alcohol use results in relaxation and tension reduction. Gender was not found to be a moderating variable between work–family conflict and frequency of alcohol use. Finally, two types of work–family conflict—work impeding family and family impeding work—were related to high rates of alcohol use, depression, and poor physical health (Frone et al., 1996).

Social Support

Compared with the large body of research on work and work–family stressors and alcohol use, a relative dearth of literature systematically examines the role of social support. Although the findings typically are complex, the available research does suggest that social support can serve as a protective factor in relation to alcohol use and the development of problem drinking, at least with certain populations and under certain conditions. In a study examining the effects of work load and job social supports on alcohol use and other health outcomes (Steptoe et al., 1998), men but not women with poor social supports consumed a greater quantity of alcohol as work load increased. McCreary and Sadava (1998) studied two samples of men and women in their 20s and 30s and found some evidence that social support moderated the relationship between certain measures of life stress and alcohol use.

Whether the moderating effect of social support is found may require taking into account specific components of social support in relation to specific sources of life stress. Peirce, Frone, Russell, and Cooper (1996), for example, examined whether tangible support moderated the relationship between financial stress and alcohol use. Results supported the buffering influence of tangible support on the financial stress–alcohol use relationship. The combination of low workplace social support and low work control contributed to higher risk for later alcoholism among a sample of young, employed men (Hemmingsson & Lundberg, 1998). The findings of this study support the need to consider multiple factors when assessing the role of social support.

One such factor is whether the employee is embedded in a drinking subculture within his or her work setting or occupational group (Trice & Sonnenstuhl, 1988). If work is a primary source of social support and the norms of the group promote drinking, then social support from work may be related to increased drinking. In a study of hospitality managers, for example, Corsun and Young (1998) found compelling evidence for the presence of an occupational subculture whose norms promoted drinking. Similarly, high levels of involvement in work-related support networks were significantly correlated with heavy drinking and drinking problems, even when employees found work intrinsically rewarding (Seeman, Seeman, & Budros, 1988). The authors concluded that work-based social networks may encourage alcohol use and abuse.

Evidence of social support as a protective factor was found in two studies of problem drinkers. Late-onset problem drinkers reported fewer social resources than non-problem drinkers (Brennan & Moos, 1990), and support from family and friends had a positive impact on drinking-behavior outcomes (Humphreys, Moos, & Finney, 1996). Finally, social support also emerged as a protective factor in relation to alcohol use in samples of college students. First-year students who reported low levels of social support demonstrated high levels of use (Zaleski, Levey-Thors, & Schiaffino, 1998), and social support was found to moderate the stress–alcohol use relationship (Steptoe, Wardle, Pollard, & Canaan, 1996).

Coping Strategies

Research on the role of coping as a correlate or precursor of problem drinking provides support for the positive effects of active coping strategies and the particularly adverse effects of avoidance coping strategies. Laurent, Catanzaro, and Callan (1997) replicated Cooper, Russell, Skinner, Frone, and Mudar's (1992) stressor vulnerability model of adult drinking in a sample of adolescents and found a pattern of results similar to those of earlier studies of adults and undergraduates. The Cooper et al. model simultaneously assesses the stress-moderating effects of gender, expectancies, and coping on alcohol use and abuse. Generally, positive expectancies for alcohol use (i.e., the individual holds more favorable beliefs about the pharmacological and behavioral effects of drinking alcohol), avoidance coping, and level of stress were predictive of frequency of alcohol use, using alcohol as a coping method, and alcohol-related problems in routine activities (Laurent et al., 1997). Late-onset problem drinkers reported higher rates of avoidance coping than non-problem drinkers (Brennan & Moos, 1990), and male alcoholics followed over a 30-month period rated active coping strategies as more important in the maintenance of abstinence than other coping strategies (McKay, Maisto, & O'Farrell, 1996). Furthermore, greater reliance on active as opposed to avoidance coping in the first 3 months predicted better drinking outcomes during the next follow-up period.

In a longitudinal study of military officers (Johnsen, Laberg, & Eid, 1998), those who used avoidance-focused coping styles scored higher on problem drinking and showed increases in problem drinking over time. In a study of production workers (Grunberg, Moore, & Greenberg, 1998), employees exhibiting an escapist coping style engaged in alcohol use and believed that drinking alcohol was an effective way to reduce stress. By comparison, those who used nonescapist coping (i.e., a greater number of active coping strategies) engaged in lower frequencies of alcohol use and believed that alcohol was not an effective means to reduce stress.

A number of other researchers have reported a relationship between avoidance coping strategies and alcohol use. Cooper et al. (1992) found that stress was highly predictive of alcohol consumption and drinking problems in men who used avoidant forms of emotional coping. Nowack and Pentkowski (1994) found that women working in dental offices who reported higher frequencies of alcohol use were more likely than women who did not drink alcohol to use avoidance coping strategies in relation to work and personal obstacles. Finally, Snow and Kline (1991) found that avoidance coping was highly related to psychological symptomatology and increased use of alcohol and tobacco among female secretarial employees.

In summary, considerable research evidence links work and family stressors, social support, and coping to alcohol use and abuse. This knowledge forms the basis for designing workplace interventions aimed at preventing problem drinking. The next section describes an intervention that builds on a risk and protective factor model and emphasizes the modification of employee coping skills.

A WORKPLACE COPING-SKILLS INTERVENTION

The Yale Work and Family Stress Project has developed a workplace intervention that is based on a tripartite conceptual model of adaptive coping behavior: attacking the problem, rethinking the problem, and managing the stress. The model is derived from Pearlin and Schooler's (1978) hierarchy of coping mechanisms: (a) responses that change the situation,

(b) responses that control the meaning of the stressful experience, and (c) responses that function to control stress after it has emerged. The aim is to teach employees behavioral, social, and cognitive coping strategies for bringing about changes in risk and protective factors for alcohol use and abuse.

The interventions in the two studies summarized in this chapter are similar. In the first study (Snow & Kline, 1995), the intervention consisted of 15 sessions, each lasting 1.5 hours, conducted at the workplace during regular work hours. The major program components of the intervention were aimed at reducing work and family stressors and the use of avoidant coping strategies while enhancing social support and the use of active behavioral, social, and cognitive coping strategies. A detailed description of the intervention used in the first study can be found in Snow and Kline (1995).

Although the major program components of the second study were the same as those of the first study, the intervention was modified in two ways: First, the intervention was increased to 16 sessions, and second, several sessions were redesigned to teach behaviors aimed more directly at decreasing AOD use as a means of stress reduction.

The first component of the intervention (sessions 1–4 and 6–9) focused on teaching employees ways to eliminate or modify the sources of stress so that the ongoing need to cope with a particular stressor was reduced. This part of the curriculum included training on the identification and analysis of stressful situations and effective problem solving (e.g., effective communication is a problem-solving skill that can change the external demands on a person and thereby modify stress at the source). An additional theme was social support and the variety of material, emotional, and instrumental benefits that people can derive from a well-developed social network.

The second component (sessions 10–11) taught techniques that do not eliminate stressors, but help modify the cognitive and appraisal processes that lead to or exacerbate the experience of stress. Such approaches are particularly necessary for stressors that cannot be directly modified. Cognitive restructuring and other methods that change how a problem is assessed and understood were central to this component.

The third component (sessions 5 and 12–15) emphasized stress management and included strategies that moderate the psychophysiological impact of stress, such as deep breathing and progressive relaxation, as well as those aimed at minimizing or eliminating the use of avoidance coping responses. Stress management techniques were taught in session 5 and were practiced for a few minutes at the beginning of each subsequent session for reinforcement purposes. The other four sessions in this component (i.e., sessions 12–15) covered alternatives to using substances to manage stress, how to identify the misuse of substances for stress reduction purposes, and effective ways of resisting AOD use.

The curriculum emphasized the development and application of skills to meet the demands encountered in employees' work and family environments. The final session of the intervention (session 16) integrated the course material by helping participants create personal stress management plans. Participants were to continue to use their plan following the completion of the intervention to extend and maintain positive program effects. A session-by-session description of this intervention is presented in Exhibit 2.1.

COPING WITH WORK AND FAMILY STRESS: STUDY 1

This first study (Snow & Kline, 1991, 1995) investigated the effectiveness of a work-based coping-skills intervention in reducing the negative psychological and behavioral consequences of work and family stressors among female secretarial employees. It was hypothesized that employees who participated in the intervention, compared with no-treatment control individuals, would report at posttest and 6-month follow up (a) lower levels of employee role, family role, and work–family stressors; (b) higher perceived social support from work and nonwork sources; (c) lower avoidance and higher behavioral and cognitive coping; and (d) lower alcohol use.

Implementation of Coping-Skills Intervention

Participants were 239 female secretarial employees at one of four job sites in Connecticut-based corporations. Site 1 was a large manufacturing company; sites 2, 3, and 4 were components of utility and telecommunications companies. Of the original sample, 136 employees participated in the intervention, and 103 served as control participants. The sample was predominantly White (83%), had completed high school or vocational training (43%) or some college (46%), had worked in the company an average of 9.4 years, and had an annual family income ranging from less than $30,000 (37%) to more than $50,000 (36%). The mean age was 40.2 years, and about half (53%) of the women had children living at home.

The posttest sample (Time 2) consisted of 205 employees, or 85.8% of the original sample. Of that number, 125 employees participated in the intervention, and 80 served as control participants. The sample at 6-month follow up (Time 3) consisted of 185 employees (77.4% of the original sample). Of those employees, 110 were intervention participants, and 75 were control participants. The proportions of intervention and control participants across each of the demographic categories remained relatively constant across all three time periods.

EXHIBIT 2.1
Managing Work and Family Stress: A Coping-Skills Intervention

Session 1. *Understanding Stress: Multiple Roles and the Stress Cycle*
Participants identify the diverse roles they assume and the kinds of pressures they face while attempting to meet the demands of each role. The causes, symptoms, and possible consequences of stress faced by working women and men are examined.

Session 2. *Solving the Problem: Examining Stressful Situations*
Participants identify problem situations from their own experiences. They learn to analyze problems as the first step in mastering them by utilizing their own individual resources as well as those of a supportive group.

Session 3. *Solving the Problem: Eight Steps*
Procedures for rational problem solving are learned and practiced. As a group, participants generate various problem-solving strategies and consider the potential costs and benefits of those strategies.

Session 4. *Solving the Problem: Using Personal Networks*
Participants consider "significant others" and members of their social networks as sources of support in time of need. Enhancement of personal networks, the costs and benefits of social support, and the group mobilization process are discussed.

Session 5. *Managing Your Stress: Deep Breathing and Muscle Relaxation*
Deep breathing and muscle relaxation are used to ameliorate the physical and psychological impact of stress. Ongoing practice of these techniques continues throughout the program so that participants will become reasonably expert with them.

Session 6. *Solving the Problem: Listening*
The benefits and elements of effective communication are discussed. Participants focus on paraphrasing and empathic responding as essential skills for resolving problems in work and related situations.

Session 7. *Solving the Problem: Responding*
Ineffective methods of communication are reviewed. Participants focus on I messages as a tool of successful problem resolution.

Session 8. *Solving the Problem: Assertive Communication*
Participants discuss the different styles of communication and learn to express their needs directly, effectively, and assertively. These skills are critical in identifying and overcoming barriers and in attacking the problem at its source.

Session 9. *Solving the Problem: Communicating for Change*
All the communication skills are brought together and practiced as means for changing conditions that may cause difficulties and stress for the individual.

Session 10. *Rethinking the Problem: Stress Reassessment*
The way one thinks about a situation often influences the severity of the stress experienced. Participants examine effective and ineffective assessment styles and practice ways of rethinking the problem.

Session 11. *Rethinking the Problem: Self-Talk*
Participants share the ways in which they have thought through recent personal situations and examine how those thoughts have influenced their self-esteem. Alternative ways of thinking about these situations are considered. Self-monitoring is introduced.

Exhibit continues

EXHIBIT 2.1 (*Continued*)

Session 12. *Managing Your Stress: Eating Patterns and Exercise*
Participants explore ways in which their eating and exercise patterns affect their individual stress levels. Participants develop exercise programs appropriate to their lifestyles.

Session 13. *Managing Your Stress: The Chemical Dependency Cycle*
Participants learn how substance use can turn to substance abuse when used as a coping strategy for stress management. After the chemical dependency cycle is examined, participants learn to identify their own social cues, triggers, and urges.

Session 14. *Managing Your Stress: Self-Monitoring*
Participants review self-monitoring and set revised, realistic goals to change their patterns and habits. Barriers to achieving these goals are discussed. Refusal techniques are practiced in small groups.

Session 15. *Managing Your Stress: Using Social Supports*
Participants learn about enabling behavior in the chemical dependency cycle. Strategies for strengthening and expanding social supports are explored.

Session 16. *Finding Your Plan: Personal Stress Management*
Problem solving, rethinking the problem, and stress-management techniques are integrated as participants consider the costs and benefits of applying each strategy to situations drawn from their own family and work experiences. A systematic procedure for choosing among these options is introduced. Participants review their accomplishments and create a personal stress management plan to follow after completion of the program. Implementation of this plan in gradual steps is discussed.

Participants were recruited first by circulating a program description to all eligible employees within each workplace inviting their participation. It was explained that half of those who volunteered would be randomly selected to receive the intervention and half would serve as control participants. It also was explained that all participants would complete a set of research measures prior to and at the completion of the intervention (4 months later) and at 6- and 22-month follow-up periods. Employees who volunteered signed a consent form and were randomly assigned within each site to the program or control conditions. The number of program and control participants as cited above (136 vs. 103) is not equal because a number of individuals assigned to the control condition withdrew from the study prior to the initial assessment once they learned they had not been assigned to the coping-skills intervention. Following the completion of Time 1 measures, program participants met in small, facilitator-led groups of approximately 10 to 12 employees for 1.5 hours each week for 15 weeks. Sessions were held at the company site and took place during work hours; each company provided release time to support employee participation.

At Time 1 (pretest), participants completed the Work and Family Stress Questionnaire, a self-report instrument that included sections on demographic information; family history of health problems; and assessments of stressors, coping, social support, psychological symptoms, and sub-stance use. The same instrument, omitting the demographic and family history items, was readministered at Time 2 (following completion of the intervention) and at the two follow-up periods. The study presented in this chapter involves the work and family stressor, coping, social support, and alcohol use variables; therefore, only those measures are discussed below. Please refer to Snow and Kline (1995) for a more extensive description of measures used in the larger study.

Work–Family Stressors

Three role stressor variables were obtained using the 48-item Role Quality Scale (Baruch & Barnett, 1986). Respondents rated the extent to which their roles as employee (e.g., "having too much to do"), spouse or partner (e.g., "conflict over housework"), and parent (e.g., "problem with children's education/school") were a source of concern or demand for them. The internal reliability of the subscales (Cronbach's α) ranges from .71 to .94 (Baruch & Barnett, 1986). The work–family stressor variable (4 items) was derived from items developed specifically for this project (α = .81). Those items (e.g., "Considering your different roles, how often do the things you do add up to being just too much?") assessed the extent to which demands from work and family were perceived as too extensive, conflictual, or overlapping.

Coping

The Health and Daily Living Form (Billings & Moos, 1982) was used to assess participants' coping strategies for addressing problem situations or events. This 33-item instrument, consisting of three subscales, provided an indication of the extent to which participants used behavioral, cognitive, and avoidant coping strategies.

Social Support

Work and nonwork social support were assessed using an adaptation of House's (1980) measure of perceived social support. Participants rated the extent to which their supervisor, coworkers, spouse or partner, family, and friends were perceived as supportive regarding difficulties both at home and at work (e.g., "How much can each of these people be relied on when things get tough at work?"). Social support from supervisor and coworkers was combined to create a measure of social support from work sources (α = .88), whereas support from spouse or partner, family, and friends was combined to create a measure of social support from nonwork sources (α = .90).

Alcohol Use

Current alcohol use was assessed using a self-report form adapted from the National Household Survey on Drug Abuse (Miller et al., 1982). Participants were asked to indicate both the frequency and the amount of use of AODs in the past 30 days. Total alcohol use was derived by multiplying the number of days in the past month the respondent reported drinking alcohol times the average number of drinks consumed on a given day when drinking occurred. In addition, one avoidance coping item (i.e., "I tried to reduce tension by drinking alcoholic beverages") from the Health and Daily Living Form was used to assess the extent to which participants used alcohol as a means of reducing tension.

Intervention Effectiveness

A relatively high level of participation in the intervention was attained. Employees completed an average of 11.7 (*SD* = 3.7) sessions. To be included in the analysis, an employee had to participate in at least 10 sessions; participants who fell below 10 sessions missed a significant portion of the intervention and did not learn many of the important skills being taught in the program. Including them could confound a true test of intervention effectiveness. Employees not reaching criterion were categorized as dropouts and were included in subsequent attrition analyses to assess threats to external and internal validity. A total of 85.2% of intervention participants completed 10 or more sessions (*M* = 13.1, *SD* = 1.4), and 14.8% attended 9 or fewer sessions (*M* = 4.4, *SD* = 3.2).

Comparisons between the intervention and control groups were made at posttest and 6-month follow up using repeated-measures analysis of variance (ANOVA).[1] Time × Condition interaction effects for both Time 1

---

[1] Repeated-measures ANOVA is a statistical procedure for evaluating treatment effects when a study uses a mixed design in which participants are randomly assigned to treatment condition and assessed longitudinally at pretest, posttest, and follow up. Critics of this approach to analysis of longitudinal treatment research have suggested that such data rarely conform to the assumptions of compound symmetry or sphericity (e.g., Gibbons et al., 1993). Compound symmetry refers to the homogeneity of variances and covariances across all time points; sphericity is a less restrictive situation requiring that variances be homogeneous. Girden (1992) notes that sphericity is the primary concern in using the repeated-measures ANOVA procedure, and describes a number of corrections to the univariate *F* test in the repeated-measures ANOVA procedures when the data violate this assumption. The Greenhouse–Geisser (1959) and Huynh–Feldt adjustments provide epsilon adjustments to the degrees of freedom prior to computing *F*-test significance levels when longitudinal data do not meet the assumption of sphericity. The Greenhouse–Geisser adjustment may be overly conservative when epsilon is between 1 and .75 (Girden, 1992); in such instances, the Huynh–Feldt adjustment is preferred (Huynh & Feldt, 1976; Ott, 1988). Epsilon adjustments reduce power to detect treatment effects, but they help protect the validity of the significance test when violations of sphericity occur in the repeated-measures ANOVA design. The epsilon values for the Greenhouse–Geisser and Huynh–Feldt procedures were in the range of .89 to 1.00 in the analyses, revealing positive intervention effects in Study 1. Use of either procedure to adjust the degrees of freedom did not alter the basic nature of the findings reported.

TABLE 2.1
Summary of Time × Condition Interaction Effects Comparing Intervention and Control Conditions from Pretest (Time 1) to Posttest (Time 2) and from Pretest (Time 1) to 6-Month Follow Up (Time 3) in Study 1

Variable	Time 1 to Time 2			Time 1 to Time 3		
	df	F	p	df	F	p
Stressor						
Employee role	1,155	4.35	.039	1,155	1.73	.191
Spouse/partner role	1,98	0.13	.718	1,98	1.09	.300
Parent role	1,79	0.13	.722	1,79	1.19	.279
Work/family	1,149	1.34	.248	1,149	3.00	.085
Social Support						
Nonwork sources	1,144	1.59	.210	1,144	0.29	.592
Work sources	1,146	6.44	.012	1,146	5.87	.017
Coping						
Behavioral	1,136	2.26	.135	1,136	2.92	.090
Cognitive	1,136	0.30	.586	1,136	0.35	.558
Avoidance	1,130	3.53	.062	1,130	5.94	.016
Alcohol Use						
No. drinks per month	1,158	0.47	.877	1,158	4.10	.045
Drink to reduce tension	1,130	1.34	.249	1,130	3.38	.068

Note. $N = 160$ (intervention $n = 96$; control $n = 64$).

to Time 2 (i.e., pretest to posttest) and Time 1 to Time 3 (i.e., pretest to 6-month follow up) were examined to determine whether greater positive changes occurred over time for the intervention group than for the control group in the stressor, social support, coping, and alcohol use variables. A summary of the F tests and significance levels for the interaction effects is shown in Table 2.1.

The intervention had limited effects on the stressor variables. Intervention participants did report a significantly greater decrease in employee role stressors from Time 1 to Time 2, although the Time 1 to Time 3 comparison indicated that by 6-month follow up, this interaction effect was no longer significant (see Figure 2.2). No effect on work–family stressors was observed from pretest to posttest, but a greater decrease in reported work–family stressors occurred for the intervention group than for the control group by 6-month follow up; this effect did not reach statistical significance. No interaction effects were observed for spouse or partner role or for parent role stressors for either time period.

Regarding the social support variables, significant Time × Condition interaction effects were observed across both time periods for social support from work. As shown in Figure 2.2, intervention participants reported an increase in social support from work from Time 1 to Time 2, an effect that was maintained at 6-month follow up. Control participants, by comparison, indicated a slight decrease in support by Time 2 and an even further decline

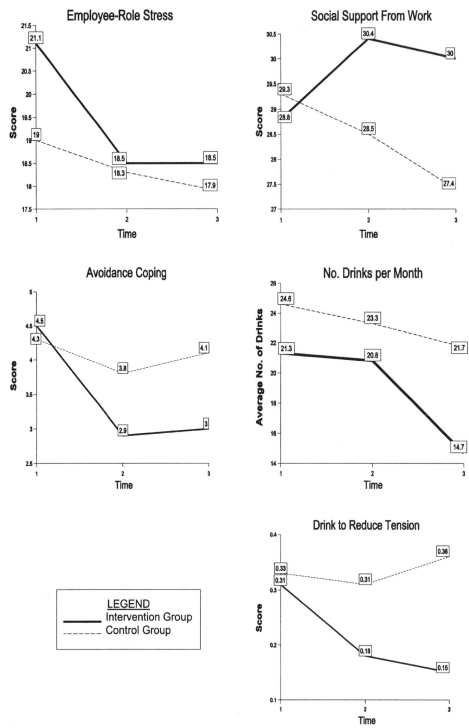

Figure 2.2. Comparisons between intervention and control groups on stressors, social support, coping, and alcohol use at Time 1, Time 2, and Time 3 for the Time × Condition interaction effects observed in Study 1.

by 6-month follow up. No effects were observed for social support from home.

The most substantial impact of the intervention on coping occurred in relation to avoidance coping. At posttest, intervention participants showed a greater decrease in the use of avoidance coping strategies than did control participants, an interaction effect that only approached significance. By 6-month follow up, however, the Time × Condition interaction effect was significant. Intervention participants continued to show the same reduction in use of avoidance coping strategies at 6-month follow up that they had reported at posttest, whereas control participants had returned to the level reported at pretest. The Time × Condition interaction for avoidance coping is also illustrated in Figure 2.2. No significant interaction effects were observed for behavioral or cognitive coping, although the changes in behavioral coping were in the predicted direction by 6-month follow up.

The effects of the intervention on alcohol use were examined in relation to two variables: number of drinks consumed in the past month and the extent to which participants used alcohol to reduce tension. For drinking in the past month, the Time × Condition interaction effect for Time 1 to Time 2 was not significant; both intervention and control participants showed little change between pretest and posttest. The interaction effect at 6-month follow up was significant, however. As shown in Figure 2.2, the extent of alcohol use in the past month among control group participants declined only modestly from pretest to 6-month follow up (declining by 2.9 drinks per month), whereas intervention participants reported a more substantial decrease in alcohol use (a decline of 6.6 drinks per month). The reduction in use primarily occurred during the 6-month period following the intervention.

The intervention showed some positive influence at 6-month follow up on participants' use of alcohol to reduce tension, although the effect did not reach statistical significance. As shown in Figure 2.2, intervention participants made less use of alcohol to reduce tension by posttest and even less use by 6-month follow up. By contrast, control participants' use of alcohol to reduce tension actually increased slightly by 6-month follow up compared with their baseline level.

Attrition Analyses

The attrition rate in this study was 14.6% at posttest and 22.6% at 6-month follow up. A significantly higher rate of attrition occurred in the control group (22.3%) than in the intervention condition (8.8%) at posttest (χ^2 = 8.55, df = 1, p = .003), but that difference did not occur at 6-month follow up. To assess potential threats to external validity, stayers and dropouts were compared at posttest and 6-month follow up on the demographic variables and on mean pretest levels for the stressor, social support, coping, and alcohol use variables. To test for potential threats to internal validity, MANOVAs were conducted using pretest scores on the study variables to assess Condition × Attrition Status interactions.

Stayers and dropouts did not differ significantly along any of the dimensions at posttest. At 6-month follow up, dropouts reported a higher level of work–family stressors, $F(1,235) = 3.42$, $p < .07$, and lower social support from work sources, $F(1,235) = 9.20$, $p < .01$, at pretest than stayers. No Condition × Attrition Status interactions were significant.

Summary and Implications of Findings

Among this sample of female secretarial employees, results suggest that the intervention helped women cope more effectively with work and family sources of stress and reduce their use of alcohol. One of the strongest effects of the intervention was on women's perceptions of social support received from their supervisors and coworkers. The structure of the intervention, in which women learned new skills and shared experiences and strategies with coworkers in small groups, likely contributed to the sustained increase women reported in social support from others in the workplace. Women who participated in the intervention reported greater social support from work than the control women did, not only just after completion of the intervention (which might be expected on the basis of their weekly group participation) but 6 months later as well. Apparently, processes had been put into effect within the workplace that helped maintain an increased level of social support over time.

The intervention also had beneficial effects in modifying participants' coping strategies. Those effects were most evident in the significant decrease in program participants' use of avoidance coping. Intervention participants also reported greater use of behavioral coping strategies, although the effect did not reach significance; the difference emerged at 6-month follow up. No effects of the intervention were found for cognitive coping. The results likely reflect differences in emphasis inherent in the intervention itself. Within the curriculum, greater attention was paid to reducing the use of avoidance coping and encouraging the use of active, behavioral coping strategies; cognitive coping strategies were less strongly emphasized. In addition, it may be more difficult, in general, to enhance participants' use of cognitive coping strategies than to modify their use of avoidant and behavioral strategies. The positive intervention effects observed were encouraging, especially given the extensive evidence identifying avoidance coping as a risk factor for alcohol abuse as well as the indications that active coping strategies, such as behavioral coping, serve a protective function.

Women who participated in the intervention also consumed significantly less alcohol than control women. Six months after the intervention ended, women in the intervention group consumed 15 drinks per month —a 29% decrease from the number of drinks they reported at pretest. In addition, the intervention had a positive effect in that it decreased the reliance on alcohol to reduce tension, although this finding did not reach significance. Interestingly, the effects became evident not at posttest, but during the 6-month period following the completion of the intervention.

Compared with reductions in drinking behavior, the intervention was less effective in modifying work and family stressors, although participants did show less employee role stress at posttest than did control individuals. Company support for the intervention and its provision of release time to participate may have contributed to the reduction in reported role stress by the completion of the intervention. At 6-month follow up, a positive but nonsignificant effect was observed for work–family stressors with intervention participants reporting less work–family stress than control individuals. The initial intervention effect of reducing employee role stress had dissipated by 6-month follow up, however. Following the intervention, employees may have found conditions related to their work relatively unchanged or discovered that they were unable to maintain changes introduced during the intervention phase. The findings suggest that the ability of individuals to make lasting changes in stressful conditions in work and family environments have certain inherent limitations. To complement individual-level efforts, workplace interventions most likely need to include components that address organization- and system-level sources of stress.

No intervention effects were observed for the other two family role stressor variables: spouse and partner role stress and parent role stress. In addition, the intervention did not help participants increase the social support they received from people outside of work. To bring about reductions in stress across both family and work domains, interventions may need to include other family members in certain components as well as focus on how to effectively manage multiple, overlapping work and family roles.

Many of the positive effects of the intervention (e.g., increased social support from work and decreased use of avoidance coping) were evident at posttest and were maintained 6 months later. This pattern of maintained effects speaks to the strength of the intervention. Other positive effects (e.g., reduced drinking, increased behavioral coping, and a reduction in work–family stress) occurred not immediately following the intervention, but 6 months afterward. The results suggest that employees require time to learn, practice, and reinforce new skills and that a relatively extensive program (15 weeks, in this case) may be necessary to bring about desired changes.

The attrition analyses support the validity of the observed results, and only limited restrictions apply to the generalizability of the findings at 6-

month follow up. The greater attrition in the control group (22.3%) than in the intervention group (8.8%) at posttest suggests that participants may have been more motivated to stay in the study because they found the intervention helpful. The control group participants, who were simply filling out measures, may have been more likely to withdraw because the study was not benefiting them personally. The results provide support for the model that guided the investigation and suggest that interventions aimed at modifying risk and protective factors can lead to positive changes in problem behaviors such as alcohol abuse.

COPING WITH WORK AND FAMILY STRESS: STUDY 2

The second study built on the initial investigation in a number of ways. First, the basic aim continued to be the modification of selected risk and protective factors through the implementation of a workplace coping-skills intervention. Certain refinements were made to the original intervention, however, so that direct attention was paid to changing employees' drinking behavior and discouraging the use of alcohol for stress management purposes. Second, the intervention again focused on helping employees develop a range of active coping strategies and discouraging the use of avoidance strategies for addressing stressors in both work and family domains. Third, because a primary objective of the intervention was to create substantive change in employees' abilities to manage work and family stressors through the acquisition of coping skills, an attention control condition was included to help determine whether a specific focus on coping-skills enhancement, rather than simply providing release time, attention, or information, was a necessary ingredient to producing changes in outcomes such as alcohol use.

Therefore, three groups were compared in the second study: a 16-session coping-skills intervention group, an 8-session attention control group, and a no-treatment control condition. Both condition and worksite were included as independent variables in a series of analyses that examined the immediate effects of the intervention at posttest (i.e., at the completion of the intervention) on the various risk- and protective-factor variables and on participants' alcohol use. Worksite was included in the analyses because of evidence that setting characteristics (e.g., tasks, processes, structures, and cultures) contribute uniquely to drinking behavior (Howland et al., 1996; Plant, 1979; Trice & Sonnenstuhl, 1988). It was of interest, therefore, to determine whether intervention effects were consistent across settings or whether worksite interacted with treatment conditions to produce differential outcomes. In addition, a subgroup of heavy alcohol users was examined to see how the intervention affected employees particularly at risk for alcohol-related problems. Given the high rate of attrition in the attention control condition (discussed below), it was not possible to conduct 6-month follow-up analyses. Data imputation methods will be used at a later time to assess long-term program effects. For the present analyses, it was hypothesized that participants in the coping-skills intervention, compared with the attention control and no-treatment control conditions, would report the following outcomes at posttest: (a) lower levels of employee role, family role, and work–family stressors; (b) higher perceived social support from work and nonwork sources; (c) greater use of active coping and less use of avoidance coping strategies; and (d) lower alcohol use and fewer indications of problem drinking. Although it was expected that the effects would hold across worksites, it was possible that certain of the effects would be stronger in some settings than in others.

Implementation of Coping-Skills Intervention and Attention Control Group

The participants were 468 male and female employees working at one of three sites in Connecticut: two large water authority companies and one manufacturing plant. The sample consisted of a cross-section of all occupational groups represented in the sites, including managerial and supervisory employees, plant and field workers, and secretarial and other support staff. Of the original sample, 171 employees participated in the coping-skills intervention, 174 participated in the attention control condition, and 123 served as control participants. The sample was predominantly White (89%) and was relatively well educated. The smallest proportion had completed high school or vocational training (18%), about a quarter had attended some college (26%), and more than half had completed college or beyond (57%). Most participants were male (71%); 11% were age 30 and younger, 37% were age 31 to 40 years, 28% were age 41 to 50, and 24% were older than age 50. The smallest proportion of participants (5%) had annual family income of less than $30,000; 28% had family incomes between $30,000 and $50,000, and 67% had family incomes of more than $50,000. Most participants were Catholic (57%); others indicated Protestant religion (27%) or other/no religious affiliation (16%). The majority were married or living with a partner (80%) and had one or more children living at home (58%).

The posttest sample (Time 2) consisted of 340 employees, representing 72.6% of the original sample. Of this number, 124 employees had participated in the intervention, 96 were in the attention control condition, and 120 were in the no-treatment control group. No significant differences were found on any of the demographic variables among the three conditions at either pretest or posttest.

Meetings were scheduled with groups of employees to present a description of the two programs being offered and their potential benefits and to invite employees to participate. The companies had already communicated their endorsement of the programs and that release time would be provided during regular work hours to facilitate employee participation. Discussions were conducted in such a way as not to reveal the essential differences between the coping-skills intervention and the attention control condition, but to present both options as interesting and potentially useful. It was explained that participants would fill out a questionnaire at four points in time: prior to and following the implementation of the two programs and at 6- and 12-month follow-up periods. Procedures to be followed to guarantee confidentiality and consent forms to be signed were carefully reviewed. Employees understood that assignment to the three conditions would be done on a random or lottery basis so that among those who volunteered, one-third would participate in each of the two programs and one-third would only be asked to complete the questionnaires. As in Study 1, the no-treatment control group had fewer participants than the other two conditions because a number of employees initially assigned to the control group indicated that they did not wish to remain in the study once they learned they would not be able to participate in one of the two programs being offered.

Program participants met at the company site in small, facilitator-led groups of approximately 10 to 12 employees. Participants in the coping-skills intervention met for 1.5 hours each week for a 16-week period. Those assigned to the attention control condition met for eight 1.5-hour sessions offered every other week . This schedule was used so that the span of time for the two programs and the time of testing were consistent across conditions. The attention control condition was limited to 8 sessions for two reasons. First, it was difficult to convince companies to provide 16 weeks of release time for more employees. Second, developing meaningful sessions for what was meant to serve as an "attention placebo" condition proved difficult, so that offering more than 8 sessions did not seem advisable. The 8-session program itself began with a description of a stress model and the identification of stress symptoms. Physical, psychological, and behavioral stress responses were described, and the social and economic costs of stress were examined. The next five sessions provided information about various patterns of substance use (including food, alcohol, and drugs) and how various substances affect physiological functioning. The seventh and eighth sessions provided information about sources of work and family stress, respectively. Types and sources of conflict were emphasized, but specific approaches to addressing work and family stressors were not included. In this way, specific stress management techniques and coping skills were not introduced or rehearsed. A general discussion of available community-based resources was conducted in the final session.

At both pretest and posttest, participants completed a modified version of the Work and Family Stress Questionnaire used in Study 1. The stressor, social support, and current alcohol use measures used in Study 2 were the same as those used in the initial study, but two changes were introduced. First, the Alcohol Use Disorders Identification Test (AUDIT; Babor & Grant, 1989; Babor, de la Fuente, Saunders, & Grant, 1989) was included to provide a broad assessment of problem-drinking behavior. The AUDIT is a 10-item screening test that was developed to detect problem-drinking behavior. In constructing and cross-validating the scale, particular attention was given to choosing items that could identify individuals at the midrange of severity; therefore, the AUDIT is suited to detecting people at risk for developing alcohol problems as well as those who are already abusing alcohol. Both the reliability of the instrument and its validity are well established (Babor et al., 1989).

Second, the Coping Strategies Inventory (Tobin, Holroyd, Reynolds, & Wigal, 1989) was administered because the psychometric properties of this instrument are superior to those reported for the Health and Daily Living Form used in Study 1. The instrument comprises eight subscales, which together allow a detailed determination of the types of changes in coping strategies that might occur as a result of participation in the intervention. Six subscales were included: Problem Solving (α = .82), Cognitive Restructuring (α = .83), and Social Support (α = .89) were treated as indexes of active coping strategies, and Problem Avoidance (α = .72), Wishful Thinking (α = .78), and Social Withdrawal (α = .81) were treated as indexes of avoidance coping strategies.

Intervention Effectiveness

A reasonably high level of participation in the intervention was attained, although somewhat lower than that of Study 1. Employees were included in the analysis if they participated in more than 50% of the intervention or attention control group sessions. Participants in the 16-session, coping-skills intervention completed an average of 10.8 sessions (SD = 4.7); 71.9% of the employees completed 9 or more sessions (M = 13.2, SD = 2.0), and 28.1% completed 8 or fewer sessions (M = 3.7, SD = 2.6). For the 8-session, attention control condition, the participation rate was lower. Participants completed an average of 4.6 sessions (SD = 2.6), and 54.0% of the employees completed 5 or more sessions (M = 6.7, SD = 1.1); 46.0% completed 4 or fewer sessions (M = 2.1, SD = 1.4). The control group maintained a high level of participation in the study: 95.9% of the sample completed the assessment at posttest.

Comparisons among the three conditions were made at posttest using repeated-measures ANOVA with time, condition, and worksite as the independent variables. The analyses were conducted for both the total sample and for a subgroup of alcohol users who scored above the mean on total drinks per month. This approach allowed comparison of program effects

TABLE 2.2

Summary of Time × Condition Interaction Effects Comparing
Intervention, Attention-Control, and No-Treatment Control Conditions
from Pretest (Time 1) to Posttest (Time 2) for Total Sample and
Subsample of Heavier Alcohol Users in Study 2

Variable	Total Sample			Heavier Alcohol Users		
	df	F	p	df	F	p
Stressor						
Employee role	2,326	1.26	.285	2,89	4.50	.014
Spouse/partner role	2,260	3.28	.039	2,77	1.74	.183
Parent role	2,236	2.14	.120	2,61	5.21	.008
Work/family	2,331	2.12	.122	2,90	0.67	.516
Social Support						
Nonwork sources	2,314	1.45	.236	2,84	0.14	.868
Work sources	2,330	0.16	.849	2,89	0.38	.684
Active Coping						
Problem solving	2,323	2.12	.121	2,88	2.32	.104
Cognitive restructuring	2,326	1.95	.144	2,89	2.83	.065
Social support	2,322	6.20	.002	2,88	4.33	.016
Total active coping	2,325	2.70	.069	2,89	3.79	.026
Avoidance Coping						
Problem avoidance	2,323	0.75	.472	2,88	2.14	.124
Wishful thinking	2,323	0.04	.958	2,88	2.31	.105
Social withdrawal	2,322	5.77	.003	2,88	2.20	.116
Total avoidance coping	2,323	0.16	.852	2,88	3.01	.055
Alcohol Use						
Alcohol factor	2,328	3.08	.047	2,88	3.14	.048
AUDIT scale[a]	2,322	1.43	.242	2,88	0.40	.669
No. drinks per month	2,322	2.64	.073	2,88	3.39	.038
Drink to reduce tension	2,322	3.63	.028	2,85	2.05	.135

Note. Total sample $N = 337$ (intervention $n = 123$; attention-control group $n = 95$; no-treatment control group $n = 119$). Heavier alcohol users $N = 98$ (intervention $n = 34$; attention-control group $n = 24$; no-treatment control group $n = 40$).
[a] AUDIT = Alcohol Use Disorders Identification Test. See Babor & Grant (1989); Babor, de la Fuente, Saunders, & Grant (1989).

over time for the three conditions (i.e., Time × Condition interaction effects) and analysis of any evidence for differential effectiveness of the intervention across worksites (i.e., Time × Condition × Worksite interaction effects). Analyses of the subgroup of heavier alcohol users explored whether the intervention was effective with employees at high risk for alcohol abuse. A summary of the F tests and significance levels for the Time × Condition interaction effects for the total sample and the subgroup of heavier alcohol users is shown in Table 2.2.

Total Sample

Intervention participants reported a significantly greater decrease in spouse or partner role stressors at posttest than participants in the attention control and no-treatment control conditions. This effect is illustrated in

Figure 2.3. No differences, however, were found for employee or parent role stressors, work–family stressors, or social support from home or work.

Highly significant intervention effects were found for two of the coping variables. Intervention participants reported a significant increase in social support coping from Time 1 to Time 2, whereas the attention control and no-treatment control group participants indicated little change in the use of this coping strategy. A significant Time × Condition × Worksite interaction effect for Time 1 to Time 2, $F(4,330) = 3.83$, $p = .005$, revealed that the impact of the intervention on social support coping was more substantial in the water authority companies than the manufacturing company. Although participants in the coping-skills intervention showed greater gains in social support coping than did the attention control group participants in all three worksites, the difference between the intervention group and the no-treatment control group was evident only in the two water authority companies. No effects were observed for problem-solving or cognitive-restructuring coping strategies.

Intervention participants also showed a significantly greater decrease in the use of social withdrawal coping from pretest to posttest than either the attention control group or the no-treatment control group. This intervention effect did not vary by worksite. No interaction effects were observed for coping strategies involving problem avoidance or wishful thinking or for the composite measure of avoidance coping. The interaction effects for social support and social withdrawal coping are illustrated in Figure 2.3.

The effect of the intervention on alcohol use was first examined in relation to an Alcohol factor obtained from a factor analysis of the outcome variables of the study (Snow, 1996). This analysis included various measures of psychological symptoms and substance use. The Alcohol factor that emerged consisted of the following variables: the AUDIT score, the total amount of alcohol use in the past month, and the extent to which alcohol was used to reduce tension. As shown in Table 2.2, the Time × Condition interaction effect for the Alcohol factor demonstrated a significant impact of the intervention on alcohol use. Coping-skills intervention participants showed a decrease in scores on this factor at posttest; both the attention control and no-treatment control groups reported higher scores at posttest as compared to pretest.

In assessing intervention effects in relation to the various components of the Alcohol factor, no Time × Condition or Time × Condition × Worksite interaction effects were observed for the AUDIT scale. Participants in the coping-skills intervention did report consuming less alcohol in the past month at posttest than at pretest, whereas those in the two control conditions showed essentially no change in alcohol consumption, although the effect did not reach statistical significance. Intervention participants indicated that they consumed an average of two fewer drinks in

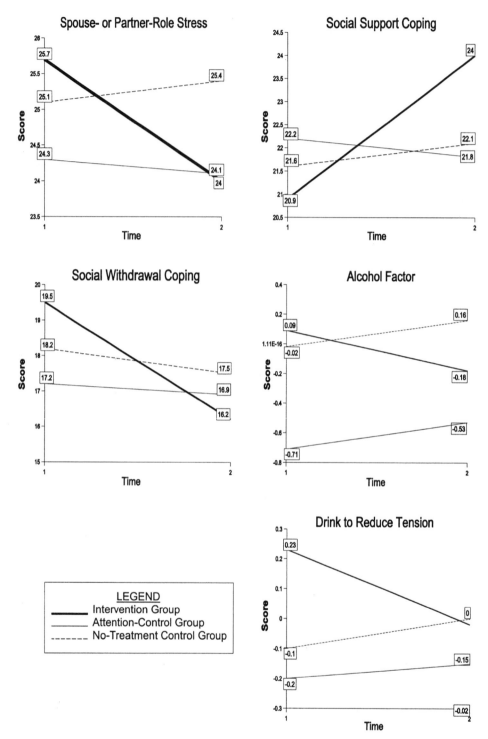

Figure 2.3. Comparisons among intervention, attention-control, and no-treatment control groups on stressors, coping, and alcohol use at Time 1 and Time 2 for the Time × Condition interaction effects observed with the total sample in Study 2.

the past month, representing a 15.7% reduction in reported alcohol use. Finally, participants in the intervention reported a significant reduction in the use of alcohol to reduce tension, but those in the two control conditions showed a modest increase in their use of alcohol for tension reduction purposes. A significant Time × Condition × Worksite interaction effect revealed that the impact of the intervention in reducing the use of alcohol to alleviate tension was evident in the manufacturing company and one of the water authority companies; no differences among the three conditions were found in the second water authority company. The interaction effects for the alcohol factor and drinking to reduce tension are also depicted in Figure 2.3.

Attrition Analyses for Total Sample

The attrition rate in this study for the total sample was 27.4% at posttest. A differential rate of attrition occurred across the three conditions —coping-skills intervention, 27.5%; attention control condition, 44.8%; and no-treatment control condition, 2.4%—that was highly significant ($\chi^2 = 65.16$, $df = 2$, $p < .001$).

Differences between stayers and dropouts were found for one demographic variable: The attrition rate was higher among White than among non-White participants ($\chi^2 = 3.92$, $df = 1$, $p = .048$). In addition, two Condition Attrition Status interactions were significant. In the no-treatment control condition at pretest, dropouts reported much greater use of problem-solving coping, $F(2,450) = 3.35$, $p = .036$, than stayers, whereas no differences emerged in the other conditions. Finally, dropouts in the intervention and no-treatment control conditions reported less use of social withdrawal coping at pretest than stayers in their respective conditions, whereas dropouts in the attention control condition reported considerably greater use of social withdrawal coping at pretest, $F(2,440) = 2.58$, $p = .077$, than stayers.

Heavier Alcohol Users

The same set of analyses was conducted for a subgroup of heavier alcohol users (i.e., the 29% of employees within the total sample who scored above the mean on total number of drinks consumed during the prior month at pretest). The average number of drinks consumed per month for the total sample was 11.4, but the average for heavier alcohol users was 31.2. Even though the study did not involve the recruitment and assignment to condition of only those who consumed greater amounts of alcohol, focusing on those employees provided an opportunity to test the effectiveness of the intervention on a group of employees at greater risk for alcohol abuse. As was the case for the total sample, no significant differences were found among the three conditions at posttest for the heavier alcohol users on any of the demographic variables.

Significant intervention effects were observed for two of the four work and family role stressor variables (see Table 2.2). Significant Time × Condition interaction effects were observed for both employee and parent role stressor variables. In both instances, as illustrated in Figure 2.4, participants in the coping-skills intervention reported a decrease in role stressors from pretest to posttest, whereas attention control participants reported an increase in role stressors and those in the no-treatment control condition showed no change. No interaction effects were observed for spouse or partner stressors or for work–family stressors. In addition, as was the case with the total sample, no effects were found for either social support from home or from work.

As shown in Table 2.2, positive intervention effects were observed for both active- and avoidance-coping strategies. A significant intervention effect was observed for social support coping: By posttest, participants in the coping-skills intervention reported a substantial increase in the use of this coping strategy, whereas attention control and no-treatment control participants showed virtually no change. No differences emerged for problem-solving coping. Finally, the Time × Condition interaction effect for the composite measure of active coping was significant. Both coping-skills intervention and attention control participants showed increased use of active coping at posttest; the intervention group reported a somewhat greater increase in use, although not significantly so. The no-treatment control group indicated decreased use of active coping at posttest. The interaction effects for the coping variables are illustrated in Figure 2.4.

No intervention effects were found for the individual measures of avoidance coping. A positive program effect was observed for the composite measure of avoidance coping, however, and the Time × Condition interaction effect approached significance. As shown in Figure 2.4, participants in the coping-skills intervention reported a substantial decrease in the use of avoidance coping at posttest. By contrast, participants in the attention control group increased their use of avoidance coping, and the no-treatment control group reported only a slight decline.

Two intervention effects on alcohol use were observed (see Table 2.2). First, the Time × Condition interaction effect for the Alcohol factor reached significance. Intervention participants showed a decrease in scores on this factor at posttest, whereas participants in the attention control condition scored higher on the factor and those in the no-treatment control group remained unchanged. Second, the intervention had a positive effect on the number of drinks consumed in the past month. Participants in the coping-skills intervention reported a substantial decrease in alcohol consumption; the attention control group showed a slight increase, and the no-treatment control group a modest decrease. Intervention participants

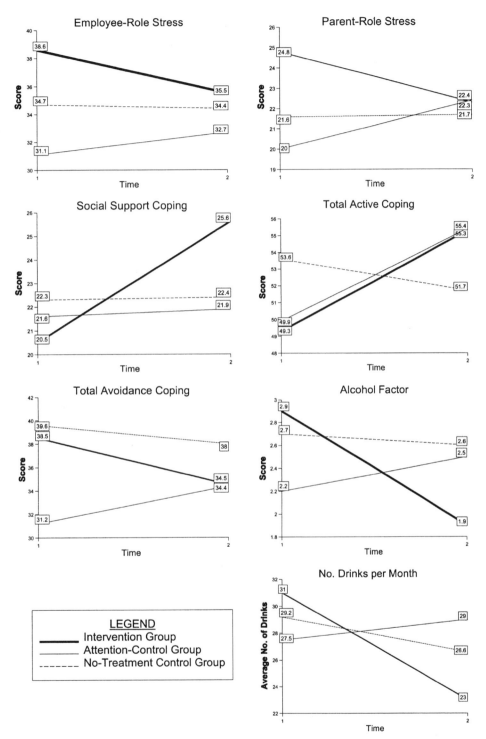

Figure 2.4. Comparisons among intervention, attention-control, and no-treatment control groups on stressors, coping, and alcohol use at Time 1 and Time 2 for the Time × Condition interaction effects observed with heavier alcohol users in Study 2.

indicated that they consumed an average of 7.9 fewer drinks per month at posttest, representing a 25.6% reduction in reported alcohol use. By comparison, the no-treatment control group reported consuming an average of 2.6 fewer drinks per month, representing only an 8.9% reduction in alcohol consumption. The interaction effects for the two alcohol measures are illustrated in Figure 2.4. Finally, no differences were found among the three conditions on the AUDIT scale or in the reported use of alcohol to reduce tension.

Attrition Analyses for Heavier Alcohol Users

The attrition rate for the heavier alcohol users was 33.8% at posttest, and the rate of attrition again was much higher in the attention control condition (61.3%) than in the intervention (27.1%) and no-treatment control (0%) conditions (χ^2 = 42.86, df = 2, p < .001). No differences between stayers and dropouts were found on any of the demographic variables. Dropouts, however, reported greater use of avoidance-coping strategies than stayers at pretest on two measures: wishful thinking, $F(1,149)$ = 3.39, p = .068, and the composite measure of avoidance coping, $F(1,146)$ = 3.39, p = .068, and they had higher scores than stayers at pretest on the AUDIT, $F(1,149)$ = 2.96, p = .088, and in the amount of alcohol consumed in the past month, $F(1,150)$ = 3.22, p = .075.

A number of Condition Attrition Status interaction effects emerged. For all four stressor variables, dropouts scored lower than stayers in the intervention condition at pretest, whereas the opposite pattern emerged in the attention control condition, in which dropouts scored higher than stayers: work–family stressors, $F(1,143)$ = 3.64, p = .058; employee role stressors, $F(1,146)$ = 11.28, p = .001; spouse or partner role stressors, $F(1,100)$ = 4.30, p = .041; and parent role stressors, $F(1,100)$ = 5.52, p = .021. Similarly, dropouts in the attention control condition reported greater use of avoidance coping at pretest than stayers on three coping variables, whereas dropouts and stayers in the intervention condition indicated relatively comparable levels of avoidance coping: problem avoidance, $F(1,145)$ = 4.23, p = .041; wishful thinking, $F(1,145)$ = 3.54, p = .062; and the composite measure of avoidance coping, $F(1,145)$ = 4.96, p = .028. Finally, on the AUDIT, $F(1,149)$ = 3.58, p = .061, dropouts in the intervention condition reported higher scores than stayers at pretest, whereas stayers and dropouts in the attention control condition reported similar pretest levels.

Summary and Implications of Findings

This study provided the opportunity to further investigate the effectiveness of a workplace coping-skills intervention. Replicating Study 1,

Study 2 again found positive effects of the intervention on employees' reported stressor levels, active- and avoidance-coping strategies, and drinking, particularly for employees who were heavier alcohol users. For the total sample, the intervention had a positive effect at posttest in reducing stressors in the role of spouse or partner. Heavier alcohol users reported reductions in both employee and parent role stressors at posttest. In addition, intervention participants as a whole reported an increase in social support coping and a decrease in social withdrawal coping at posttest. Heavier alcohol users participating in the intervention also showed an increase in social support coping as well as increased use of active-coping strategies and a general decrease in the use of avoidance-coping strategies. Finally, all intervention participants reported less alcohol use at posttest than the attention control and no-treatment control participants did. This effect was particularly strong for heavier alcohol users.

Some effects of the intervention proved to be consistent across the two studies. Reported reductions in employee role stressors at posttest occurred in the intervention group in Study 1 and for heavier alcohol users in Study 2. Decreases in the use of avoidance-coping strategies by program participants were observed in both studies. On measures of alcohol use, including drinking to reduce tension and number of drinks per month, participants in the coping-skills intervention reported greater reductions following the intervention in both studies.

The results of Study 2 differed in some ways from Study 1. Spouse or partner role stressors were not significantly affected by the intervention in Study 1, but program participants in Study 2 reported reduced levels of spouse or partner role stressors at posttest. Parent role stressors also were unaffected by the intervention in Study 1, yet heavier alcohol users in Study 2 who participated in the intervention reported reduced parental role stressors at posttest. The increased impact on family role stressors in Study 2 may have been due in part to a change in the intervention. In both studies, employees were asked to give examples of role stress situations they encountered and to think about effective coping strategies they could use to deal with those situations. The experience in the first study was that group members tended to mainly provide examples about their work experiences. In Study 2, facilitators made a conscious effort to elicit a better balance of both work *and* family stressors to address in the group sessions.

Although Study 1 found highly significant increases in social support from supervisors and coworkers for intervention participants, Study 2 found no impact of the intervention on work social support. Gender may have contributed to these differing outcomes: Study 1 involved a female sample, whereas the Study 2 sample was 71% male. Women participating in small groups over a period of weeks may be more likely to bond with and offer support to one another than mixed-gender, primarily male groups. Second, participants in Study 1 were all from the same occupational group (i.e., secretarial staff), but in Study 2 they were from diverse occupational groups. The intervention brought employees together on a weekly basis, but differences in roles, locations, and work-related concerns might have made it more difficult for participants to connect with each other in a supportive way.

Despite the fact that Study 2 intervention participants did not report increases in social support from work or nonwork sources, they did report significantly greater use of social support coping and a decrease in social withdrawal coping at posttest than attention control or no-treatment control participants did. Differences in measurement may account for this discrepancy. Many of the social support coping items described seeking support from a particular individual (e.g., "I talked to someone that I was very close to"). In contrast, the scale assessing social support from work and nonwork sources was more general. On this scale, respondents indicated the extent to which supervisors, other people at work, spouses, friends, and relatives can be relied on when things get tough at work. The intervention may have helped participants seek support from certain people, but it did not increase support from their broader social network. This area is deserving of further research to tease out the various interrelated dimensions involving individual perceptions and use of social networks. Certainly, one intention in promoting changes in social support and social withdrawal coping is to increase participants' social involvement and use of social resources. The pattern of findings that emerged in Study 2 concerning social support again suggests that interventions may need to target broad organizational changes and involve employees' families to have a stronger impact on employees' social networks and their perceived usefulness.

Related to the focus on organization-level factors, worksite was included as an independent variable to assess differential effectiveness of the intervention across the three work settings. For the most part, the observed effects of the intervention did not vary by worksite, suggesting that the effects are quite robust. Even so, significant Time × Condition × Worksite interaction effects did emerge in two instances, one involving social support coping and the other the use of alcohol to reduce tension. In both cases, significant intervention effects were observed in two sites but were either less pronounced or absent in the third. Although limited to only these two variables in this study, the findings, along with the limited effects the intervention had on stressor and social support variables, do suggest that it would make sense to pay greater attention to how setting characteristics might operate to either promote or limit intervention effectiveness.

The different attrition rates across conditions raised some issues worthy of note. One issue concerns the dropout rates in the no-treatment control groups across studies. In Study 1, 22.3% of the no-treatment control group dropped out by posttest, and in Study 2, only 2.4% of control group participants dropped out. Because of the dropout rate in Study 1, greater care was taken in Study 2 to encourage control group participants to stay involved in the study.

Differences also occurred in dropout rates between the intervention and attention control groups in Study 2. Although the participation rate in the coping-skills intervention was relatively high (nearly three-fourths of the participants completed nine or more sessions), almost half of the employees assigned to the attention control condition dropped out without completing at least five of eight sessions. The proportion dropping out of the attention control condition was even greater among the subgroup of heavier alcohol users, whereas that was not the case for the intervention and no-treatment control conditions. Facilitators leading the groups reported that participants in the attention control condition became increasingly dissatisfied as they realized that the program described stressors and their impact but did not teach them skills for coping with stress. In fact, attention control group dropouts had significantly higher scores on all four stressor variables and reported greater use of avoidance coping than did those who stayed in this condition. By comparison, the coping-skills intervention was more effective in sustaining employees' involvement; among heavier alcohol users, those who stayed actually reported higher levels of stressors and greater alcohol consumption than dropouts. Taken together, the differential participation rates, including those among heavier alcohol users, add some credibility to the perceived usefulness to employees of the coping-skills intervention. Such characteristics are essential if employees are to be effectively engaged in preventive interventions within the workplace.

For the total sample, the attrition analyses support the external validity of the observed results with only limited restrictions to the generalizability of study findings. In contrast, attrition analyses for the subgroup of heavier alcohol users revealed that at pretest, those who dropped out reported greater use of avoidance coping, heavier alcohol use, and more problem drinking than stayers. Therefore, for the analyses pertaining to the heavier alcohol users, the generalizability of the findings is restricted to those who show less extreme patterns of problem drinking and avoidance coping.

The attrition analyses lend support to the internal validity of the results for both the total sample and the subgroup of heavier alcohol users. For the total sample, the Condition Attrition Status interaction effect involving social withdrawal coping revealed that employees in the intervention and no-treatment control groups who had lower scores were more likely to drop out of the study, whereas the opposite was true for those in the attention control condition. This pattern suggests that the positive impact of the coping-skills intervention on social withdrawal was likely more substantial than the findings indicated. Likewise, for heavier alcohol users, interaction effects demonstrated that people with higher stress levels were more likely to stay in the intervention, but those with higher levels of stress and avoidance coping were more likely to drop out of the attention control group. Therefore, the positive effects of the intervention in reducing stressors and avoidance coping may be even stronger than the results suggest. The remaining attrition analyses did not reveal any threats to the internal validity of the positive effects of the coping-skills intervention in reducing the amount of alcohol consumption among heavier users.

SUMMARY AND FUTURE DIRECTIONS

The results of the two studies provide support for the risk- and protective-factor model that guided the workplace interventions. In both investigations, the intervention had a positive effect in modifying certain risk and protective factors related to alcohol use and in reducing alcohol consumption and reliance on alcohol for tension reduction purposes. The effects have now been demonstrated across diverse work settings and with employees who have diverse occupational and demographic characteristics. Although corresponding changes in risk and protective factors and alcohol use did occur, future research is needed to more clearly determine whether changes in stressor, social support, and coping variables are causally linked to changes in drinking behavior. The inclusion of an attention control condition in the second study allowed an assessment of whether intervention effects can be attributed to the emphasis on modification of coping skills, beyond simply attention and release time. The pattern of findings quite consistently revealed substantially greater changes in predicted directions for the coping-skills intervention than for both the attention control and no-treatment control conditions, lending considerable support to this contention.

The observed effects with heavier alcohol users on stressor, coping, and alcohol dimensions were encouraging, given the potential for serious alcohol-related problems among this subgroup of employees. At the same time, it was apparent that the employees with the most extreme alcohol problems, who also relied heavily on avoidance-coping strategies, dropped out of the study at higher rates than others. It is not unusual for higher-risk participants to drop out of interventions at a greater rate than those at lower risk (Snow, Tebes, & Arthur, 1992). The ongoing challenge is to identify ways to effectively recruit *and* retain those at greater risk, and to consider the types of interventions that might be best suited for this group of employees. Clearly, the factor of company "buy in," as exemplified in the commitment of resources, (e.g., release time from work), was essential to the level of participation achieved in the two studies. The results underscore the critical work that needs to be done to form partnerships with companies in developing comprehensive and sustained workplace preventive interventions.

The coping-skills intervention presented in this chapter has been used to date as a person-centered approach to prevention in the workplace. It seeks to promote change in individual workers and to provide them with skills to create changes in their environment. The risk- and protective-factor model that underlies this intervention also can be used to design complementary strategies involving organization-level and cross-domain (i.e., work and family) interventions. Although the findings reported above are encouraging, they also reveal the inherent limitations of a person-centered approach and underscore the need to test alternative intervention designs. Other related models, which emphasize the role of the organization, person, and person–organization interactions, have been articulated (Ivancevich, Matteson, Freedman, & Phillips, 1990; Kahn & Byosiere, 1990). The application of these models involves the design of multilevel, workplace interventions aimed at both systemic and individual change (Heaney & van Ryn, 1990). In addition, integrative models of the work–family interface have been advanced (e.g., Frone, Yardley, & Markel, 1998) that provide a framework for developing interventions across multiple systems. Clearly, moving in these directions will enhance the effectiveness of workplace preventive interventions, although doing so will require addressing the barriers to examining and altering the systemic factors encountered when entering worksites.

REFERENCES

Babor, T. F., de la Fuente, J. R., Saunders, J., & Grant, M. (1989). *The Alcohol Use Disorders Identification Test: Guidelines for use in primary health care.* Geneva: World Health Organization.

Babor, T. F., & Grant, M. (1989). From clinical research to secondary prevention: International collaboration in the development of the alcohol use disorders identification test (AUDIT). *International Perspectives, 13,* 371–374.

Baruch, G. K., & Barnett, R. C. (1986). Role quality, multiple role involvement, and psychological well-being in midlife women. *Journal of Personality and Social Psychology, 51,* 578–585.

Billings, A. G., & Moos, R. H. (1982). Stressful life events and symptoms: A longitudinal model. *Health Psychology, 1,* 99–118.

Bray, R. M., Fairbank, J. A., & Marsden, M. E. (1999). Stress and substance use among military women and men. *American Journal of Drug and Alcohol Abuse, 25,* 239–256.

Brennan, P. L., & Moos, R. H. (1990). Life stressors, social resources, and late-life problem drinking. *Psychology and Aging, 5,* 491–501.

Cohen, S., Schwartz, J. E., Bromet, E. J., & Parkinson, D. K. (1991). Mental health, stress, and poor health behaviors in two community samples. *Preventive Medicine, 20,* 306–315.

Coie, J. D., Watt, N. F., West, S. G., Hawkins, J. D., Asarnow, J. R., Markman, H. J., et al. (1993). The science of prevention: A conceptual framework and some directions for a national research program. *American Psychologist, 48,* 1013–1022.

Cooper, M. L., Russell, M., Skinner, J. B., Frone, M. R., & Mudar, P. (1992). Stress and alcohol use: Moderating effects of gender, coping, and alcohol expectancies. *Journal of Abnormal Psychology, 101,* 139–152.

Corsun, D. L., & Young, C. A. (1998). An occupational hazard: Alcohol consumption among hospitality managers. *Marriage and Family Review, 28,* 187–211.

Crum, R. M., Muntaner, C., Eaton, W. W., & Anthony, J. C. (1995). Occupational stress and the risk of alcohol abuse and dependence. *Alcoholism: Clinical and Experimental Research, 19,* 647–655.

Ehrensaft, D. (1980). When women and men mother. *Sociological Review, 49,* 37–73.

Ferguson, D. (1974). A study of occupational stress and health. In A. T. Welford (Ed.), *Man under stress* (pp. 83–98). New York: Wiley.

Frone, M. R., Russell, M., & Barnes, G. M. (1996). Work-family conflict, gender, and health-related outcomes: A study of employed parents in two community samples. *Journal of Occupational Health Psychology, 1,* 57–69.

Frone, M. R., Russell, M., & Cooper, M. L. (1993). Relationship of work–family conflict, gender and alcohol expectancies to alcohol use/abuse. *Journal of Organizational Behavior, 14,* 545–558.

Frone, M. R., Russell, M., & Cooper, M. L. (1995). Job stressors, job involvement and employee health: A test of identity theory. *Journal of Occupational and Organizational Psychology, 68,* 1–11.

Frone, M. R., Russell, M., & Cooper, M. L. (1997). Relation of work-family conflict to health outcomes: A four-year longitudinal study of employed parents. *Journal of Occupational and Organizational Psychology, 70,* 325–335.

Frone, M. R., Yardley, J. K., & Markel, K. S. (1998). Developing and testing an integrative model of the work-family interface. *Journal of Vocational Behavior, 50,* 145–167.

Gibbons, R. D., Hedeker, D., Elkin, I., Waternaux, C., Kraemer, H. C., Greenhouse, J. B., et al. (1993). Some conceptual and statistical issues in analysis of longitudinal psychiatric data: Application to the NIMH Treatment of Depression Collaborative Research Program dataset. *Archives of General Psychiatry, 50,* 739–750.

Girden, E. R. (1992). *ANOVA repeated measures* (Sage University Paper Series on Quantitative Applications in the Social Sciences, Series No. 07-084). Newbury Park, CA: Sage.

Grant, B. F. (1997). Prevalence and correlates of alcohol use and DSM–IV alcohol dependence in the United States: Results of the National Longitudinal Alcohol Epidemiologic Survey. *Journal of Studies on Alcohol, 58,* 464–473.

Greenhaus, J. H., & Parasuraman, S. (1986). A work-nonwork interactive perspective of stress and its consequences. *Journal of Organizational Behavior Management, 8,* 37–60.

Greenhouse, S. W., & Geisser, S. (1959). On methods in the analysis of profile data. *Psychometrika, 24,* 95–112.

Grunberg, L., Moore, S., & Greenberg, E. S. (1998). Work stress and problem alcohol behavior: A test of the spillover model. *Journal of Organizational Behavior, 19,* 487–502.

Hanna, E. Z., & Grant, B. F. (1997). Gender differences in DSM–IV alcohol use disorders and major depression as distributed in the general population: Clinical implications. *Comprehensive Psychiatry, 38,* 202–212.

Harford, T. C., Parker, D. A., Grant, B. F., & Dawson, D. A. (1992). Alcohol use and dependence among employed men and women in the United States in 1988. *Alcoholism: Clinical and Experimental Research, 16,* 146–148.

Harwood, H. J., Napolitano, D. M., Kristiansen, P. L., & Collins, J. J. (1984). *Economic costs to society of alcohol and drug abuse and mental illness: 1980.* Research Triangle Park, NC: Research Triangle Institute.

Havlovic, S. J., & Keenan, J. P. (1991). Coping with work stress: The influence of individual differences. *Journal of Social Behavior and Personality, 6,* 199–212.

Hawkins, J. D., Catalano, R. F., & Miller, J. Y. (1992). Risk and protective factors for alcohol and other drug problems in adolescence and early adulthood: Implications for substance abuse prevention. *Psychological Bulletin, 112,* 64–105.

Heaney, C. A., & van Ryn, M. (1990). Broadening the scope of worksite stress programs: A guiding framework. *American Journal of Health Promotion, 4,* 413–420.

Heller, K. (1996). Coming of age of prevention science: Comments on the 1994 National Institute of Mental Health-Institute of Medicine prevention reports. *American Psychologist, 51,* 1123–1133.

Hemmingsson, T., & Lundberg, I. (1998). Work control, work demands, and work social support in relation to alcoholism among young men. *Alcoholism: Clinical and Experimental Research, 22,* 921–927.

Hollinger, R. C. (1988). Working under the influence (WUI): Correlates of employees' use of alcohol and other drugs. *Journal of Applied Behavioral Science, 24,* 439–454.

House, J. S. (1980). *Occupational stress and the mental and physical health of factory workers.* Ann Arbor, MI: Institute for Social Research.

Howland, J., Mangione, T. W., Kuhlthau, K., Bell, N., Heeren, T., Lee, M., & Levine, S. (1996). Worksite variation in managerial drinking. *Addiction, 91,* 1007–1017.

Humphreys, K., Moos, R. H., & Finney, J. W. (1996). Life domains, alcoholics anonymous, and role incumbency in the 3-year course of problem drinking. *Journal of Nervous and Mental Disease, 184,* 475–481.

Huynh, H., & Feldt, L. S. (1976). Estimation of the Box correction for degrees of freedom from sample data in randomized block and split-plot designs. *Journal of Educational Statistics, 1,* 69–82.

Ivancevich, J. M., Matteson, M. T., Freedman, S. M., & Phillips, J. S. (1990). Worksite stress management interventions. *American Psychologist, 45,* 252–261.

Jasinski, J. L., Asdigian, N. L., & Kantor, G. K. (1998). Ethnic adaptations to occupational strain: Work-related stress, drinking, and wife assault among Anglo and Hispanic husbands. *Journal of Interpersonal Violence, 12,* 814–831.

Johnsen, B. H., Laberg, J. C., & Eid, J. (1998). Coping strategies and mental health problems in a military unit. *Military Medicine, 163,* 599–602.

Kahn, R. L., & Byosiere, A. (1990). Stress in organizations. In M. Dunnette (Ed.), *Handbook of Industrial and Organizational Psychology* (pp. 571–650). Chicago: Rand-McNally.

Kjerheim, K., Haldorsen, T., Anderson, A., Mykletun, R., & Aasland, O. G. (1997). Work-related stress, coping resources, and heavy drinking in the restaurant business. *Work and Stress, 11,* 6–16.

Kunda, G. (1992). *Engineering culture: Control and commitment in a high-tech corporation.* Philadelphia: Temple University Press.

Laurent, J., Catanzaro, S. J., & Callan, M. K. (1997). Stress, alcohol-related expectancies and coping preferences: A replication with adolescents of the Cooper et al. (1992) model. *Journal of Studies on Alcohol, 58,* 644–651.

McCreary, D. R., & Sadava, S. W. (1998). Stress, drinking, and the adverse consequences of drinking in two samples of young adults. *Psychology of Addictive Behaviors, 12,* 247–261.

McKay, J. R., Maisto, S. A., & O'Farrell, T. J. (1996). Alcoholics' perceptions of factors in the onset and termination of relapses and the maintenance of abstinence: Results from a 30-month follow-up. *Psychology of Addictive Behaviors, 10,* 167–180.

Mensch, B. S., & Kandel, D. B. (1988). Do job conditions influence the use of drugs? *Journal of Health and Social Behavior, 29,* 169–184.

Miller, J. D., Cisin, I. H., Gardner-Keaton, H., Harrell, A. V., Wirtz, P. W., Abelson, H. I., et al. (1982). *National household survey on drug abuse: Main findings 1982* (DHHS Pub. No. ADM 83-1263). Washington, DC: U.S. Government Printing Office.

Moos, R. H., Fenn, C. B., Billings, A. G., & Moos, B. S. (1989). Assessing life stressors and social resources: Applications to alcoholic patients. *Journal of Substance Abuse, 1,* 135–152.

Nowack, K. M., & Pentkowski, A. M. (1994). Lifestyle habits, substance use and predictors of job burnout in professional working women. *Work and Stress, 8,* 19–35.

Ott, L. (1988). *An introduction to statistical methods and data analysis*. Boston: PWS-Kent.

Parker, D. A., & Brody, J. A. (1982). Risk factors for alcoholism and alcohol problems among employed women and men. In *Occupational alcoholism: A review of research issues* (NIAAA Research Monograph No. 8, pp. 99–128). Washington, DC: U.S. Government Printing Office.

Parker, D. A., & Farmer, G. C. (1988). The epidemiology of alcohol abuse among employed men and women. In M. Galanter (Ed.), *Recent developments in alcoholism* (Vol. 6, pp. 113–130). New York: Plenum.

Parker, D. A., & Harford, T. C. (1992). The epidemiology of alcohol consumption and dependence across occupations in the United States. *Alcohol Health and Research World, 16*, 97–105.

Pearlin, L. I., & Schooler, C. (1978). The structure of coping. *Journal of Health and Social Behavior, 19*, 2–21.

Peirce, R. S., Frone, M. R., Russell, M., & Cooper, M. L. (1996). Financial stress, social support, and alcohol involvement: A longitudinal test of the buffering hypothesis in a general population survey. *Health Psychology, 15*, 38–47.

Plant, M. A. (1979). *Drinking careers: Occupations, drinking habits and drinking problems*. London: Tavistock.

Ragland, D. R., Greiner, B. A., Krause, N., Holman, B. L., & Fisher, J. M. (1995). Occupational and nonoccupational correlates of alcohol consumption in urban transit operators. *Preventive Medicine, 24*, 634–645.

Regier, D. A., Myers, J. K., Kramer, M., Robins, L. N., Blazer, D. G., Hough, R. L., et al. (1984). The NIMH epidemiologic catchment area program. *Archives of General Psychiatry, 41*, 934–941.

Reiss, D., & Price, R. H. (1996). National research agenda for prevention research: The National Institute of Mental Health report. *American Psychologist, 51*, 1109–1115.

Rutter, M. (1985). Resilience in the face of adversity: Protective factors and resistance to psychiatric disorder. *British Journal of Psychiatry, 147*, 598–611.

Seeman, M., & Seeman, A. Z. (1992). Life strains, alienation, and drinking behavior. *Alcoholism: Clinical and Experimental Research, 16*, 199–205.

Seeman, M., Seeman, A. Z., & Budros, A. (1988). Powerlessness, work and community: A longitudinal study of alienation and alcohol use. *Journal of Health and Social Behavior, 29*, 185–198.

Shapiro, S., Skinner, E. A., Kessler, L. G., Von Korff, M., German, P. S., Tischler, G. L., et al. (1984). Utilization of health and mental health services: Three epidemiologic catchment area sites. *Archives of General Psychiatry, 41*, 971–978.

Snow, D. L. (1996, April). *A workplace coping skills intervention: Effect on alcoholism*. Paper presented at the Working Group on Research on Alcohol Problems in the Worksite: Moving toward Prevention Research, National Institute on Alcohol Abuse and Alcoholism, Washington, DC.

Snow, D. L., & Kline, M. L. (1991). A worksite coping skills intervention: Effects on women's psychological symptomatology and substance use. *Community Psychologist, 24,* 14–17.

Snow, D. L., & Kline, M. L. (1995). Preventive interventions in the workplace to reduce negative psychiatric consequences of work and family stress. In C. M. Mazure (Ed.), *Does stress cause psychiatric illness?* (pp. 221–270). Washington, DC: American Psychiatric Press.

Snow, D. L., Tebes, J. K., & Arthur, M. W. (1992). Panel attrition and external validity in adolescent substance use research. *Journal of Consulting and Clinical Psychology, 60,* 804–807.

Steptoe, A., Wardle, J., Lipsey, Z., Mills, R., Oliver, G., Jarvis, M., et al. (1998). A longitudinal study of workload and variation in psychological well-being, cortisol, smoking, and alcohol consumption. *Annals of Behavioral Medicine, 20,* 84–91.

Steptoe, A., Wardle, J., Pollard, T. M., & Canaan, L. (1996). Stress, social support and health-related behavior: A study of smoking, alcohol consumption and physical exercise. *Journal of Psychosomatic Research, 41,* 171–180.

Taggart, R. W. (1989). Results of the drug testing program at Southern Pacific Railroad. In S. W. Gust & J. M. Walsh (Eds.), *Drugs in the workplace: Research and evaluation data* (NIDA Research Monograph 91, DHHS Pub. No. ADM 89-1612, pp. 97–108). Washington, DC: U.S. Government Printing Office.

Tobin, D. L., Holroyd, K. A., Reynolds, R. V., & Wigal, J. K. (1989). The hierarchical factor structure of the Coping Strategies Inventory. *Cognitive Therapy and Research, 13,* 343–361.

Trice, H. M. (1992). Work-related risk factors associated with alcohol abuse. *Alcohol Health & Research World, 16,* 106–111.

Trice, H., & Roman, P. (1971). Occupational risk factors in mental health and the impact of role change experience. In J. Jody (Ed.), *Compensation in psychiatric disability and rehabilitation* (pp. 145–202). Springfield, IL: Charles C Thomas.

Trice, H. M., & Sonnenstuhl, W. J. (1988). Drinking behavior and risk factors related to the workplace: Implications for research and prevention. *Journal of Applied Behavioral Science, 24,* 327–346.

Voss, H. L. (1989). Patterns of drug use: Data from the 1985 National Household Survey. In S. W. Gust & J. M. Walsh (Eds.), *Drugs in the workplace: Research and evaluation data* (NIDA Research Monograph 91, DHHS Pub. No. ADM 89-1612, pp. 33–46). Washington, DC: U.S. Government Printing Office.

Watts, D. W., & Short, A. P. (1990). Teacher drug use: A response to occupational stress. *Journal of Drug Education, 20,* 47–65.

Zaleski, E. H., Levey-Thors, C., & Schiaffino, K. M. (1998). Coping mechanisms, stress, social support, and health problems in college students. *Applied Developmental Science, 2,* 127–137.

3

INTEGRATING SUBSTANCE ABUSE PREVENTION INTO HEALTH PROMOTION PROGRAMS IN THE WORKPLACE: A SOCIAL COGNITIVE INTERVENTION TARGETING THE MAINSTREAM USER

ROYER F. COOK, ANITA S. BACK, JAMES TRUDEAU, AND
TRACY McPHERSON

For the past dozen years, our research team has been developing and testing substance abuse prevention programs and materials for the workplace, typically cast in a health promotion framework and rooted in social cognitive theory (Cook & Youngblood, 1990; Cook, Back, & Trudeau, 1996a, 1996b). Our efforts have been based on the belief that workers' attitudes toward and practices involving alcohol and other drugs (AODs) can be shaped by interventions that are congruent with prevailing psychological theories of behavior change and that health promotion programs in the workplace are a logical and appropriate vehicle for substance abuse prevention programs. Although the authors view these interventions as entirely compatible with sociocultural perspectives (as reflected in the work of Sonnenstuhl and his colleagues, 1996) and interventions that focus on changes in work group norms (as in the work of Bennett and Lehman, 1998), they draw heavily on social cognitive theory and concepts and are focused primarily on attempts to change the behavior of individual workers.

In this chapter we first discuss the rationale for the health promotion–oriented prevention strategies along with the conceptual and practical foundations of the approach. We then summarize the field tests of the first two interventions in this program of research, which were conducted in the early 1990s. The remainder of the chapter is devoted to the findings from our recently completed field test of the *Connections* program; it ends with some tentative conclusions and implications of this approach.

FOUNDATIONS OF THE HEALTH PROMOTION APPROACH

If AOD abuse prevention programs were to be found in the workplace, one might expect to find them within the growing number of health promotion programs in industry, programs that encourage the development of healthful practices through preventive means. Yet as our research team has conducted periodic examinations of worksite health programs over the past 12 years—including some of the most comprehensive programs—we have consistently found that with rare exception, prevention of drug and alcohol abuse is not part of those efforts (Cook, in press; Cook & Youngblood, 1990, Cook et al., 1996a).

In part, the reason for this omission may be that health promotion programs see substance abuse as the purview of employee assistance programs (EAPs), and EAPs see prevention as the purview of health promotion programs. As Shain and his associates have suggested, health promotion programs mainly reach the "conspicuously well," whereas EAPs touch the lives of the "walking wounded." The "ragged and the frayed" are left unattended (Shain, Suurvali, & Boutilier, 1986). Miller took a similar position: People who use alcohol excessively, consume illicit drugs, and misuse prescription drugs do not necessarily progress, as in a disease paradigm of alcoholism, to become addicts. Several estimates place this employee group of excessive and inappropriate AOD users at approximately 20% of all employees—two to three times more than those in late-stage substance dependence. Employers and their managed care organizations neglect these workers at their peril. They are the "farm team" from which the seriously troubled drinkers and drug users are drafted. Those who do not progress to an addictive state (the majority) drift in and out of problem categories, drinking too much, experimenting with drugs, damaging their health, and draining energy from the workplace for much of their working lives. As Miller and his associates suggested, the cumulative effect of these problems is a diffuse disruption of organizational functioning (Miller et al., 1985).

Workplace substance abuse prevention activities should be conducted within health promotion programs for several reasons:

1. Substance abuse is closely linked to health status. Mounting evidence indicates that drug and alcohol abuse are health hazards. Excessive alcohol use is associated with increased risk of death from cancer and heart disease, and the health hazards of illicit drug use (e.g., overdose deaths) are well documented.

2. The use of drugs and alcohol affects nearly all the main components of a health promotion program. If a person is a drinker or drug user, the way in which alcohol or drugs are used can have a substantial impact on stress management, weight control, physical exercise, nutrition, and mental wellbeing. For millions of working adults, drinking and drug use are a chief means of managing stress; they need to be led away from this practice as well as to learn healthful ways of reducing stress. Developing a program of after-work exercise activities has little chance of succeeding if after-work drinking habits are ignored. Monitoring caloric intake for weight control purposes makes little sense if it does not include the 300 to 400 calories in the two or three drinks many workers consume daily.

3. Health promotion programs can serve as a needed positive vehicle for the prevention of drug and alcohol abuse. One of the chief obstacles to the successful implementation of worksite prevention programs is the stigma attached to the topic. It is the rare, courageous employee who is willing to be seen entering a workshop carrying the label "Drug and Alcohol Abuse Prevention!" At a broad level, many corporations are reluctant to embrace serious alcohol abuse prevention as an independent activity because it seems to fly in the face of a corporate culture in which drinking is deeply embedded and ritualized. Health promotion programs have no such problems. Their goals of boosting health and energy are highly congruent with the typical corporate culture, and in most companies workers who enroll in a program to improve their health—to lose weight, get fit, and so forth—are applauded. By integrating substance abuse prevention into a company's health promotion program, the troublesome cultural and individual stigmata are bypassed.

4. Health promotion programs can provide needed secondary prevention of drug and alcohol abuse. Many people who are heavy drinkers or occasional drug users—but not yet in se-

rious trouble—can be reached through a health promotion program. They may be highly resistant to participating in a drug and alcohol abuse program, but they will have little reluctance to enroll in a health promotion program (see the research evidence summarized below). In this way programs can reach employees who are engaging in hazardous and productivity-lessening substance abuse but who are unlikely to come to the attention of the EAP, at least until much later.

5. The promotion of healthful lifestyles and the control of drug and alcohol use are mutually reinforcing. Preventing and reducing substance abuse helps people engage in healthful activities. Pursuing a healthier lifestyle makes it easier for people to reduce their consumption of alcohol and drugs.

6. A health promotion program that addresses substance abuse can serve as a valuable outreach service for the EAP. The substance abuse portion of the health promotion program, can inform employees about the warning signals of substance abuse and the advantages of seeking assistance through their EAP.

Despite the many reasons for integrating substance abuse prevention into worksite health promotion, significant obstacles remain. The sources of this resistance can be found within health promotion programs and EAPs as well as in certain general perceptions and attitudes of management. In interviews with scores of corporate officials over the years, our group has found a consistent reluctance to address squarely the issue of alcohol abuse prevention in the workplace, mainly because of the role alcohol use continues to play in many corporate cultures. Although the "three-martini" business lunch is facing extinction, other forms of heavy drinking—the nightly drinking bouts at annual sales meetings, the "reward" of several rounds of drinks after an especially arduous period of work, the promotion celebrations, and so on—remain an expected and valued ritual of corporate existence.

In all of those situations, heavy drinking (defined as 5 or more drinks on 5 or more occasions in the last 30 days) is not only condoned but encouraged as an effective means of both relieving stress and strengthening the social bonds that promote teamwork and company loyalty. Some people may fear that alcohol abuse prevention programs in the workplace are aimed at taking away a worker's pleasurable activity while jeopardizing the valued bonding and teamwork of the work unit. To counter such concerns, alcohol abuse prevention programs in the workplace should make it clear that they are not a temperance movement, only a force for moderation, and that they are not designed to eliminate social bonding events, simply to help ensure that the drinking at such events does not reach damaging dimensions.

One source of resistance to integrated efforts is often the health promotion program itself. Program staff may perceive or anticipate a lukewarm reception by management if prevention of alcohol and drug abuse is included in the health promotion activities. Programs typically prefer to trumpet the positive, pleasurable consequences of the healthful lifestyle, rather than address the complex issue of substance abuse, with all its attendant stigma and social ramifications. EAPs, however, generally claim substance abuse prevention as part of their mission, although the "prevention" efforts of EAPs are typically confined to the tertiary end of the prevention continuum (i.e., the identification and treatment of troubled employees). In Roman and Blum's (1996) review of the impact of worksite interventions (mostly EAPs and the like) on health behavioral outcomes, nearly all of the 24 studies that the authors reviewed focused on the effectiveness with which employees were identified and treated for alcohol problems. In their recent description of six workplace functions served by EAPs, virtually all are treatment oriented; none of the specified functions includes prevention (Roman & Blum, 1999). This rather exclusive focus on treatment-related functions may be entirely appropriate; the Roman and Blum review indicated (and most observers would agree) that the EAPs perform valuable functions for the work force. It is also likely that they operate as a generalized, diffuse force for the prevention of substance abuse by raising awareness of the risks of substance abuse and nudging norms toward more responsible drinking. Nonetheless, it is the rare EAP that actively pursues genuine prevention strategies with the mainstream of workers (i.e., strategies designed to alter drinking practices, halt experimentation with illicit drugs or the misuse of prescription drugs before dependence develops, or help keep their children from substance abuse). Such primary and secondary prevention targets seem to be off the radar screen of virtually all EAPs.

The central theoretical basis for our approach, as well as for several other theories and practices in the health behavior field, is the social cognitive theory (SCT; also known as cognitive–behavioral theory), which was articulated first and most fully by Bandura (1977, 1986). Although the roots of SCT are more than half a century old, it only began to have a major influence in health behavior research in the 1980s. Exhibit 3.1 provides a brief primer on SCT, including the implications of the major concepts for the shape and direction of interventions. The development of our conceptual framework, as well as the shape of specific interventions, has been heavily influenced by SCT and its implications.

An Evolving Conceptual and Theoretical Framework

In 1990, Cook and Youngblood developed a preliminary conceptual model to guide the development of workplace substance abuse prevention

EXHIBIT 3.1
Social Cognitive Theory: A Brief Primer

History

The roots of social cognitive theory (also known as cognitive–behavioral theory) originated in the social learning theory of Miller and Dollard (1941), which they developed to explain imitation behavior. In 1977 Bandura published his seminal work, *Social Learning Theory*, which incorporated cognitive elements into the theory. In that same year Farquhar and his associates reported the first communitywide intervention for heart disease prevention that was based on social learning theory. In 1986, Bandura published a comprehensive framework for understanding human social behavior, renaming it Social Cognitive Theory (SCT; Baranowski, Perry, & Parcel, 1997).

Major Concepts and Their Implications

SCT emphasizes the reciprocal interaction of cognitive, behavioral, and environmental determinants. Among the crucial personal factors are a person's ability to symbolize behavior, to learn by observing others, to have confidence in performing a behavior, to self-regulate behavior, and to reflect on and analyze experience (Bandura, 1986). Baranowski and his associates (1997) listed the major concepts in social cognitive theory and their implications for interventions; selected concepts from their list are presented below:

Concept	Definition	Implications for Interventions
Behavioral capability	Knowledge and skill to perform a behavior	Promote mastery learning through skills training
Self-control	Personal regulation of goal-directed behavior	Provide opportunities for self-monitoring and goal-setting
Self-efficacy	Confidence in performing a particular behavior	Approach behavior in small steps; be specific about the changes sought
Observational learning	Learning that occurs by watching the actions and outcomes of others	Include credible role models of the targeted behavior
Expectancies	The values placed on a given outcome	Present outcomes that have functional meaning
Emotional coping responses	Strategies that are used to deal with emotions	Provide training in problem-solving and stress management
Situation	Person's perception of the environment	Correct misperceptions and promote healthful norms

interventions. The model was designed to draw on existing health behavior theories and constructs, including the work of Abrams et al., 1986; Bandura (1977, 1986), and Rosenstock, Strecher, & Becker (1988) on the health belief model and Cook's (1985) biopsychological model of healthful alternatives to drug abuse. This preliminary model (Figure 3.1) viewed AOD use as a type of unhealthful behavior and held that at any point in time, people possess a particular level of awareness, motivation, and knowledge

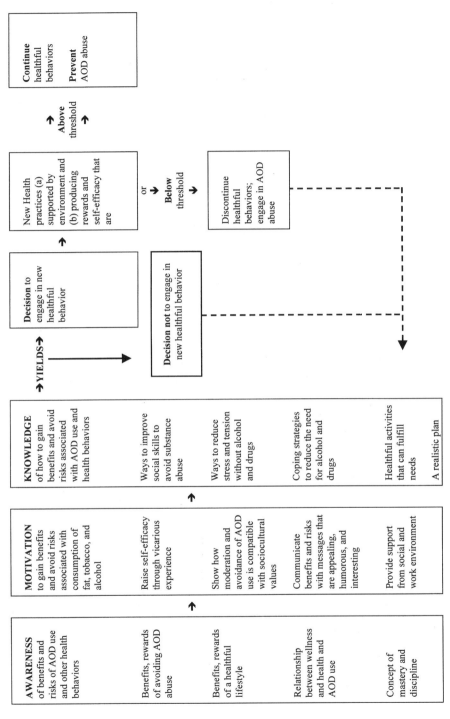

Figure 3.1. A preliminary conceptual model for workplace health promotion and prevention of alcohol and other drug (AOD) abuse.

about the risks and benefits of drug and alcohol use and other health practices. The three components were seen as combining in multiplicative fashion (i.e., if any component is missing or below threshold, the person will not engage in the healthful behavior). For example, one must be sufficiently aware both of the risks of substance abuse and of the benefits of avoiding substance abuse to be motivated, and without the needed knowledge or skills (e.g., monitoring alcohol consumption, refusing drinks, and so forth), one is less likely to avoid substance abuse. The model suggested that by raising awareness, motivation, and knowledge with respect to healthful behavior, people would be less likely to engage in substance abuse (i.e., that healthful behavior and substance abuse tend to be negatively correlated, although only moderately so). As people begin adopting healthful practices—eating better, getting regular exercise, and so on—they are less likely to engage in substance abuse. Stated somewhat differently, as one becomes more committed to a healthful lifestyle, one typically becomes less likely to engage in health-damaging substance abuse.

The model contained two decision points, one at which health behavior is begun or decided against, and one at which the behavior is continued or dropped. Compatible with the stages-of-change theory of Prochaska, DiClemente, & Norcross (1992), the model recognized that most people do not make all-or-nothing, permanent decisions about health behavior (e.g., drinking practices and exercise). If negative decisions are made, they may be reversed later as the necessary components reach threshold levels. Similarly, a decision to engage in a healthful behavior can be reversed if the rewards and supports become insufficient (e.g., if the person is placed in a work environment that is unsupportive of the healthful behavior or experiences an overload of stress and tension).

Support from the social environment at work and at home is seen as a significant element in both stages. Organizational support for avoidance of substance abuse can be demonstrated in a variety of ways, from personal statements by the CEO, to a display by managers of moderation in their drinking habits, to provision of nonalcoholic alternatives at company social functions. Because other healthful behavior generally reinforces the avoidance of substance abuse, any support the organization provides to a health promotion program also helps prevent substance abuse (e.g., the employer might encourage participation in stress management seminars). Finally, management must consider the degree to which its own policies and corporate culture are contributing to unhealthy employee behavior, particularly any dynamics (e.g., pressure and work overload) that may contribute to substance abuse.

A worksite substance abuse prevention program that is based on this model looks quite different from most other such programs, despite the inclusion of central elements such as self-efficacy and social support. First, the program is positive: It emphasizes the benefits of healthful behaviors rather than stress the dangers of substance abuse, although it also covers harmful effects. In contrast to the "scare tactics" approach, the program materials are designed to be appealing, partly by emphasizing healthful activities that are fun and rewarding and by presenting the program in ways that engage the audience's interest. This approach is exemplified by the use of video segments that contain dramatic vignettes designed to catch and hold the interest of the audience. The video also mixes verbal messages of an on-screen narrator with behavioral modeling, as the vignettes show people practicing healthful behaviors, cutting down on their drinking, and refusing drugs.

The Cook and Youngblood (1990) model served as the conceptual basis for the authors' first two workplace substance abuse prevention programs, and their field tests are summarized below. The programs contained print and video materials that emphasized the rewards of healthful behavior and avoidance of substance abuse and described the risks of substance abuse. On the basis of the results of the field tests and the work of other investigators (e.g., Ames, 1993; Lehman, Farabee, Holcom, & Simpson, 1995), Cook and his colleagues expanded the conceptual model to include an explicit recognition of the role of the work environment and the impact of job stress and workplace culture on patterns of AOD use (Cook et al., 1996a).

The new model (Figure 3.2) is designed to (a) identify the major determinants of work force substance abuse, (b) specify prevention interventions that can affect workers' substance use, and (c) specify mediating variables that are directly affected by the interventions and which, in turn, reduce the amount of substance abuse in the work force. According to the model, the major work and employee characteristics determining work force substance use include perceived stress and work culture. The key interventions designed to prevent substance abuse are stress management programs that include substance abuse prevention materials and training programs designed to influence the work culture. Those key interventions are designed to reduce stress; raise awareness, motivation, and knowledge related to substance use; and alter the norms and beliefs of the work culture, thereby reducing the prevalence of substance abuse in the work force. The new model retains the three-component dynamics of the original model (see "AOD Attitudes and Beliefs" on Figure 3.2) as well as the feedback loop by which changes in individual substance use can influence the norms and beliefs of the work culture. In the new model, however, the preventive interventions occupy a prominent place and role, and the particular mediating variables by which the interventions affect substance use are specified. In addition, the model suggests that a particular type of health promotion program—a stress management program containing substance abuse prevention materials—can be an especially effective form of workplace intervention. The central role of stress and stress management in the

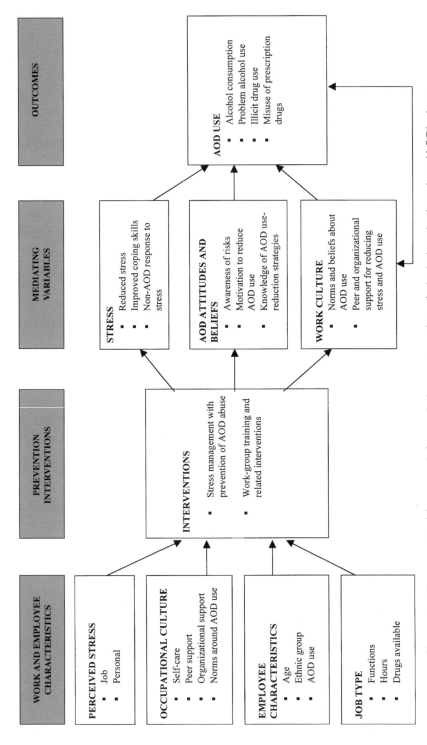

Figure 3.2. A conceptual framework for workplace prevention of alcohol and other drug (AOD) abuse.

model has occurred in part as a result of the recently completed field test of the *Stress Management Connection* program, which is described in detail below.

SUMMARY OF INITIAL FIELD TESTS

Using the preliminary conceptual framework as a guide, two workplace substance abuse prevention programs were developed and field tested in the early 1990s: SAY YES! Healthy Choices for Feeling Good and Working People: Decisions About Drinking. Both programs were based on the original Cook and Youngblood (1990) model: They were rooted in cognitive–behavioral principles of self-efficacy enhancement, bolstering of social support, and providing opportunities for behavioral modeling, mainly through specially developed video segments. Both programs emphasized the short-term rewards and broad benefits of adopting a healthful lifestyle and avoiding substance abuse.

In constructing the program, the research team was guided by pragmatic considerations as well as the conceptual model and the other issues discussed above. In particular, we believed that it was important to develop interventions that realistically could be adopted by organizations without requiring a major upheaval in their operations. Those considerations led us to create interventions that were relatively brief (i.e., not requiring large amounts of employee time away from the job) and transportable (i.e., wherein the major elements of the program would exist in video and print form).

The initial programs and the main findings of their field tests are summarized below. Detailed descriptions of methods and results may be found in Cook et al. (1996a, 1996b).

The SAY YES! Program

The *SAY YES! program* was a classroom series with a multisegment video and corresponding booklet. The purpose of the intervention was twofold: (a) to improve health attitudes and practices and (b) to reduce substance abuse. The program was delivered by a trainer in three sessions, the contents of which are summarized below:

- *Session 1: Introduction (45 minutes).* The central concepts of the program were presented and discussed, including healthful lifestyle and well-being, personal choices and lifestyle, and the impact of alcohol and drug use on health and well-being.
- *Session 2: Drugs, Alcohol and Healthy Choices (1.5 hours).* This session included an examination of the messages of alcoholic

beverage advertising and the social-emotional needs targeted by advertising. Didactic presentation, video vignettes, and group exercises enabled examination of the rewards and costs associated with drug and alcohol use compared with healthful choices, such as relaxation exercises, physical exercise, and recreational activities. Behavioral guidelines for moderate alcohol consumption, responsible use of alcohol, and refusing unwanted alcohol and drugs were presented, demonstrated in the form of video vignettes, and discussed.

- *Session 3: Healthy Choices Into Action (45 minutes)*. The final session focused on a stepwise process of behavior change that included a plan to decrease alcohol consumption. Video testimonials described how "real people" have implemented healthful behaviors such as regular exercise, relaxation, and reducing their alcohol consumption. The group was guided in setting realistic health behavior goals and encouraged to proceed in manageable increments toward their goals.

The design was a randomized trial: a pretest–posttest experimental design in which 371 employees of a manufacturing facility in the northeastern United States were randomly assigned to an experimental group, which received the program, or a control group, which did not. Both groups were assessed at pretest and posttest on a self-administered Health Behavior Questionnaire (HBQ),[1] which contained four measures of health attitudes and practices and four measures of alcohol attitudes and practices. (The questionnaire also contained measures of illicit drug use, but reported use at pretest was so low—approximately 4%—that the data were not analyzed further.)

The experimental group showed improvements on measures of Health Control and Work Control, subscales that measure the extent to which the respondent feels in control of his or her health and work life, respectively. The experimental group also showed improvement on the measure of Health Efficacy, whereas the control group did not. A multivariate analysis testing the effect of the program on all four health measures found that the program group showed significant improvement across the cluster of measures, but the control group did not.

No differences were found between the experimental and control groups on measures of alcohol consumption. On the measure of Desire to Reduce Drinking, however, a significant Group × Time interaction was found: The program group exhibited an increase and the control group

---

[1] The Health Behavior Questionnaire (HBQ) is the label applied by the authors to a varying collection of measures used across several studies. In all instances, the HBQ contained a core set of measures of health and substance abuse; however, in each study, other measures are added or deleted depending on the purposes and content of the programs being tested.

showed a decrease on the measure. A significant Group × Time interaction also was found on the Drinking Problems subscale, but in this instance the result was attributable to a decrease in drinking among the control group.

This study found that when a substance abuse prevention program was combined with a general program promoting healthier lifestyles, substantial improvements occurred in health attitudes and practices, but little change occurred in attitudes toward or practices involving substance use. The substantial amount of material on adopting a healthful lifestyle clearly was effective with this population, and no evidence indicated that combining the substance abuse prevention with health promotion topics hindered improvements in the general health domain.

The Working People Program

Working People: Decisions About Drinking was a four-session program delivered in 30-minute, small-group sessions over a period of 4 weeks. In contrast to the SAY YES! program, Working People focused specifically on reducing alcohol abuse, rather than illicit drug use, and contained less emphasis on improving health practices. Contents of the sessions are described below:

- *Session 1: A Closer Look at Drinking.* This session served to introduce the series; it provided an overview of some of the health and safety risks and potential negative social and lifestyle effects of heavy or irresponsible alcohol use. The dangers and costs of "alcohol abuse" were contrasted with the positive messages of television and print media advertising designed to appeal to social and emotional needs and desires. Didactic presentation, video vignettes, and group discussion enabled examination of the rewards and costs associated with alcohol use and abuse. The idea of "cutting down" and potential rewards of decreasing alcohol consumption were introduced through video testimonials and group discussion. Participants were cautioned that people who have difficulty cutting down or feel that they have a problem with alcohol should seek help as a first step. Materials describing access to the company's EAP were distributed to all participants in this session, as was a pamphlet summarizing the major topics of the session.
- *Session 2: Some Important Facts About Alcohol.* This session centered on a lecture-style video, which presented factual information regarding the properties of alcohol; health risks associated with heavy alcohol consumption; safety implications of working under the influence of alcohol; definitions of al-

cohol misuse, "abuse," and dependence; and signs and symptoms of alcohol dependence. Participants discussed the concept of moderate drinking (defined as not more than two drinks per day for men and not more than one drink per day for women, except for pregnant women), and they were encouraged to begin thinking about their own alcohol consumption in terms of amount, frequency, and so on. All participants were given a copy of the session's video, *Some Important Facts About Alcohol*, to take home for review and for showing to family members.

- *Session 3: One More Pitcher?* This session focused on decision-making processes and alcohol consumption, setting personal limits, and practical ways to cut down. Video and print materials provided behavioral guidelines for moderate drinking for drinkers who can safely drink. The positive effects of responsible drinking and healthful choices were discussed and were demonstrated in the video segment. Guidelines for cutting down on alcohol use in social situations were discussed, and obstacles were identified along with strategies for overcoming them. Refusal skills demonstrated in a video vignette were analyzed, and participants were asked to demonstrate how they might refuse in a social situation. Printed materials describing the signs and symptoms of a problem with alcohol were distributed, and people believing that they might have a problem were encouraged to seek help.

- *Session 4: It's About Choices: Building Personal Power.* The final segment focused on positive alternatives to alcohol abuse. A video vignette demonstrated the negative effects of drinking to relieve stress and then provided modeling opportunities for using healthful alternatives, such as sports and exercise, to relieve tension. Video testimonials featured "real people" describing how they used healthful alternatives and cut down on alcohol consumption. Print materials included a stepwise process for cutting down on alcohol consumption and engaging in healthful alternative behaviors. A secondary focus of this segment was on parenting and setting a positive example for children. Participants discussed a range of alternatives that they might use in meeting social and emotional needs and ways in which they could provide a positive example to their children.

The research design was a pretest–posttest, quasi-experimental design involving 108 employees of a medium-sized printing company. Thirty-eight employees who participated in Working People were compared with two groups who did not participate in the program. The first comparison group consisted of 26 employees and was located in the same facility as the program group; the second comparison group consisted of 44 employees and was located at a branch facility. Both groups were assessed on the Health Behavior Questionnaire, which contained many of the same measures as used in the SAY YES! field test, with the addition of two stages-of-change measures.

The program group showed significant decreases on two out of three measures of alcohol consumption ("number of drinking days in the past 30 days" and "number of days having 5 or more drinks in the past 30 days"), whereas the comparison groups showed no such decreases. The program group also showed significant increases on two measures of motivation to reduce drinking in relation to the comparison groups. Drawn from stage-of-change theory, the measures asked respondents where they were "right now" with respect to cutting back on their drinking in terms of five stages, from "not even thinking about it" to "just started cutting back." One item asked the question in reference to the amount individual respondents drank at any one time; the other in reference to the amount they drank weekly. No differences were found between the groups on two measures of health attitudes.

This study showed that a workplace alcohol abuse prevention program can produce desired, significant changes in participants' alcohol consumption and their motivation to reduce their drinking. The program appeared to have no effect on health attitudes, though. The findings are in some contrast to the SAY YES! findings, which showed substantial changes on health measures but not on substance use measures. This finding perhaps is not surprising in that the health–substance abuse emphasis was reversed in the Working People program. In addition, the samples in the Working People field test were self-selected: An intervention with "drinking" in the title is likely to attract more employees with an interest in possibly changing their drinking practices and perhaps likely to repel employees who are either uninterested in such change or fearful of the stigma of attending such a program in the workplace.

INTEGRATING SUBSTANCE ABUSE PREVENTION INTO WORKPLACE HEALTH PROMOTION: A RANDOMIZED FIELD TEST

In designing a substance abuse prevention program for the workplace with a health promotion orientation, one option is to construct an entirely new program that includes substance abuse prevention, as in the SAY YES! program. As the results of the SAY YES! field test indicate, such a program may attract sizable numbers of employees (thereby overcoming the substance abuse stigma) and move them toward healthier lifestyles, but its impact on substance use appears limited. When the health promotion aspects of the program are deemphasized within a program that is openly labeled as a substance abuse prevention program (as in the Working People program), a substantial impact on AOD use can be achieved for those who participate, but such a program succeeds in attracting only a small number of workers.

With the creation of the Make the Connection program, our research team tested a third way to reach employees with substance abuse prevention messages. Substance abuse prevention materials (print and video) were created especially for insertion into existing workplace health promotion programs. Make the Connection included three sets of video and print materials, called The Stress Management Connection, The Healthy Eating Connection, and The Active Lifestyle Connection.

This study tested the impact of The Stress Management Connection and The Healthy Eating Connection when the materials were inserted into an existing stress management program and a nutrition and weight management program, respectively. The main purpose of the study was to test the effects of the substance abuse prevention materials on the attitudes toward and practices involving AOD use of workers who participate in health promotion programs. A secondary purpose was to assess the ancillary effects of inserting such materials in health promotion programs, including whether the substance abuse prevention materials would dilute the central impact of the health promotion programs. Workplace stress management and healthful-eating and nutrition programs have been shown to have beneficial effects on workers (Glanz, Sorensen, & Farmer, 1996; Murphy, 1996); the beneficial effects should not be hindered by the insertion of substance abuse prevention materials.

Methods

The central design of the research was a randomized trial: a pretest–posttest experimental design in which employees of an insurance company who volunteered to participate in a health promotion program were randomly assigned to one of two health promotion conditions: health promotion only (HP) or health promotion plus substance abuse prevention (HP + SAP). The classes and materials were identical across conditions except that in the HP + SAP condition, the participants also received specially developed substance abuse prevention messages and materials tailored to the particular health promotion topic. Participants were assessed on a version of the HBQ, with certain measures added to reflect the specific purposes and content of the two health promotion programs, as described below. The HBQ was given to participants before the classes began and at approximately 1 and 10 months after the class ended.

The research consisted of two studies, each involving a specific type of health promotion program. In the first study, the health promotion classes were devoted to the topic of stress management; participants in the HP condition received only stress management materials, and participants in the HP + SAP condition received the same stress management materials along with substance abuse prevention materials. In the second study, the classes were devoted to the topic of healthful eating (a combination of nutrition and weight management), and participants were randomly assigned to the HP or the HP + SAP condition.

The two main research questions were, (a) Do employees in the HP + SAP condition show greater improvements than employees in the HP condition in attitudes toward and behaviors involving substance abuse? and (b) Do employees in the two programs show positive gains in health practices and attitudes (either stress management or healthful eating), regardless of whether they are in the HP condition or the HP + SAP condition? The central measures of substance abuse attitudes were perceptions of health risks associated with AOD use and the extent to which substance use and health were seen as interconnected. Substance abuse behavior was measured mainly by self-reports of AOD consumption.

All employees (approximately 1,800) were notified about the stress management and healthy-eating classes through a letter from the CEO, followed by notices sent through company mail. The notices informed them that the health promotion programs would be accompanied by research activities that included the administration of a questionnaire before and after the classes and that all participants would receive a colorful T-shirt on completion of the classes and the questionnaire administration. A total of 209 employees signed up for the stress management classes and took the pretest questionnaire; 161 completed the initial posttest questionnaire, and 116 completed the posttest 2 questionnaire. A total of 215 employees signed up for the healthy-eating classes and completed the pretest questionnaire; 126 completed the initial posttest questionnaire, and 64 completed the posttest 2 questionnaire.

The demographic characteristics of participants in both programs generally reflected the composition of the work force: They were mostly white (88% in the stress management classes; 75% in the healthy-eating classes) women (86% in stress management; 83% in healthy eating) in their mid-30s, married, with some college. Nearly all the nonwhite participants were African American.

The research procedures were virtually identical for the two types of programs. All employees who signed up for a program were asked to complete the self-administered HBQ in the context of an individual interview. (In previous methodological studies by the author, the use of a self-administered questionnaire within an individual interview had been found to be the best approach to gathering self-report data on substance use among workers; Cook, Bernstein, Arrington, Andrews, & Marshall, 1995; Cook, Hersch, & McPherson, 1999.) Participants were then randomly assigned to either the experimental group (HP + SAP) or a control group (HP) to receive the intervention. Within 1 month following the completion of the classes, participants completed the HBQ a second time, again in individual interviews. The HBQ was administered a third time by company mail approximately 10 months after the completion of the intervention.

The HBQ contained several measures of alcohol consumption, attitudes and intentions about alcohol use, use of illicit drugs, perceived risks of AOD use, health beliefs, and views on the connections between substance use and health. The HBQ completed by participants in the stress management program also contained three measures of stress. The HBQ completed by healthy-eating program participants also contained five measures of eating practices and attitudes as well as brief measures of exercise practices and attitudes. Most of the measures of substance use and health beliefs contained in the questionnaire were developed and used by the research team in previous workplace research projects and had shown evidence of reliability and validity.

The specific measures are described below:

1. *Demographics:* 6 items assessing age, sex, race, education, marital status, and number of sick days taken in the past 12 months
2. *Drinking Quantity and Frequency:* 4 items assessing whether the respondent had a drink in the past 12 months, the number of days in the past 30 days on which the respondent had had a drink, the number of drinks usually drunk on those days, and the number of days the respondent had had five or more drinks at one time
3. *Connections Between Health and Substance Use:* a 13-item subscale that assessed the degree to which the respondent perceived connections between health and substance use (α = .86)
4. *Risks of AOD Use:* a 14-item subscale that assessed the extent to which the respondent thought people risk harming themselves by using AODs (α = .76)
5. *Drinking Reduction Self-Efficacy:* 2 items assessing how confident the respondent felt about being able to reduce alcohol consumption
6. *Intention to Reduce Drinking:* 1 item that asked whether the respondent intended to reduce his or her alcohol consumption
7. *Drug Use Checklist:* a checklist assessing the frequency of use of eight major drugs of abuse in the past 30 days

8. *Health and Job Control:* a 12-item subscale that assessed the degree to which the respondent felt in control of his or her health and work life ($\alpha = .72$).

The HBQ given to the stress management program participants also contained the following five subscales:

1. *Work Pressures:* a 10-item subscale assessing the frequency with which the respondent felt pressures from work during the past 30 days ($\alpha = .85$)
2. *Personal Pressures:* a 10-item subscale assessing the frequency with which the respondent felt pressures from personal life during the past 30 days ($\alpha = .82$)
3. *Symptoms of Distress:* a 15-item subscale assessing the frequency of specific physical and emotional distress symptoms during the past 30 days ($\alpha = .80$)
4. *Coping with Stress:* a 12-item subscale assessing the respondent's perceived ability to cope with stress ($\alpha = .82$)
5. *Substance Use Stress Relief:* a 10-item subscale assessing the frequency with which the respondent used AODs to relieve stress ($\alpha = .67$).

The HBQ given to the healthy-eating program participants also contained the following five subscales:

1. *Nutritional Patterns:* a 10-item scale assessing the nutritional content of the respondent's typical daily diet ($\alpha = .64$)
2. *Attitudes Toward a Healthy Diet:* an 18-item subscale assessing the respondent's attitudes toward healthful eating practices ($\alpha = .70$)
3. *Eating Patterns:* a 10-item subscale assessing the frequency with which the respondent engaged in healthful eating practices ($\alpha = .63$)
4. *Exercise Habits:* a 3-item subscale assessing the frequency and intensity with which the respondent engaged in physical exercise ($\alpha = .76$)
5. *Exercise Self-Efficacy:* a 3-item subscale assessing the respondent's confidence in being able to engage in regular exercise ($\alpha = .69$).

Interventions

All participants in the stress management program attended three 45-minute sessions, which took place during lunch hour in groups of approximately 15 employees over a 3-week period. Sessions were led by a trainer who was experienced in conducting stress management training and who was also given training by the research team in the presentation of the special substance abuse prevention materials. The program focused on the identification of personal stressors at home and at work, analysis of personal choices, and development of healthful behaviors for the management of stress.

Experimental group members received the stress management information, supplemented by materials that were developed especially for insertion into stress management programs. At each session, a substance abuse module was presented, consisting of a video segment, print materials, and a brief discussion. The video segments presented "testimonials"—personal stories of people who had successfully reduced their drinking or other drug use and learned to manage stress through healthful means—along with dramatic vignettes that showed working adults and their families encountering and overcoming situations involving stress and substance abuse. The video segments were designed to engage participants while presenting opportunities for observational learning, behavioral modeling, and boosting self-efficacy. The video segments also contained skills-training materials (e.g., drink-refusal skills) that were designed to improve behavioral capabilities related to control of drinking and drug use. At each session, participants were given a pamphlet containing additional information on substance abuse and its connection to stress management.

In the initial session, the use of alcohol as a stress management tool was contrasted negatively with the use of healthful methods, such as relaxation techniques and gaining social support. Behavioral guidelines for limiting or reducing alcohol intake were discussed and demonstrated. In the second session, the materials focused on drug abuse (including misuse of prescription drugs) as a counterproductive behavior, in contrast to the healthful stress management methods. The process of drug dependency (the "drug trap") was presented and discussed. The final session focused on a video segment that showed a woman using both relaxation and assertiveness techniques to reduce the stress of family demands, contrasting these techniques with the use of alcohol.

The healthy-eating program was presented in three 45-minute classes to groups of approximately 15 participants over a 3-week period. Nutrition trainers who had been trained in the use of the specially developed substance abuse prevention materials led the classes. The nutrition and weight management content was the same for the experimental and control groups, and it covered the benefits of good nutrition; how to use the Food Guide Pyramid (USDA, 1992); and skills for using food labels, decreasing dietary fat, increasing intake of fruits and vegetables, modifying recipes, setting goals, and overcoming obstacles.

The experimental group received the specially developed substance abuse prevention materials (video, print, and brief discussion), which presented AOD use as significant obstacles to reaching dietary and weight management goals. Dramatic vignettes modeled healthful choices (e.g., refusal of drinks, exercise for tension relief, and so on), and testimonials provided insights into strategies for improving diet and avoiding AODs. Guidelines were presented for limiting and reducing alcohol intake. Unlike the stress management program, the healthy-eating experimental condition presented all the substance abuse prevention material in the last session. This change was made after reviewing participant evaluations from the stress management program, which indicated that some participants felt that too much time was devoted to substance abuse material.

Randomization and Attrition Effects

The success of the random assignment to the experimental or control groups was assessed by examining possible differences between the two groups on both demographics and central dependent measures at pretest. Chi-square analyses showed no differences on demographics between experimental and control groups for either the stress management or the healthy-eating programs.

Similarly, tests of mean differences between experimental and control groups at pretest on the Perceived Risks of AOD Use subscale and on the Connections Between Health and Substance Use subscale found significant differences only on the Risks measure for the stress management groups; the experimental group showed higher scores on perceived Risks of AOD Use than the control group at pretest ($t = 2.22$, $p = .03$). No other differences were found between the two groups; therefore, the randomization was judged a success.

As indicated above, noticeable attrition occurred from pretest to posttest 2, particularly in the healthy-eating group, an outcome that could have implications for the interpretation of the findings. In the stress management program, greater attrition occurred among men than among women in both the control and experimental groups. In the experimental group, one third of the men had dropped out by the posttest 1, and only 15% of the women had dropped out ($\chi^2 = 4.01$, $p = .04$). In the control group, significantly more men than women dropped out at both the posttest 1 ($\chi^2 = 5.23$, $p = .02$) and at posttest 2 ($\chi^2 = 7.79$, $p = .005$). In the healthy-eating group, greater attrition in the experimental group occurred among workers ages 20 to 29 than among older workers at posttest 2 ($\chi^2 = 14.4$, $p = .001$), and greater attrition in the control group occurred among participants with "some college" than among lesser or more highly educated participants at posttest 1 ($\chi^2 = 6.31$, $p = .04$). No other demographic differences in attrition were found in either group.

To determine whether baseline scores on dependent variables differed between participants who dropped out and those who remained, three dependent measures (Risk of AOD Use, Connections Between Health and

Substance Use, and Number of Drinking Days in Past 30 Days) were dichotomized, and dropouts were compared with the remaining participants on proportions above and below the median at each posttest. Chi-square tests of the proportions for all three measures at each posttest for both stress management and healthy-eating program participants were nonsignificant. Thus, the main impact of attrition was to deplete the proportion of male participants in the stress management program and to erode statistical power at posttest 2, especially in the healthy-eating groups.

Results

Post hoc estimates of statistical power were conducted for selected analyses and measures, following Lipsey (1990). Alpha was set at .05, and effect size was calculated as the ratio of the difference between the intervention and the control groups to the common standard deviation, adjusted for the correlation between the dependent variable and the covariate. Power analyses were conducted for two attitudes and perceptions measures and an alcohol-use measure (i.e., drinking days).

Power analyses of the Connections measure generally showed moderate to weak statistical power. For the stress management program, power for pretest to posttest 1 analysis was .68, but it fell to .45 at posttest 2. For the healthy-eating program, power was low at the first (.20) and second (.15) posttests. For the AOD Risks subscale, power at posttest 1 was only .24, but it rose to .60 by posttest 2 because a larger effect size (.40 vs. .15) more than compensated for reduced samples. Power for the number of drinking days in the past 30 days was low for the combined groups (.17 at posttest 2 and .27 at posttest 2—only slightly better). The analyses indicated that statistical power would be limited for the attitude and perception measures, particularly at posttest 2, and low for the substance use measures.

The effects of the substance abuse prevention materials on stress management program participants were assessed through analysis of covariance (ANCOVA), which compared the experimental group (HP + SAP) with the control group (HP) on posttest measures using the pretest measure as a covariate. The results, shown in Table 3.1, indicated that few differences existed between the two groups at either posttest 1 or posttest 2. Among the substance abuse measures, significant differences between the experimental and control groups were found only on the measure of Substance Use Stress Relief at posttest 2; the group receiving the substance abuse prevention materials showed less frequent AOD use to relieve stress. In addition, the control group showed more significant gains on the Coping with Stress measure at posttest 1 than the experimental group did, although both groups showed substantial gains.

To assess the efficacy of the stress management program, the experimental and control groups were combined, and the effects on HBQ

TABLE 3.1
Comparison of Stress Management Program Experimental and Control Groups

Measure	Pretest	N	Mean (SD) Posttest 1	N	Posttest 2	N	Posttest 1 ANCOVA With Group F	p	Posttest 2 ANCOVA F	p
Health attitudes										
Health and job control										
Experimental	3.48 (.55)	99	3.60 (.55)	81	3.76 (.53)	60	1.70	.19	1.45	.23
Control	3.39 (.53)	105	3.61 (.56)	73	3.58 (.52)	53				
Substance abuse										
Connections between health and substance use[a]										
Experimental	1.46 (.36)	97	1.32 (.29)	81	1.34 (.35)	60	1.54	.22	1.78	.19
Control	1.53 (.38)	104	1.43 (.38)	76	1.45 (.40)	55				
Risks of alcohol and drug use										
Experimental	3.74 (.23)	97	3.77 (.25)	82	3.78 (.23)	56	.03	.87	2.19	.14
Control	3.62 (.46)	105	3.72 (.25)	74	3.70 (.32)	55				
Substance use stress relief[a]										
Experimental	1.64 (.41)	95	1.52 (.30)	80	1.51 (.28)	61	.17	.68	4.01	.05
Control	1.68 (.46)	107	1.56 (.39)	74	1.61 (.34)	56				
Stress										
Work pressure[a]										
Experimental	1.61 (.54)	99	1.39 (.64)	82	1.15 (.59)	61	1.39	.24	1.59	.21
Control	1.62 (.54)	104	1.38 (.61)	74	1.34 (.60)	56				
Personal pressure[a]										
Experimental	1.21 (.61)	98	1.06 (.53)	81	.96 (.54)	61	.67	.41	2.33	.13
Control	1.26 (.63)	105	1.08 (.62)	76	1.12 (.58)	56				
Symptoms of distress[a]										
Experimental	1.46 (.54)	96	1.19 (.56)	76	1.02 (.57)	56	.03	.87	2.61	.11
Control	1.41 (.53)	102	1.23 (.56)	71	1.13 (.61)	53				
Coping with stress										
Experimental	1.98 (.35)	98	2.11 (.33)	81	2.19 (.32)	59	3.95	.05	.01	.93
Control	1.93 (.36)	102	2.13 (.37)	73	2.13 (.41)	51				

[a] Lower is better.
Note. ANCOVA = analysis of covariance.

measures were analyzed through repeated-measures analysis of variance (ANOVA). As shown in Table 3.2, significant improvements were shown at posttest 1 on all Stress Measures, Health and Job Control, Connections Between Health and Substance Use, and Substance Use Stress Relief subscales. Most of the improvements continued through posttest 2, although by that point the changes in the two substance abuse perception measures had become nonsignificant. No effects were found on the Drinking Reduction Self-Efficacy or Intention to Reduce Drinking subscales.

As shown in Table 3.1, the improvements on the stress measures occurred in both the experimental and control groups (i.e., the presence of the substance abuse prevention materials did not appreciably dilute the impact of the stress management program). Only on the Coping With Stress measure did the control group improve significantly more than the experimental group, although both groups showed gains. Moreover, the stress management program itself showed unexpected effects on the substance abuse measures, indicating that stress management may have indirect, but substantial, effects on attitudes toward and practices involving substance abuse. Consequently, further analyses were conducted on AOD use for all stress management program participants.

Because an examination of changes in drinking measures revealed that most of the drinkers had reduced their drinking from pretest to posttest, a Wilcoxon Matched-Pairs Sign Test (Siegel, 1956) was used to determine whether more participants reduced their drinking than stayed the same or increased (the ANOVA had tested the significance of mean drinking levels). Among the stress management participants who were drinkers (i.e., who had had an alcoholic beverage in the past 12 months), 44 reduced the number of drinking days in the past month at posttest 1, whereas 21 increased the number and 35 stayed the same. Applying a Wilcoxon test to the data revealed a significant effect of the program at posttest 1 ($z = -1.99$, $p = .047$). The changes on this measure from pretest to posttest 2 were not significant. Reduction in drinking was further assessed using an estimate of the number of drinks in the past 30 days (the product of the number of drinking days and the average number of drinks per drinking day). Applying the Wilcoxon test to this measure showed that the change from pretest to posttest 1 was significant (51 decreased, 20 increased, and 29 stayed the same; $z = -2.68$, $p = .007$), as was the change from pretest to posttest 2 (33 decreased, 18 increased, and 17 stayed the same; $z = -2.00$; $p = .045$). These reductions are displayed in Figure 3.3.

Among the stress management program participants, 25 reported using illicit drugs at any one of the three data collection points. Of the 16 participants who reported using drugs at pretest, 11 reported no use, and 5 reported they were still using at posttest 1 (McNemar test significant, $p = .02$). By posttest 2, data were available on 9 of the 16 participants, 7 of whom reported not using drugs and 2 of whom were still reporting use

TABLE 3.2
Effects Over Time of the Stress Management Program on Combined Groups (Experimental and Control)

Measure	Combined Sample Mean (SD)							Repeated-Measures ANOVA				
	Pretest	N	Posttest 1	N	Posttest 2	N		Posttest 1		Posttest 2	
								F	p	F	p
Health attitudes											
Health and job control	3.43 (.56)	204	3.61 (.55)	154	3.67 (.53)	113		40.44	.001	19.70	.001
Substance abuse											
Connections between health and substance use[a]	1.49 (.37)	201	1.37 (.34)	157	1.39 (.38)	115		10.70	.001	2.67	.11
Risks of alcohol and drug use	3.68 (.37)	202	3.74 (.25)	156	3.74 (.28)	111		4.29	.04	.12	.74
Substance use stress relief[a]	1.66 (.42)	202	1.54 (.34)	157	1.56 (.31)	117		24.36	.001	4.41	.038
Stress											
Work pressure[a]	1.62 (.54)	203	1.39 (.62)	156	1.24 (.60)	117		37.47	.001	41.98	.001
Personal pressure[a]	1.23 (.62)	203	1.07 (.57)	157	1.04 (.57)	117		19.46	.001	8.13	.005
Symptoms of distress[a]	1.44 (.53)	198	1.21 (.56)	147	1.08 (.59)	109		43.04	.001	44.71	.001
Coping with stress	1.95 (.36)	200	2.12 (.35)	154	2.16 (.37)	110		60.50	.001	36.58	.001
Alcohol consumption											
No. of drinking days in the past 30 days	4.76 (5.81)	144	4.30 (5.42)	106	4.17 (4.93)	75		2.39	.125	4.13	.046
No. of drinks per day	1.92 (1.99)	142	1.81 (2.42)	106	1.93 (1.34)	56		.02	.885	1.40	.243
No. of heavy drinking days	.67 (1.64)	142	.61 (2.07)	103	.67 (1.81)	55		2.78	.099	.59	.446

[a]Lower is better.
Note.   ANOVA = analysis of variance.

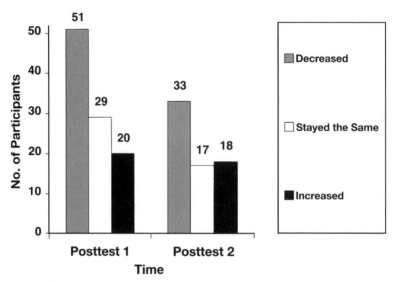

Figure 3.3. Change in the number of drinks consumed in the past 30 days among participants in the stress management program.

(McNemar test, n.s.). Although the findings indicate that the impact of the stress management program itself on stress and substance use was rather sweeping—with or without the substance abuse prevention materials—it should be noted that this facet of the design was relatively nonrigorous (i.e., it did not include a comparison to a group of employees who did not receive the stress management classes; Figure 3.4).

The effects of the substance abuse prevention materials on healthy-eating program participants also were assessed through ANCOVA that compared the experimental group (HP + SAP) and control group (HP)

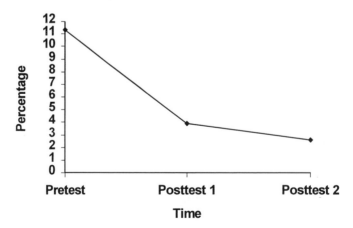

Figure 3.4. Change in the percentage of participants in the stress management program reporting illicit drug use.

on posttest measures and used the pretest measure as a covariate. Table 3.3 displays the results of these analyses. In some contrast to the stress management program participants, the healthy-eating program participants exposed to the substance abuse prevention materials showed significant gains at posttest 1 on both the measure of Connections Between Health and Substance Use and the measure of Risks of Alcohol and Drug Use, whereas the control group participants showed none. The improvements by the experimental group on the Risks measure held through posttest 2, but their gains on the Connections measure did not. No differences were found between the two groups on the measures of alcohol consumption. As indicated by the analysis of combined groups, the Health Attitudes measure showed gains by both groups, and as expected, no difference was found between the two groups.

The impact of the healthy-eating program on both experimental (HP + SAP) and control (HP-only) participants from pretest to posttest 1 and posttest 2 also was assessed by repeated measures ANOVA. As shown in Table 3.4, the program had a significant impact on the central measures of healthy eating, but not as much impact on the health and substance abuse measures. All five measures of eating and weight management showed significant gains from pretest to posttest 1. At posttest 2, the gains on the Nutritional Patterns and Attitudes About a Healthy Diet subscales had diminished somewhat, but they remained significantly better than at pretest. The gains on the measure of Eating Patterns held constant through posttest 2. Participants exhibited significant improvement on the measure of Connections Between Health and Substance Use at posttest 1, but this improvement had disappeared by posttest 2. No change was found at posttest 1 on the measure of Health and Job Control, but significant improvement occurred by posttest 2. (We repeat the caution that because of a lack of a no-treatment control, this kind of delayed late improvement could very well be a function of events outside the healthy-eating program.) No effects were found on the Drinking Reduction Self-Efficacy or Intention to Reduce Drinking subscales.

As shown in Table 3.3, the significant improvements in the eating and weight management measures occurred in both the experimental and the control groups, indicating that the presence of the substance abuse prevention materials did not dilute the impact of the Healthy Eating program.

Neither the ANOVA nor the Wilcoxon test detected any significant changes in alcohol consumption over time for the combined groups of healthy-eating program participants. Among the healthy-eating program participants, 15 reported using illicit drugs at any of the three points of data collection. Of the 12 participants who reported illicit drug use at pretest, 6 reported no use by posttest 1, and 2 reported they were using at

TABLE 3.3
Comparison of Healthy-Eating Program Experimental and Control Groups

	Mean (SD)						Posttest 1 ANCOVA With Group		Posttest 2 ANCOVA	
Measure	Pretest	N	Posttest 1	N	Posttest 2	N	F	p	F	p
Health attitudes: Health and job control										
Experimental	3.61 (.47)	102	3.66 (.53)	61	3.72 (.36)	30	.06	.81	1.35	.25
Control	3.64 (.46)	109	3.68 (.49)	63	3.84 (.46)	30				
Substance abuse										
Connections between health and substance use[a]										
Experimental	1.48 (.37)	103	1.37 (.33)	62	1.45 (.32)	29	5.73	.018	.38	.54
Control	1.45 (.35)	109	1.40 (.33)	61	1.39 (.34)	34				
Risks of alcohol and drug use										
Experimental	3.69 (.25)	103	3.77 (.22)	58	3.80 (.20)	30	7.16	.009	4.34	.04
Control	3.74 (.24)	107	3.75 (.23)	63	3.73 (.26)	34				
Eating and weight management										
Nutritional patterns										
Experimental	2.37 (.36)	100	2.57 (.33)	59	2.47 (.37)	28	1.47	.23	.31	.58
Control	2.35 (.35)	107	2.58 (.30)	59	2.49 (.28)	31				
Attitudes about a healthy diet[a]										
Experimental	2.51 (.39)	102	2.39 (.42)	59	2.52 (.37)	29	.70	.41	1.21	.28
Control	2.52 (.37)	106	2.20 (.44)	60	2.28 (.39)	31				
Eating patterns										
Experimental	2.63 (.38)	95	2.77 (.40)	57	2.80 (.39)	24	.64	.43	2.37	.13
Control	2.58 (.43)	98	2.70 (.36)	51	2.68 (.29)	28				
Exercise habits										
Experimental	2.92 (.95)	87	3.18 (.87)	56	2.75 (.92)	19	.08	.79	3.30	.08
Control	2.85 (.88)	85	3.09 (.84)	53	2.96 (.91)	22				
Exercise self-efficacy[a]										
Experimental	2.15 (.81)	94	1.92 (.85)	59	2.41 (1.19)	23	.82	.37	1.21	.28
Control	2.18 (.91)	99	1.94 (.76)	56	2.20 (.96)	28				

[a]Lower is better.
Note. ANCOVA = analysis of covariance.

124 COOK ET AL.

TABLE 3.4
Effects Over Time of the Healthy-Eating Program on Combined Groups (Experimental and Control)

Measure	Combined Sample Mean (SD)						Repeated-Measures ANOVA			
							Posttest 1		Posttest 2	
	Pretest	N	Posttest 1	N	Posttest 2	N	F	p	F	p
Health attitudes										
Health and job control	3.63 (.46)	211	3.67 (.51)	124	3.78 (.41)	60	.64	.43	4.64	.04
Substance abuse										
Connections between health and substance use[a]	1.46 (.36)	212	1.38 (.33)	123	1.42 (.33)	63	9.42	.003	.57	.45
Risks of alcohol and drug use	3.71 (.24)	210	3.76 (.22)	121	3.76 (.23)	64	.65	.42	.59	.45
Eating and weight management										
Nutritional patterns	2.36 (.36)	207	2.57 (.31)	118	2.48 (.32)	59	77.37	.001	5.47	.02
Attitudes about a healthy diet[a]	2.52 (.38)	208	2.26 (.42)	119	2.33 (.41)	60	41.04	.001	10.20	.002
Eating patterns	2.60 (.41)	193	2.74 (.40)	108	2.73 (.34)	52	20.22	.001	6.79	.012
Exercise habits	2.88 (.91)	172	3.13 (.85)	109	2.87 (.91)	41	20.84	.001	1.04	.32
Exercise self-efficacy[a]	2.17 (.86)	193	1.93 (.80)	115	2.29 (1.04)	51	11.98	.001	.94	.34
Alcohol consumption										
No. of drinking days in the past 30 days	3.77 (5.72)	131	4.14 (5.78)	75	3.97 (7.00)	37	1.75	.19	.98	.33
No. of drinks per day	2.19 (1.64)	98	1.95 (2.15)	74	1.64 (.90)	25	.17	.68	1.87	.19
No. of heavy drinking days	.74 (1.92)	93	.99 (2.71)	74	.73 (2.18)	26	.28	.62	2.71	.12

[a]Lower is better.
Note. ANOVA = analysis of variance.

TABLE 3.5
Participant Evaluations: Comparisons of Stress Management and
Healthy-Eating Groups (Combined Experimental and Control Groups)

Program Element	Mean (SD)		t	p
	Stress Management	Healthy Eating		
Trainer	3.76 (.89)	4.31 (.75)	5.49	.001
Course	3.36 (.98)	4.10 (.78)	7.01	.001
Substance abuse content	3.26 (1.03)	3.78 (.93)	3.21	.002

posttest 1 (the remaining 4 participants did not complete the posttest). The McNemar test of the changes was nonsignificant.

As part of posttest 1, participants rated program elements on a scale of 1 to 5 (where 5 was favorable). A shown in Table 3.5, the healthy-eating program received significantly higher ratings than the stress management program on all three elements. No differences were found between the experimental and control groups on ratings of the three program elements.

When experimental-group participants were asked about the amount of substance abuse material in future programs, 64% of the healthy-eating program participants recommended having "the same amount" of materials, and 29% recommended having more information on substance abuse. In contrast, among stress management program participants, only 36% recommended "the same amount" of material on substance abuse, and 46% recommended having less such material. (The stress management program included substance abuse material in each session, whereas the Healthy Eating program limited the substance abuse materials to the final session.)

Discussion

This study shows that substance abuse prevention materials can be inserted into workplace health promotion offerings without diluting the impact of such programs. The improvements in stress and in eating and exercise measures occurred regardless of whether the substance abuse prevention materials were included in the program, and they were virtually unaffected by the presence of the materials. Because the improvements were registered in the context of a design that did not include a "no-treatment" control group, it is not entirely clear that the gains were a function mainly of the program experiences or of some outside influences. Nonetheless, the apparent gains are congruent with the typical positive outcomes generated by similar workplace interventions directed toward stress and eating practices, at least in the short-term (Glanz et al., 1996; Murphy, 1996). Note that the substance abuse materials were carefully crafted and specially tailored to the particular health promotion subject matter, and most of the program time was devoted to the stress management or healthy-eating topic, not to substance abuse. Indeed, it appears that when a workplace health promotion program focuses mainly on substance abuse, many participants react negatively to the relatively heavy dose of substance abuse material and messages, as participants indicated by their evaluations in the stress management program.

The substance abuse components themselves were found to have mixed effects. In the stress management program, participants exposed to the substance abuse prevention materials relied less on AODs to relieve their stress, an effect that was registered several months after the program classes ended. Although not an especially dramatic finding, it is nonetheless important. Millions of people use alcohol and a variety of prescription and illicit drugs for reasons that are at least partly stress related. In this instance, a significant proportion of participants reported that they now viewed chemical means of stress relief as less desirable and had chosen to use behavioral approaches.

In the healthy-eating program, the positive impact of the substance abuse prevention materials was reflected in both the Risks of AOD Use and in the Connections Between Health and Substance Use subscales. These results also were viewed as important because the measure of perceived risks of AOD use often has been associated with drug use, and the perceived connections between drug use and health were a theme of the substance abuse prevention materials. With the important exception of the Substance Use Stress Relief measure, however, the specific impact of the substance abuse prevention materials was confined to measures of substance abuse attitudes and perceptions; no effects were reflected in the direct self-reports of AOD use. This finding was at least partly attributable to the fact that heavy drinking and illicit drug use was relatively uncommon in this group of workers when they came into the programs, leaving little opportunity for demonstrating the effects of the prevention materials on substance use. Indeed, post hoc power analyses indicated that with this particular combination of sample sizes, effect sizes, and substance use practices, significant intervention effects would be difficult to demonstrate, particularly on AOD use.

The impact of the stress management program itself (i.e., with or without the substance abuse prevention materials) on attitudes toward and behavior involving substance use was not unanticipated, but it was nevertheless surprising in its strength and breadth. In both experimental and control conditions, participants reported significant improvements in attitudes and perceptions along with reductions in the use of AODs. Although the validity of the findings is weakened somewhat by the lack of a no-treatment control group, the healthy-eating control group (which was also assessed on the same substance use measures and showed no such decreases) could be considered a comparison group against which the Stress Management program can be contrasted. Moreover, the effects of stress management on substance use shown in this research parallel the findings of similar past research. The work of Snow and his associates (see chapter 2, this volume) has shown that workplace stress management programs have multiple beneficial effects on participants' adjustment and coping skills, including reductions in alcohol and tobacco use, even though the programs contained little explicit discussion of the hazards of tobacco and alcohol (Kline & Snow, 1994; Snow & Kline, 1995). In the present study, the participants may have changed their attitudes and reduced their AOD use as a function of adopting new stress management beliefs and skills. The stress management programs tested by Snow and Kline were of greater intensity and duration than the program in the present study, typically involving 12 to 15 one-hour sessions, in contrast to the three 45-minute sessions in this study. Although the present study should be replicated with a stronger design, when viewed in the light of the Snow and Kline studies, stress management programs appear to offer particular promise as effective vehicles for substance abuse prevention in the work force.

Note that although the methodology of this study was generally quite rigorous, several potential weaknesses of design and measurement remain that could diminish the validity of the findings. In addition to the cautions expressed above, other methodological concerns include effects of attrition and the validity of self-reports. As noted, attrition was substantial, particularly by posttest 2. Because men dropped out of the stress management posttests at a faster rate than women and were a small minority at the beginning, the findings have little generalizability to working men. Workers younger than age 30 tended to drop out of the healthy-eating posttests faster than older workers, but significantly so only by posttest 2. It is also important that no differential attrition was noted by outcome measures at pretest. Consequently, with the possible exception of gender and loss of statistical power, the effects of attrition on the findings appear negligible.

Another potential limitation of the study is that because all participants were volunteers, virtually all of them entered the programs with some level of motivation to change—a level that would not be present in employees who chose not to participate in the programs. Because of the randomized design, however, one might reasonably assume that the motivation to change was roughly equal between experimental and control participants.

In any study of substance abuse that relies solely on self-reports, the validity of self-reported substance use is of concern. Our research has consistently found that respondents in the workplace typically underreport their drug use and that some proportion of heavy drinkers and drug users (perhaps as much as one third) do not disclose their use accurately or at all. As with the motivation to change, however, no evidence indicates that the lack of disclosure is differentially distributed between randomized groups. Therefore, it is unlikely that underreporting of substance use affected the results, other than further reducing statistical power on substance use outcome measures.

IMPLICATIONS AND CONCLUSIONS

The three field tests conducted to date provide qualified support for the view that relatively brief interventions in the workplace can achieve changes in substance use attitudes and behavior and that health promotion programs can be effective vehicles for such interventions. Shain and his associates (1986) found similar effects on health and drinking practices in their research on the Take Charge program at Champion Spark Plug. The research of Heirich (see chapter 4, this volume) also has provided evidence for the effectiveness of a substance abuse intervention that is housed within a workplace cardiovascular disease prevention program. Further support for the effectiveness of social cognitive workplace prevention interventions outside of a larger health promotion program was generated by Kishuk and her associates (1994) when they field tested their worksite program (in a randomized design) promoting "healthy alcohol consumption." They found that the program was effective in promoting socially responsible attitudes toward drinking practices and in reducing self-reported weekly consumption of alcohol.

Although the interventions tested by our group included messages urging seriously dependent alcohol users to seek help (as well as a self-test to assess the degree of one's alcohol problem), the interventions are targeted at the mainstream of users—moderate-to-heavy drinkers, occasional users of illicit drugs, and people who may misuse psychoactive prescription drugs—who have not reached debilitating dependency. The social cognitive approaches used in the interventions (i.e., self-examination of thoughts and behavior, boosting of self-efficacy, goal setting, training in substance use control, and consideration of healthful alternatives to substance use) are similar in concept (although not intensity) to the treatment strategies tested and advocated by Miller and his colleagues, including brief interventions, motivational enhancement therapy, and behavioral self-control training (Harris & Miller, 1990; Heather, 1995; Miller and Sanchez, 1994). These strategies have been found to be highly successful in the treatment of substance abuse (Moyers & Hester, 1999); perhaps it should not be surprising that interventions with similar conceptual roots show promise in preventing substance abuse as well.

For numerous reasons, stress management programs appear to be especially promising vehicles for workplace substance abuse prevention. Because much substance abuse is a form of self-medicating for stress and tension, substance abuse topics can be easily and naturally woven into stress management programs, although if the proportion of substance abuse material becomes too great, doing so can be counterproductive. Stress management programs are increasingly popular in a broad variety of work forces, with the rise in working couples and ever-increasing pressures to improve productivity. Other health promotion topics, such as nutrition and weight management, are somewhat less natural vehicles for the inclusion of substance abuse material, but the findings from the healthy-eating program field test indicate that the insertion of the materials can be effectively accomplished with such topics, resulting in positive reactions from participants as well as significant changes in substance use attitudes and perceptions. Parenting programs for workers are also promising vehicles for the presentation of substance abuse prevention messages to workers. In particular, programs designed to help working parents keep their children healthy and drug free can provide excellent opportunities for both broaching the subject of worker substance use and providing potentially powerful interventions for adolescent substance abuse prevention.

Much research remains to be conducted on integrated substance abuse–health promotion programs; different combinations of topics, organizational settings, delivery mechanisms, worker characteristics, and program structures need to be tested. Future research on this issue should also use large samples and comprehensive measurements of substance use to improve the internal validity and avoid Type II error. Of particular, immediate interest would be research that includes three conditions: stress management alone, stress management with substance abuse prevention, and a no-treatment control.

Despite the considerable amount of research still needed on this issue, the results of research to date, both from our group and from others, strongly support the inclusion of carefully crafted substance abuse prevention materials into popular worksite health promotion programs. Yet the obstacles to this approach discussed at the beginning of this chapter remain, and the health promotion community (a vast and diverse group) continues to exclude substance abuse topics from their main agenda. A fruitful area of research would involve the exploration of strategies designed to move the health promotion community toward accepting and promoting the inclusion of substance abuse into their programs and activities. (Our group is just beginning a project, in conjunction with leading health promotion associations and groups, to develop and test a computer-based program to train health promotion professionals in substance abuse prevention.)

Health promotion and disease prevention are receiving increased attention from employers and their managed care organizations as they seek to improve worker health and productivity and contain rising health care costs. Substance abuse prevention and related issues of behavioral health should be an integral part of these efforts.

REFERENCES

Abrams, D. B., Elder, J. P., Carleton, R. A., Lasater, T. M., & Artz, L. M. (1986). Social learning principles for organizational health promotion: An integrated approach. In M. F. Cataldo & T. J. Coates (Eds.), *Health and industry: A behavioral medicine perspective*. New York: John Wiley & Sons.

Ames, G. (1993). Research and strategies for the primary prevention of workplace alcohol problems. *Alcohol Health and Research World, 17,* 19–27.

Bandura, A. (1977). *Social learning theory.* Englewood Cliffs, NJ: Prentice Hall.

Bandura, A. (1986). *Social foundations of thought and action: A social cognitive theory.* Englewood Cliffs, NJ: Prentice Hall.

Baranowski, T., Perry, C., & Parcel, G. (1997). How individuals, environments, and health behavior interact: Social cognitive theory. In K. Glantz, F. Lewis, & B. Rimer (Eds.), *Health behavior and health education: Theory, research and practice* (pp. 153–178). San Francisco, CA: Jossey-Bass.

Bennett, J. B., & Lehman, W. E. K. (1998). Workplace drinking climate, stress, and problem indicators: Assessing the influence of teamwork (group cohesion). *Journal of Studies on Alcohol, 59,* 608–818.

Cook, R. F. (1985). An evaluation of the alternatives approach to drug abuse prevention. *International Journal of the Addictions, 19,* 767–787.

Cook, R. F. (in press). Drug abuse prevention in the workplace. In W. Bukoski & Z. Sloboda (Eds.), *Handbook of drug abuse prevention theory, science and practice.* New York: Plenum.

Cook, R. F., Back, A. S., & Trudeau, J. (1996a). Substance abuse prevention in the workplace: Recent findings and an expanded conceptual model. *Journal of Primary Prevention, 16,* 319–338.

Cook, R. F., Back, A. S., & Trudeau, J. (1996b). Preventing alcohol use problems among blue-collar workers: A field test of the Working People program. *Substance Use and Misuse, 31,* 255–275.

Cook, R. F., Bernstein, A. D., Arrington, T. L., Andrews, C. M., & Marshall, G. A. (1995). Methods for assessing drug use prevalence in the workplace: A comparison of self-report, urinalysis and hair analysis. *International Journal of the Addictions, 30,* 403–426.

Cook, R. F., Hersch, R., & McPherson, T. (1999). Drug assessment methods for the workplace. In T. Mieczkowski (Ed.), *Drug testing methods: Assessment and evaluation* (pp. 255–282). Boca Raton, FL: CRC Press.

Cook, R. F., & Youngblood, A. (1990). Preventing substance abuse as an integral part of worksite health promotion. *Occupational Medicine: State of the Art Reviews, 5,* 725–738.

Glanz, K., Sorensen, G., & Farmer, A. (1996). The health impact of worksite nutrition and cholesterol intervention programs. *American Journal of Health Promotion, 10,* 453–470.

Harris, K. B., & Miller, W. R. (1990). Behavioral self-control training for problem drinkers: Competence and efficacy. *Psychology of Addictive Behaviors, 4*, 82–90.

Heather, N. (1995). Brief intervention strategies. In R. Hester & W. Miller (Eds.), *Handbook of alcoholism treatment: Effective alternatives* (2nd ed., pp. 105–122). Needham Heights, MA: Allyn & Bacon.

Kishuk, N., Peters, C., Towers, A., Sylvester, M., Bourgault, C., & Richard, L. (1994). Formative and effectiveness evaluation of a worksite program promoting healthy alcohol consumption. *American Journal of Health Promotion, 8*, 353–362.

Kline, M., & Snow, D. (1994). Effects of a worksite coping skills intervention on the stress, social support and health outcomes of working mothers. *Journal of Primary Prevention, 15*, 105–121.

Lehman, W. E. K., Farabee, D. J., Holcom, M. L., & Simpson, D. D. (1995). Prediction of substance use in the workplace: Unique contributions of personal background and work environment variables. *Journal of Drug Issues, 25*, 253–274.

Lipsey, M. W. (1990). *Design sensitivity: Statistical power for experimental research.* London: Sage.

Miller, N., & Dollard, J. (1941). *Social learning and imitation.* New Haven, CT: Yale University Press.

Miller, R., Shain, M., & Golasewski, T. J. (1985). The synergism of health promotion and restoration in the prevention of substance abuse in the workplace. *Health Values, 9*(5), 50–58.

Miller, W. R., & Sanchez, V. C. (1994). Motivating young adults for treatment and lifestyle change. In G. Howard & P. E. Nathan (Eds.), *Alcohol use and misuse by young adults* (pp. 55–81). Notre Dame, IN: Notre Dame Press.

Moyer, T., & Hester, R. K. (1999). Outcome research: Alcoholism. In M. Galanter & H. D. Kleber (Eds.), *Textbook of substance abuse treatment* (2nd ed., pp. 423–435). Washington, DC: American Psychiatric Press.

Murphy, L. R. (1996). Stress management in work settings: A critical review of the health effects. *American Journal of Health Promotion, 11*, 112–135.

Prochaska, J. O., DiClemente, C. C., & Norcross, J. C. (1992). In search of how people change: Applications to addictive behaviors. *American Psychologist, 47*, 1102–1114.

Roman, P., & Blum, T. (1996). Alcohol: A review of the impact of worksite interventions on health and behavioral outcomes. *American Journal of Health Promotion, 11*, 136–149.

Roman, P., & Blum, T. (1999). Employee assistance programs and other workplace interventions. In M. Galanter & H. D. Kleber (Eds.), *Textbook of substance abuse treatment* (2nd ed., pp. 423–435). Washington, DC: American Psychiatric Press.

Rosenstock, I. M., Strecher, V. J., & Becker, M. H. (Summer, 1988). Social learning theory and the health belief model. *Health Education Quarterly, 15*(2), 175–183.

Shain, M., Suurvali, H., & Boutilier, M. (1986). *Healthier workers: Health promotion and employee assistance programs*. Lexington, MA: Lexington Books.

Siegel, S. (1956). *Nonparametric statistics and the behavioral sciences*. New York: McGraw-Hill.

Snow, D., & Kline, M. (1995). Preventive interventions in the workplace to reduce negative psychiatric consequences of work and family stress. In C. M. Mazure (Ed.), *Does stress cause psychiatric illness?* (pp. 220–270). Washington, DC: American Psychiatric Press.

Sonnenstuhl, W. (1996). *Working sober: The transformation of an occupational drinking cutlure*. Ithaca, NY: Cornell University Press.

4

HELPING AT-RISK DRINKERS REDUCE THEIR DRINKING: CARDIOVASCULAR WELLNESS OUTREACH AT WORK

MAX HEIRICH AND CYNTHIA J. SIECK

Worksite substance abuse prevention programs can have a strong and measurable impact on alcohol consumption. This chapter describes the Wellness Outreach at Work model for behavior change and shows how it applies current understandings of the processes involved in acknowledging health risks and subsequently changing problematic health behaviors including alcohol abuse. The model has been implemented in more than 100 worksites; the recent applications described here use it both for the pre-

Portions of this chapter were adapted from "Worksite Cardiovascular Wellness Programs as a Route to Substance Abuse Prevention," by M. A. Heirich, and C. J. Sieck, 2000, *Journal of Occupational and Environmental Medicine, 42,* pp. 47–56. Copyright © 2000 by Lippincott Williams & Wilkins. Adapted with permission.

Successful disease prevention and health improvement efforts need to use a different model for health delivery than is used for more conventional disease care. One intervenes at a different point on the health–disease continuum, before pain or discomfort motivates people to seek out the services of a health professional. Thus one must be proactive rather than reactive, seeking out those who need services, alerting them to their own health issues, and motivating and empowering them to change health behaviors. These studies of the Wellness Outreach at Work model's use for alcohol prevention demonstrate its potential while alerting us to limits of this approach. It is not a panacea, but it offers entrée to populations normally unresponsive to alcohol education.

vention of alcohol abuse and for intervention with people whose alcohol use now puts their health at risk.

The fear of being labeled an alcoholic or a drug abuser may make it difficult for workers to look at their own alcohol consumption and its possible impact on health and well-being. Because of the stigma attached to alcohol and other drug (AOD) abuse, many employees avoid addressing their AOD-related issues until work performance deteriorates or serious health problems develop. The Wellness Outreach at Work model originally was developed to address cardiovascular disease (CVD) prevention, a non-stigmatizing health problem of concern to a wide segment of the work force. It involves strategies for reaching and assessing the entire work force, determining individual readiness to attempt behavior changes that address various health risks, and creating ongoing counseling relationships with workers. The structure of those ongoing relationships is designed to motivate, empower, and socially reinforce workers as they attempt health behavior changes and then incorporate them into their lifestyle. The outreach strategies have proven useful for alcohol abuse prevention as well as for cardiovascular risk reduction.

This chapter presents a general model for health behavior change, shows its relevance for alcohol abuse prevention at various levels of risk, and discusses three studies that have examined its applicability for use with workers at quite different levels of risk for alcohol abuse. The studies demonstrate the impact that the Wellness Outreach at Work model can have on individual alcohol consumption behavior and highlight both the intervention's potential for influencing the broad culture of work and its limitations. The first study, which involved the most limited application of the model, illustrates the relevance of proactive follow up for working with employees known to be at high risk for alcohol abuse. The second study shows the model's usefulness for general prevention of alcohol abuse in a program directed at an entire work force. The third study describes research currently underway that is attempting to extend this model to be a part of broader health care provision.

The strategic approach underlying the Wellness Outreach at Work model is of particular interest because of its ability to produce desired outcomes in a variety of institutional contexts and with workers at all degrees of risk for substance abuse. In the first study, a 3-year demonstration project, 70% of employee assistance program (EAP) clients with alcohol problems avoided recurrence of alcohol use, the problem that had brought them to the EAP (Root & Sieck, 1998). In a second 3-year study, which included workers at all levels of alcohol risk, half of the people who initially drank at levels that could negatively affect their health over time, including many people who were not yet alcohol dependent, reduced their alcohol consumption. Most employees who were drinking at levels not likely to damage their health remained so or became abstinent (Heirich & Sieck, 2000).

Comparable results have been obtained in a third study, now under way, which uses the organizational strategies underlying the earlier, successful programs.

The studies described in this chapter all used a proactive outreach strategy, which differs in important ways from the traditional health care delivery model that guides many alcohol education and management programs. American health care traditionally has depended on self-referred patients, who come for help when disease or discomfort disrupts their ability to carry on life as usual. In health care, especially for alcohol-related problems, this strategy is inefficient. Alcohol abuse prevention efforts in the work force often target employees who have drinking problems severe enough to be damaging their work performance or actively threatening their current health. Once physical or psychological dependence on alcohol has developed, the problem becomes more difficult for alcohol abusers to address. Programs focused on alcohol-dependent workers are expensive, and most find that about half of the workers relapse to problematic drinking levels (Allsop, Sannders, & Philips, 2000; Anton, Mook, Waid, Malcolm, & Dias, 1999; Basset & Levental, 2000; Foster, Marshall, Hooper, & Peter, 2000; Greenfield et al., 2000; Tempesta, Janir, Bignenmimi, Cliabac, & Pogieter, 2000). Clearly, such workers need attention and assistance with health behavior change. If cost-effective ways can be found to identify potential problems and intervene before work performance or health deteriorates, however, both workers and management gain.

The proactive outreach and follow-up counseling strategy described in this chapter intervenes at a different stage and in a different way from the traditional disease model for health care delivery. Prevention intervenes *before* something goes wrong (or, in the case of EAP clients, before something goes wrong again). Because no immediate warning signs can motivate the worker or client to seek assistance, the most effective prevention efforts reach out actively to an entire work force and persistently direct attention to health issues. They motivate people over a period of time to attempt health behavior changes, and they provide social reinforcement that helps improved health behaviors become habit.

A GENERAL MODEL OF HEALTH BEHAVIOR CHANGE

How do people successfully change behaviors that affect their health? The research literature on health behavior change suggests that the processes involved when adopting new behaviors to improve one's health and sense of well-being differ from those that are involved when one attempts to change a current habit. For example, it is easier to start taking walks daily than to stop smoking or reduce one's level of alcohol consumption.

The process of adopting new behaviors that improve health and a sense of well-being is relatively simple and often involves four steps: First, a person becomes aware of the potential benefits of a health behavior change and assesses them against the costs or inconvenience that may be involved in making the change. Next, if that balance is positive, and especially if other people join that person in making the change or encourage it, he or she is more likely to view the new behavior favorably. Third, proactive outreach often is needed before a person actually adopts the new behavior. Finally, social reinforcement of the new behaviors helps make them habitual (Kelly, Zyzanski, & Alemagno, 1991; Rosenstock, Strecher, & Becker, 1994).

When current behaviors carry health risk and therefore must be replaced with healthier behaviors, the process of health behavior change is more complex. Awareness of health risk becomes the first step in a process of risk reduction (Rosenstock et al., 1994). That awareness, however, must develop in a manner that is not so frightening that it encourages denial. The person at risk must come to view the risk as relevant for immediate behavior choices. Awareness alone is rarely sufficient to produce behavior change: Behaviors that put one's health at risk often are pleasurable (at least in the short-term), and they may have social benefits. Therefore, once a person becomes aware of a health risk, he or she must become motivated to care about the risk, rather than deny or ignore it. Those at risk also must have—or must develop—self-confidence and a belief that they can change the risky behavior, and then they must become committed to making that change. If new health behaviors bring immediate improvement in one's sense of well-being or if they involve other gains that can be experienced in the present, replacing one behavior with another becomes easier. In situations involving simple health improvement or risk reduction, people who receive social reinforcement as they attempt to change their habitual behavior have the highest chance of success (Center for AIDS Prevention Studies, 1996; Kelly et al., 1991).

At any point in time, people are at quite different stages of readiness to make health behavior changes (Prochaska, DiClemente, & Norcross, 1992). Consequently, general information programs aimed at prevention often are effective with only a small portion of their target population. In health education, no single message at any given point in time will reach the entire target population. Rather than seek the "ideal" information package, truly effective programs adapt the message to the particular situation of each recipient.

PROACTIVE INTERVENTION: THE WELLNESS OUTREACH AT WORK MODEL

The Wellness Outreach at Work model uses a five-element model of health behavior change:

1. Assessment of individual risk and stage of readiness to change risky behaviors
2. Proactive, individualized follow-up counseling
3. Assurances of confidentiality for workers
4. Social reinforcement of healthy behaviors
5. Periodic reassessment of the health status of the population.

Proactive, individualized outreach programs identify problematic behaviors at an early stage and make an initial assessment of where each person is on a continuum of readiness to change particular behaviors. The initial health screening also helps establish personal rapport between individual clients and the wellness professionals conducting the screening. After the initial screening, wellness professionals obtain permission to continue counseling in the future. Once people learn of their health risks, regularly scheduled, brief counseling sessions help them move forward until desired health behavior changes are attempted and successfully incorporated into their ongoing habits. Counseling sessions are individualized to the situation of each client, and efforts are made to respect the lifestyle and concerns of each client. Through information sharing, emotional engagement and support, and joint assessment of goals and strategies for reaching those goals, a partnership is established between the counselor and the client to create self-empowerment for health improvement. As this process occurs, social support is mobilized to help ensure the success of efforts to change health behaviors, and gains are reinforced. If recidivism occurs, counselors help clients reassess their strategies and try again until they successfully incorporate their new behaviors into their lifestyle.

Health delivery ethics and the need to gain and retain the cooperation of the work force require information about individual workers' health risks and health changes needs to be kept confidential and not made available to the employer. Workers, of course, have the right to share information about themselves with whomever they choose, but health counselors must not discuss individual worker's health status with others. When employees are able to maintain total control over what information is given to others about themselves, most are surprisingly candid and open with health counselors (Erfurt, Foote, Brock, & Heirich, 1995; Heirich & Sieck, 2000).

For some people, an initial health intervention will create awareness of the need for change. Others who already are aware that their behavior is problematic will need motivation to change their behavior. Still others will need to develop confidence that it is possible for them to change. To maximize impact, one must seize the moment and discover the circumstances that will help a person decide that now is the time to change—and then reinforce attempts at behavior change.

Health behavior changes become easier and are more likely to be sustained over time if the worksite culture develops health behavior norms that reinforce individual change efforts. For example, if the worksite actively encourages individual health improvement efforts that become visible to other workers; it becomes clear that the worksite welcomes employees' concerns about health and attempts to improve it. Social reinforcement both from health professionals *and* from fellow workers as health behavior changes are attempted also increases a program's impact. Cooperative efforts to improve health help focus attention on the desirability of new health behaviors and establish new cultural norms at the worksite for building health. A rescreening of the population every 3 to 5 years allows assessment of a health improvement program's impact on the health status of the population. It also allows identification of changes in program strategy that may be appropriate as health risks change. If screening can be combined with evaluation of changes in health care costs, one can begin to assess both the health and the economic impact of a program.

THE IMPACT OF PROACTIVE WELLNESS PROGRAMS

Beginning in the mid-1970s, Jack Erfurt and Andrea Foote, who for many years codirected the Worker Health Program of the University of Michigan's Institute of Labor and Industrial Relations, developed a series of worksite-based demonstration and evaluation research studies addressing health issues of workers. The interdisciplinary research that they and their colleagues developed addressed worksite strategies for either dealing with substance abuse or preventing CVD. Their early work developed protocols and monitoring strategies for the effective operation of EAPs; parallel studies evaluated the most effective ways to reduce CVD risks. A series of quasi-experimental designs, which used separate manufacturing plants (similar in demographic and other characteristics) as sites for different kinds of interventions and a control site where only initial screening and end-of-study rescreening were done, provided the evidence. The studies set standards for the field: An independent reviewer at the National Institutes of Health (NIH) cited the studies as models for research (Pelletier, 1997). The National Heart, Lung, and Blood Institute commissioned Erfurt, Foote, and their colleagues to write a step-by-step guide for proactive outreach at worksites (Erfurt et al., 1995). That guide, in turn, became the heart of recommended guidelines for worksite health promotion that were developed with the cooperation of 19 national and regional organizations and adopted officially in 1999 by the Association for Worksite Health Promotion (1998).

The intervention projects that Erfurt, Foote, and their colleagues introduced had a strong impact on the health status of the work forces where the projects were implemented. Moreover, at sites where data on health benefits expenditures were available, reductions in health spending could be seen within 3 to 5 years of the introduction of the proactive outreach strategies, more than offsetting the costs for the additional services. Gradually, the Worker Health Program team came to realize that the model "Wellness Outreach at Work" could be as relevant for the prevention of substance abuse as for CVD prevention.

MAKING THE MODEL RELEVANT
FOR ALCOHOL BEHAVIOR CHANGE

The same steps that are involved in changing other health risk behaviors affect alcohol risk reduction, although the ways in which physiological or psychological addiction affect motivations to change behavior create additional challenges. Like other prevention efforts to change habits that put health at risk, alcohol abuse prevention involves changing a risky behavior that often gives pleasure or comfort. Not surprisingly, calling attention to a potential risk often is not sufficient motivation to change the health behavior that is in question. Moreover, because of the social stigma attached to alcoholism, getting people to pay attention to their own drinking patterns is not easy. People who consume alcohol at levels similar to those of their friends or who drink alone often do not notice that they are drinking at levels that can create problems for them. Once forced to acknowledge a problem with AOD use, many employees find it easy to slip back into earlier behavior patterns. Recidivism rates following rehabilitation programs are high.

Data from the more than 100 worksites that have implemented the Wellness Outreach at Work model consistently show significant reductions in health risks when proactive outreach and ongoing follow up are systematically implemented (Erfurt et al., 1995). From 65% to 85% of employees at the various worksites participated in the initial, voluntary health screenings. Over a 3-year period, more than half of the employees with an identified health risk worked actively to change their behaviors affecting that health risk. At rescreening 3 years after initial screening, in a typical site two thirds of the people attempting health behavior changes had been successful. The risk profiles of the plant population showed striking improvement (Erfurt et al., 1995). Where medical costs were tracked over time, worksites that had implemented the Wellness Outreach at Work program had lower health benefits costs than the control sites where the program had not been implemented (Foote & Erfurt, 1984, 1991; Erfurt, Foote, & Heirich, 1994b; see also the NIH monograph developed by the Worker Health Program team, Erfurt et al., 1995). Most of the worksites had wellness programs that focused on CVD risks and paid only passing attention to alcohol consumption. This chapter examines whether the same approaches can include alcohol abuse prevention as a part of an outreach model that generally has focused on reduction of cardiovascular health risks.

The first two studies to be discussed in this chapter were designed by Erfurt and Foote before their deaths and were further modified by their colleagues when implemented. The third study extended the logic of the demonstration projects by seeking ways to institutionalize effective practices among health care providers and employers. All three studies build on information gathered previously at worksites that had implemented this model for CVD risk reduction.

STUDY 1: USING PROACTIVE APPROACHES WITH EAP CLIENTS

This 3-year study, conducted from 1991 through 1994, was sponsored by the National Institute on Alcohol Abuse and Alcoholism and was limited to employees of a large public utility who sought out the services of the company's EAP either on their own or at the requirement of their supervisor. (In contrast, the Wellness Outreach proactive approach screens the entire work force to identify not only workers who recognize their health risks but also those who may not be aware of their risks.) The company's internal EAP had been in existence for 12 years prior to the study but did not include regular follow up with clients or formal outreach to families as part of the existing protocol.

All employees who sought out the services of the EAP were invited to participate in the study, except for those whose reasons for seeking EAP services were limited in nature (e.g., simple requests for information). Clients who agreed to participate were randomly assigned to one of four groups and followed for a period of 2 years. Group 1 received only the standard EAP services. Group 2 received regular, proactive follow-up visits with the EAP counselor in addition to the standard services. Clients in Group 3 received the standard EAP services and were asked to identify a family member the EAP could contact for follow-up visits without the employee's direct participation. Group 4 clients received both client follow up and follow up with a family member.

During 1991, 517 EAP clients agreed to participate in the study. Their demographic makeup was representative of a typical EAP population in any given year at this company. The most common reason for the EAP visit was a job-related problem (33% of the caseload). Clients with diagnoses related to substance abuse, the main focus of the study, constituted 26% of the caseload. This percentage is considerably smaller than that anticipated when the study was designed and approved; at that time, AOD-related diagnoses accounted for 50% of the company's EAP caseload. One possible explanation is that the company experienced a major downsizing and reorganization during this period, and employees may have been leery of revealing a drinking problem to their employer during this period, when doing so might have made them especially vulnerable to layoff.

EAP clients who agreed to participate in the study received follow-up counseling sessions at scheduled intervals, mainly to review the client's progress and discuss any relevant behavioral goals. A detailed discussion of the content of the follow-up visits has been published elsewhere (Foote et al., 1994).

The main outcome variable of interest was recurrence of the problem that had brought the employee to the EAP. Information about problem recurrence was obtained from the employee in a confidential telephone interview conducted at the end of the study. Participants were asked whether the problem that brought them to the EAP had occurred again in the previous 2 years. A total of 62% of the EAP clients who agreed to participate in the study made themselves available for these confidential telephone interviews at the end of the study. No significant differences were found in demographics between those who agreed to the phone interview and those who refused.

Table 4.1 shows the impact of the proactive outreach and follow-up program on recurrence. This table collapses Groups 1 and 3, which received no client follow up, and Groups 2 and 4, which received client follow up. Proactive outreach, whether offered to the employee alone or to the employee and a family member, resulted in similar and lower recidivism rates for all the employees.

The study included the entire EAP caseload, not simply employees who had been identified as alcohol dependent. The proactive outreach and follow-up method worked equally well for the entire EAP clientele. Almost identical results were found whether analysis included only employees who had gone through AOD rehabilitation programs or all EAP clients, in-

TABLE 4.1
The Impact of Proactive Outreach and Follow-up on Recidivism Rates
Among Employee Assistance Program (EAP) Clients

	No Follow-up Counseling	Follow-up Counseling	Total
Entire EAP Caseload			
Recurrence (%)	66 (44)	53 (31)	119 (37)
No Recurrence (%)	84 (56)	117 (69)	201 (63*)
AOD Clients Only			
Recurrence (%)	19 (44)	14 (30)	33 (37)
No Recurrence (%)	24 (56)	33 (70)	57 (63**)

Note. AOD = alcohol and other drug.
*$p < .05$.
**$p > .05$.

cluding those whose original presenting problems were not for AOD abuse. Because the sample size for employees with AOD problems was small (N = 90 employees), the impact of proactive counseling is not statistically significant. A similar result, however, was found when analyzing recidivism patterns for the entire EAP caseload. This almost identical difference in patterns of recidivism between those counseled proactively and those not counseled was statistically significant. This finding lends support to the argument that proactive outreach was responsible for the difference in patterns of recidivism among clients with AOD problems.

This small study demonstrates that the outreach and follow-up techniques that encourage health behavior change in a general population also work to stabilize new health behaviors and prevent recidivism even among those who have a history of AOD dependence (Root & Sieck, 1998)

Can these methods for encouraging and reinforcing health behavior change work equally effectively to prevent development of alcohol abuse among employees who are not yet alcohol dependent and have not had to face an immediate health crisis? If so, how can one gain the attention and participation of employees not in crisis? Prevention programs focusing on cardiovascular risk reduction and general wellness provide a clear answer to those questions.

Alcohol consumption has wide-ranging effects on CVD risk factors (e.g., hypertension, obesity, smoking, high cholesterol, stress) and other health risks of great concern to workers. Wellness programs that address nonstigmatized risks easily attract attention and gain widespread participation. The programs described below have found that including alcohol education as part of efforts to assess and control other health risks is a simple and effective way to reach and motivate people with problematic alcohol consumption. Conducting such programs effectively, however, involves a systematic strategy of proactive outreach and continuing brief assessment and counseling with workers. Workers must develop ongoing trust relationships with health professionals and, sometimes, with fellow workers for the programs to succeed.

STUDY 2: AFFECTING ALCOHOL BEHAVIOR THROUGH CARDIOVASCULAR WELLNESS PROGRAMS

This 3-year study sponsored by the National Institute on Drug Abuse was designed to determine the effectiveness of cardiovascular wellness programs as a route to alcohol abuse prevention, as measured by lowered levels of alcohol consumption. It also compared the impact of proactive individual outreach and regular follow-up counseling on alcohol use with the effects of health education classes.

All employees in a large manufacturing plant were offered an initial cardiovascular wellness screening that took place near their work location. This screening served both to recruit participants into the study and to establish baseline health measures, including levels of alcohol consumption. Alcohol consumption was measured by the following questions:

- "Do you ever drink alcoholic beverages such as beer, wine, or liquor?"
- "If yes, in an average week, on how many days do you drink something alcoholic?"
- "On the days that you drink, how many drinks do you have?"

Health screenings continued until the desired sample size was reached. A total of 2,229 employees—more than half of the plant population—participated in this initial screening. An additional 607 employees sought out wellness screening throughout the course of the project. A description of the sample is shown in Table 4.2.

Participants were randomly assigned to one of two study groups. Group 1 employees, the counseling group, received outreach from the wellness staff periodically and were offered proactive individual counseling as a follow up to their initial health screening. The study protocol called for proactive contact with participants for about 20 minutes once every 6 months, or more often during times when a counseling session suggested that the client might be ready to move forward along the behavior change continuum, when he or she was attempting changes in health behavior, or when recidivism occurred. The counselor's assessment of how much reinforcement or other assistance was needed during these times of potential change determined the frequency of counseling. All the counseling sessions focused on the employee's health risks and steps the employee could take to ameliorate those risks. Alcohol risk was addressed in relation to CVD risk.

Group 2 employees received periodic invitations to participate in

TABLE 4.2
Cardiovascular Wellness Study Sample

	Group 1 (Follow-up Counseling)	Group 2 (Classes Only)
Total participants	1,128	1,101
% Male	82	82
% White	56	54
% Hourly	89	94
Mean age (years)	44	45
Mean no. drinks per week	6.5	6.5
% Safer drinkers	71	72
% Potentially problematic drinkers	15	13
% Binge or heavy drinkers	12	13
% Rescreened	44	38

health education classes relevant to their personal health risks, such as smoking cessation and weight management. Alcohol education was included in each class.

Alcohol risk level was determined by the Centers for Disease Control and Prevention's definitions of "safe," "at-risk" or "problematic," and "binge or heavy" drinkers (Table 4.3). In the health education classes on high blood pressure, weight loss, stress, and other CVD risks, information was given about how alcohol consumption affects the health problem and recommendations were given about safer and less safe levels of alcohol consumption. This information also was included in the individual counseling sessions.

Studies of the Worker Health Program in comparable settings used quasi-experimental designs and found major differences in CVD risk reduction in study sites where individual counseling occurred, but not in those offering CVD-oriented health education classes or in control sites. Quasi-experimental designs use an independent site as control for before and after measurements, thus guaranteeing that the behavior of people who serve as the controls will not be affected by contact with participants who are receiving the interventions being studied. When a quasi-experimental design is used, however, one cannot be certain that unidentified differences in worksite cultures do not account for the differences in health outcomes seen in plants where contrasting intervention strategies have been used. Instead of the multisite, quasi-experimental design of the Worker Health Program's earlier research, this study used a single site and randomly assigned participants to the two interventions. The study design allowed comparisons of participation and health behavior change in the two groups within a single worksite. Given the earlier findings from Study 1, current use of a comparison group, rather than a strict control group, would be sufficient to demonstrate that the proactive outreach, rather than unknown differences in worksite cultures, produced the outcomes observed. If CVD

TABLE 4.3
Classification of Alcohol Consumption Risk

	Safer Drinker	At-Risk Drinker	Binge or Heavy Drinker
Men	Fewer than 3 drinks per day and fewer than 12 drinks per week	3 to 4 drinks per day	5 or more drinks per day or 15 or more drinks per week
Women	Fewer than 2 drinks per day and fewer than 9 drinks per week	2 to 4 drinks per day	5 or more drinks per day or 15 or more drinks per week

From National Institute on Drug Abuse and Alcoholism (NIDAA) Web site Guidelines for alcohol consumption.

risks diminished and alcohol consumption patterns improved as well, the findings would also demonstrate that cardiovascular wellness can be an effective route to alcohol abuse prevention. Final proof that CVD wellness interventions had made the difference in drinking behavior, of course, would require replication in a study that included a control group or site.

The design for this study involved its own risks: A quasi-experimental design strategy originally had been chosen to prevent contamination of study interventions because people in real-life situations often make their own decisions about what kinds of help they would like to receive, independent of the intentions of researchers, and this may not cooperate with a research study design. To minimize that risk in this single-plant study, employees were contacted by letter and phone calls to their homes; for the convenience of workers, before- and after-work classes and counseling sessions were provided at the worksite at locations that could not be easily observed by other workers.

Changes in the nature of work in this location, such as downsizing of the work force and speed-ups of the assembly line and overtime work, made it difficult to engage workers in before- or after-work classes or counseling. The intervention protocol therefore was modified to include shorter, more accessible classes that could be taken during the work day at break times and direct outreach to workers at their work stations for those slated for proactive outreach and counseling. Soon the visibility of proactive counseling posed a challenge to the original research design: Once workers saw the wellness counselors circulating around the plant floor and making contact with some employees, a number of people refused to stay in the study group to which they had been assigned. Many workers assigned to the classes-only intervention, as well as others who had not participated in the original screening, began requesting one-to-one sessions with the wellness counselors. To refuse them risked alienating the union and jeopardizing access to work stations. Consequently, the study protocol was altered to allow counselors to respond to requests for counseling but not add those workers to their caseload for future outreach. When rescreening was conducted at the end of the study, the workers who had refused to stay in their assigned intervention group would form a separate group for analysis. Once this modified plan was put into operation, however, so many people requested individual counseling that it became difficult to see everyone in the outreach sample as frequently as planned.

At the end of the intervention period, half of the employees who had been screened at the beginning of the study were rescreened. Budget limitations precluded rescreening the total sample. It had been necessary to initially screen and work with a significant portion of the worksite population to gain acceptance and create an environment of social support. To document study results stastically, however, rescreening half of the participants would provide sufficient evidence of differences in impact while maintaining reasonable research costs. Rescreening of participants was conducted randomly within each department and continued until half of the participants had been rescreened.

As the results were analyzed, employees in Group 1, to whom wellness counselors had been instructed to reach out proactively, could be divided according to their actual contact with the wellness counselors. Consequently, Group 1 participants who were rescreened were subdivided into those who had been seen regularly and those who had been seen rarely because of increased demand for individual counseling. Within Group 2, which was to receive only invitations to classes, 56% of those rescreened had sought out wellness counseling services on their own, many repeatedly doing so, thus creating a group of workers not seen for counseling and a group who did receive follow-up counseling at their own request. As a result, the study population was divided into the following four groups: counseling group seen regularly for follow up, counseling group seen rarely for follow up, classes group seen for follow up, and classes group not seen for follow up. No differences among the groups were found in demographic characteristics or initial health risks. The initial profiles reported in Table 4.3 continued to fit each subgroup. The changes however, allowed for two additional comparisons: Participants who received regular follow-up counseling initiated by project staff were compared with those who received only occasional follow-up counseling initiated by the participants. Changes in alcohol and CVD risks also were compared for participants who received follow-up counseling and those who received only the initial and final health screenings. Because it does not distort response patterns found among the four subgroups, the presentation of results is simplified by reporting comparisons between workers who were counseled and those who were not counseled.

Significant Study Results

Access to At-Risk Drinkers

Table 4.4 shows that CVD risk screening and counseling was an effective way to gain access to the adult population for alcohol education. When brief screenings and counseling sessions were offered in locations easily accessible to work stations, most of the work force participated. As Table 4.4 also shows, a sizable proportion of at-risk drinkers also had cardiovascular risks. Once alerted to CVD risks, most workers welcomed continuing information and assistance with lowering their risks. CVD risk screening was an effective way to contact problematic and not yet problematic drinkers and focus their attention on health.

TABLE 4.4
The Effectiveness of Cardiovascular Risk Screening for Engaging Problem Drinkers

Percentage of Drinkers With at Least One CVD Risk (n)	Percentage of Drinkers With at Least One CVD Risk Who Were Drinking at Risky Levels (n)
75 (1,026)	45 (461)

CVD Risk	Drinkers With at Least One CVD Risk (N = 1,026)	
	n With Risk	% Drinking at Risky Levels (n = 461)
Hypertension	160	50
Hypercholesterolemia	358	43
Low HDL cholesterol	160	46
Smoking	270	54
Overweight	291	44

Impact on Alcohol Abuse

In addition to assessing how well a program like this provides access to drinkers, one must also consider its actual effect on lowering or preventing alcohol abuse. As Table 4.5 shows, by the end of the study, 43 percent of the workers who had been identified as at-risk drinkers at the initial screening were either abstemious (12.5%) or had reduced their alcohol consumption to levels that no longer put them at risk (30.6%). Moreover, although the research intervention was focused on helping at-risk drinkers reduce their risks, total alcohol consumption in this work force decreased. In addition, risks to health diminished among all study groups. Both primary and secondary alcohol prevention efforts (i.e., the prevention

TABLE 4.5
Changes in Drinking Patterns for the Entire Study Sample

	At-Risk Drinkers n (%)	Safer Drinkers n (%)	Nondrinkers n (%)
Stopped drinking	29 (12.5)	37 (14.2)	—
Remained nondrinkers	—	—	247 (76.5)
Became safer drinkers	71 (30.6)	—	56 (17.3)
Remained safer drinkers	—	166 (63.6)	—
Decreased their drinking but still at risk	12 (5.2)	—	—
Became at-risk drinkers	—	58 (22.2)	20 (6.2)
Did not change their drinking	120 (51.8)	—	—
Total	232	261	323

$p < .001$, using one-tailed z test.

of potentially problematic drinking behaviors among employees not yet at risk and movement away from problematic behaviors by those currently at some risk) seem to have been effective. Although about 1 in 5 initially safe drinkers reported an increase in alcohol consumption, most did not. In addition to workers who reported that they no longer drank alcohol, the clear majority reported levels of drinking that kept them within safe limits. Moreover, half of the clearly at-risk drinkers reported a reduced level of alcohol consumption.

Table 4.5 makes it clear that the program had areas of failure as well: 25% of the rescreened employees had unfavorable drinking outcomes. A total of 120 employees who initially drank at risky levels had not lowered their alcohol consumption, and another 12 initially at-risk drinkers were drinking less alcohol than at the start of the program but still were not at levels considered safe. Moreover, 78 employees who initially did not drink or who drank at safe levels were drinking at levels that clearly put them at risk. Many employees, of course, had not received counseling beyond that provided at the initial screening.

Among employees who received counseling, 43 percent of those whose initial drinking level put them at risk were either abstinent or drinking at safe levels 3 years later ($n = 62$). Among counseled employees who initially were not at risk for alcohol-related problems, 88.6% were still not at risk 3 years later ($n = 302$). Thirty-nine counseled workers who initially were not at risk for alcohol-related problems, however, reported drinking at problematic levels at the end of the study. These outcomes clearly count as failures for the program, along with the 82 at-risk drinkers who received counseling but still drank at risky levels 3 years later.

A closer look at the employees' CVD risk factors suggests why some workers' drinking may have been unaffected by cardiovascular wellness counseling. Twenty-nine of the "failures" were among people who had no cardiovascular risks identified at screening and who therefore might pay little attention to information about the relation between drinking and cardiovascular risks. Fifty-two of the "failures" had only one cardiovascular risk, but 29 of the initially at-risk drinkers whose drinking levels still put them at risk 3 years later had two or more cardiovascular risks, as did 22 of the initially safe drinkers and the nondrinkers who later drank at risky levels.

Did frequency of contact make the difference? Apparently not. The number of visits with a health counselor did not predict the degree of health improvement, either for alcohol consumption or for other CVD risks. This outcome is to be expected given that a variety of factors affected the frequency with which employees were counseled. Some people were seen frequently because they themselves sought out the health counselor. Others were seen more frequently because counselors believed they were especially at risk or needed more than the usual encouragement at moments of recidivism or potential readiness to change. Thus one would not expect to find a one-to-one correspondence between frequency of visit and behavior change. In short, the evidence from Table 4.5 and the more fine-grained analyses reported above suggest that cardiovascular wellness programs are an effective way to identify alcohol consumption problems at an early stage and that they effectively encourage many at-risk drinkers to modify their drinking behavior.

Table 4.6 suggests that at-risk drinkers took their cardiovascular risks more seriously than did safe drinkers or nondrinkers with the same cardiovascular problem. All the participants with hypertension, in theory, could have lowered their blood pressure, but the at-risk drinkers made greater gains in blood pressure control than other participants with hypertension did. Safe drinkers were intermediate in their blood pressure improvement, whereas nondrinkers made the least improvement. Significantly, both safe and at-risk drinkers who reported lowering their level of alcohol consumption made greater gains in blood pressure control than did their counterparts who continued to drink at the levels they had before.

Individual Counseling vs. Health Education Classes

The two interventions being tested, individual counseling and classes, were not equally effective. Only 5% (49) of those assigned to the classes-only group took part in a class, despite regular offerings and repeated invitations. Fifty-six percent of this same group (224), however, sought out the services of the wellness counselors. Therefore, although the classes provided useful behavior change information, not enough employees took part in them to affect employee health. Ironically, the refusal of many employees to stay in their assigned intervention, which at first appeared to invalidate the intended comparison of the intervention strategy's effects on outcomes, made one finding indisputably clear: For real-life applications, proactive outreach counseling gains the interest of workers and actively engages them at a different level from that of health education classes. Because of the low participation in classes and high rate of seeking out counseling services, the results here are discussed either in terms of the study sample as a whole or by comparing those who received counseling with those who did not.

Health Improvements

Health risks improved for the entire work force. Of those who had high blood pressure at the initial screening, 53% showed controlled blood pressure at rescreening. Twenty-seven percent of those with high cholesterol initially had lowered their cholesterol to normal levels by the end of the study in 1997. Finally, among those who were 20% or more overweight at the beginning of the study, 31% had lost 3 to 9 pounds and 19% had

TABLE 4.6
Comparison of Changes in Blood Pressure (bp) Among Hypertensives With Changes in Reported Drinking From Initial Screening to Final Rescreening

Changes in Biometric Measures	Nondrinkers	Drinkers Not At-Risk Whose Drinking		At-Risk Drinkers Whose Drinking	
		Stayed the Same	Reduced	Stayed the Same	Reduced
Systolic bp	+0.30	+1.88	+1.30	−4.33*	−5.18*
Diastolic bp	−1.15	+1.30	+2.30	−1.62	−2.91

*p < .05, using one-tailed t test.

TABLE 4.7
The Impact of Counseling on Alcohol and Other Drug Use

	Counseled	Not Counseled
Smokers and former smokers at screening who were not smoking at rescreening (%)	65	53*
Drinkers at highest risk who lowered their drinking to a safe level (%)	38	22**

*$p < .001$.
**$p < .10$, using one-tailed t test.

lost 10 or more pounds. Not surprisingly, counseled smokers and heavy drinkers succeeded in reaching and maintaining goals about alcohol consumption and smoking cessation in higher proportions than their coworkers with similar health problems who did not receive counseling after the initial screening (Table 4.7).

Unanticipated Effects of the Intervention

For most health risks measured, improvements occurred among workers whose health risks were identified at screening, regardless of whether they worked directly with a counselor thereafter. Previous studies had used a separate plant as the control group, which precluded influence from others receiving the health intervention being studied. At control sites, health improvements found at rescreening were minimal. In contrast, in this study even those who received only screening and rescreening showed significant health improvements.

Something clearly had happened in this work force. A striking improvement occurred in the health of most workers—but was the intervention responsible for this? If not, could a broad cultural change in public understanding of health risks and appropriate behaviors account for these findings? Did reductions in health risks occur in other, comparable plants that had not had a wellness outreach program? These questions led to a more extensive analysis of possible explanatory conditions. However, no company policies or practices were instituted, and no new personnel implemented older practices that could account for these findings. On-site personnel responsible for employee's health were convinced that it was the intervention, not other factors, that made the difference. No similar health improvements occurred during this period at other plants with comparable populations (as determined through telephone interviews with personnel keeping records on plants within the corporation. Health costs went up elsewhere; they went down in this plant.)

The high visibility of the proactive outreach counseling may have helped the entire plant population focus its attention on health risks and the desirability of health improvement, thereby stimulating conversations far beyond the impact of the confidential, one-to-one counseling sessions themselves. As far as the health professionals doing the counseling were concerned, all information about individual clients was confidential. The employees themselves, however, were under no compunction to keep their health information secret, and it seems clear that many did not. Other employees saw their fellow workers being released from the assembly line to talk with a health counselor. Many workers, especially those who were pleased by improvements in their own health risks, probably told their fellow workers about their health progress. Such conversations direct the attention of noncounseled workers to health issues and help them realize that it is *possible* to lose weight, lower blood pressure, and cut down on drinking and that one feels better when one does so. Moreover, because the workers are talking directly with a peer, it is possible to discover *what* the peer is doing to achieve that success and consider trying it oneself. In short, a high-visibility outreach strategy, born of necessity, may have demonstrated a more cost-effective way to affect the behavior of an entire work force. If future research proves this scenario to be correct, the contamination of an original study design will have produced a serendipitous outcome that increases the cost-effectiveness of this intervention strategy.

Limitations of the Intervention

In making the above claims about the effectiveness of the outreach model in this manufacturing plant study, it should be emphasized that the evidence is primarily associative rather than providing logistic regressions or other tests of causal inference. However, this plant was experiencing changes in health behaviors and reductions in health care costs that were not occurring in comparable plants within the same corporation, and no evidence was found of other possible causes for the change. Moreover, knowledgeable local personnel insisted that the outreach intervention was the only change of note that had occurred in the plant's health and alcohol practices or policies during this time. Thus, it is not unreasonable to assert that the intervention was creating the changes. This assertion, however, does not establish the causal claim, and the use of this intervention at only one site raises additional questions about whether the same results would be found if the intervention were replicated.

The Wellness Outreach at Work model has consistently produced CVD risk reductions comparable to those reported here (Erfurt, Foote, Heirich, & Gregg, 1990; Erfurt et al., 1991a). The study cited above demonstrates that alcohol abuse prevention can be an important focus of such programs without reducing the focus on CVD risk reduction. The best ways to interest worksites and health care providers in making proactive prevention services available, however, are less clear. One-to-one outreach is labor intensive, and the costs of such outreach must be added to health budgets before savings are realized in lowered utilization of disease care services. A time lag of 2 to 5 years may occur before cost savings are seen; meanwhile, the cost of reaching employees not likely to have an immediate, costly health crisis must be added to existing operating expenses. Employers, whose budgeting often is for 1- to 3-year planning stages, often hesitate to commit funds whose payoff will come later. Moreover, unless it includes total health benefits utilization as part of its calculus of costs and gains, management may not recognize savings that occur.

Managed health care providers that rely on fixed capitation rates might have more interest than employers in prevention services that can produce major reductions in high-cost services later. With 20 percent or more of patients disenrolling from their managed care plans each year, many health management executives hesitate to invest new funds in health promotion, lest the investment be made in patients who will shift to other plans before the managed care plan has recouped those additional costs (National Committee for Quality Assurance, 1999). What is needed is a demonstration of short-term costs and benefits of providing such services. A study currently underway, sponsored by the worksite managed care program of the Center for Substance Abuse Prevention, is exploring those issues.

STUDY 3: COOPERATION BETWEEN MANAGED CARE AND THE WORKSITE

This 3-year intervention program, which is similar to the wellness example described above but limited to university employees who are enrolled in a managed care health plan, is now nearing completion. In this study, one group received proactive outreach and counseling (with possible referral to an alcohol management program), whereas the other group received only an initial and final health screening (although referral to an alcohol management program also was possible). This variation in design allowed use of a control group, making it possible to demonstrate conclusively that the cardiovascular wellness counseling was making the difference in alcohol consumption.

To minimize possible on-site contamination, a random sample of worksite locations on the university campus were first randomly assigned to intervention (i.e., proactive outreach) or control status (i.e., screening and rescreening only). All employees within a specific worksite who were enrolled in the managed care plan were invited to participate. The worksites are physically separated from one another, minimizing the probability that participants assigned to the control group will become aware of ongoing health counseling that is being made available to other employees.

A random sample of employees who were enrolled in the managed care plan was invited to participate in a free health screening. Logistical problems involved in contacting and screening a subset of employees in many, widely scattered worksites increased research costs sufficiently to reduce the number of people actually screened. (Because only the employees at each site who were enrolled with the managed care company being studied were eligible to be included, proven screening strategies that maximize participation could not be used.) Eventually about 1,300 employees participated in the health screenings. Table 4.8 shows the characteristics of this sample.

An early finding of this study is that initial screening and response rates are much higher, and the cost of contacting employees much lower, if everyone at a worksite is eligible for screening outreach. Setting up individual appointments for initial screening, rather than inviting everyone in an area to participate at his or her convenience, limits initial intake. Despite the limitations that this selective screening design imposed, the study design kept open the opportunity for peer influence to reinforce professional counseling outreach: Including all managed care enrollees at a particular worksite leaves open the possibility that employee-to-employee reinforcement of health behavior norms will develop as an outgrowth of the one-to-one outreach counseling by health professionals.

This study hopes to document the influence of alcohol counseling on the drinking behavior, health care utilization, and health costs of employees when a worksite and a managed care company cooperate to identify people at risk and encourage them to modify their relevant health behaviors. Therefore, in addition to the random sample of employees invited to the health screening, the study also includes employees who seek out alcohol services on their own.

Prior to this study, the managed care plan offered its members partial coverage for participation in an alcohol management program, DrinkWise, which was also one of the resources being used for alcohol abuse prevention in this study. Employees enrolled in the managed care plan who participate in DrinkWise were invited to participate in the study. DrinkWise clients

TABLE 4.8
Worksite Managed Care Substance Abuse Prevention Demonstration Project Study Sample

	Group 1 (Follow-up Counseling)	Group 2 (Screening Only)
% Male	38	32
% White	84	78
% Hourly	26	26
Mean age (years)	43	43
Mean no. drinks per week	3	3
Total participants	652	653

who agreed to participate were then randomly assigned either to proactive follow-up intervention or to control status in the same manner as those in the random sample. Participants who entered the study through their contact with DrinkWise were appropriately flagged for later analysis.

Preliminary results show a positive effect on alcohol consumption and other CVD risk factors for the *intervention* group, similar to the findings in Study 2. This report is being written before comparisons of rescreening results for participants in the intervention and control groups are complete. Therefore, results (Tables 4.9, 4.10, and 4.11) come only from the follow-up records for those who are part of the outreach intervention (Group 1). The records trace employees' willingness to participate, their movement along stages of readiness to change health behaviors, and their actual self-reported behavior changes. They also include biometric measures of changes in health status that can be affected by alcohol consumption. Most employees identified at the initial screening as safe drinkers, at-risk drinkers, and binge or heavy drinkers have made themselves available for follow-up counseling (Table 4.9). Moreover, as Table 4.10 makes clear, people who have alcohol risk factors are as likely to participate in follow-up health counseling as employees who have other CVD risk factors. The only CVD risk group that has a higher participation rate in follow-up counseling than those with alcohol risks are people with high blood pressure, who directly benefit from periodic blood pressure monitoring. More than two thirds of the employees with identified alcohol risks are taking part in the follow-up counseling.

Proactive outreach counseling is making a difference in drinking behaviors (Table 4.11). Half of the employees who at initial screening were binge or heavy drinkers have decreased their drinking; 25% are now drinking at safer levels, and 42% of the potentially problematic drinkers have now reached a safe level of alcohol consumption. Moreover, only 1% of the initially safe drinkers have increased their alcohol consumption to levels that could put their health at risk. Once again, the evidence is consis-

TABLE 4.9
Participation in Follow-up Counseling by Initial Alcohol Risk Level in the Managed Care Substance Abuse Prevention Demonstration Project

	Safer Drinkers n (%)	At-Risk Drinkers n (%)	Binge or Heavy Drinkers n (%)
0 visits (could not be reached for follow-up counseling)	49 (8)	1 (3)	4 (17)
1+ visits	438 (74)	26 (72)	15 (63)
Refused follow-up counseling	65 (11)	6 (17)	3 (13)
Left study	40 (7)	3 (8)	2 (7)
Total	592 (100)	36 (100)	24 (100)

TABLE 4.10

Participation in Follow-Up Counseling by Risk Factor in the Worksite Managed Care Substance Abuse Prevention Demonstration Project

	Alcohol n (%)	Hypertension n (%)	High Cholesterol n (%)	Overweight n (%)	Smoking n (%)
0 visits (could not be reached for follow-up counseling)	5 (8)	15 (10)	10 (14)	21 (10)	5 (9)
1+ visits	41 (68)	116 (76)	49 (66)	147 (68)	37 (64)
Refused follow-up counseling	9 (15)	13 (9)	11 (15)	28 (13)	9 (16)
Left study	5 (8)	8 (5)	4 (5)	20 (9)	7 (12)
Total	60 (100)	152 (100)	74 (100)	216 (100)	58 (100)

TABLE 4.11
Changes in Drinking Behavior for the Intervention Group in the Worksite Managed Care Substance Abuse Prevention Demonstration Project

Behavior Change	At-Risk Drinkers n (%)	Binge or Heavy Drinkers n (%)	Safer Drinkers n (%)
Became safe drinkers	6 (25)	15 (42)	—
Remained safe drinkers	—	—	413 (70)
Decreased their drinking but were still at risk	6 (25)	3 (9)	—
Did not change their drinking	1 (4)	7 (19)	—
Became at-risk drinkers	—	—	8 (1)
Could not be reached for follow-up counseling	6 (25)	4 (11)	92 (16)
Refused follow-up counseling	5 (21)	7 (19)	79 (13)

tent with the argument that proactive counseling is superior to a health screening–rescreening control group, but we cannot draw final conclusions until rescreening data allow comparison with other groups. As this chapter goes to press, additional evidence strengthens the argument for effectiveness. First, logistic regression analysis finds no explanatory impact from such covariates as age, race, gender, or initial readiness to change in alcohol consumption behavior for the proactive counseling group. Second, the rescreening results show positive effects from proactive, ongoing counseling beyond that seen from initial screening. Finally, a third group from the same study population, initially screened as the other two groups were being rescreened, shared the initial profiles found in the intervention and control groups. Thus the changes that were found after the intervention were not seen more generally in this study population. The consistency of results across the three studies provides increasingly strong evidence that ongoing, proactive outreach and follow-up counseling, in the context of general health improvement, achieves real health behavior change.

In addition, two new foci are present but not yet available for analysis. First, in addition to analysis of alcohol and CVD risk outcomes, an evaluation is underway of strategies most effective for mobilizing worksite personnel and various kinds of health care providers to address substance abuse *prevention* as part of their daily tasks. Second, analysis will include differences in health benefit utilization by the intervention and control samples of this work force. At a later date it should be possible to report the impact of this kind of prevention program on short-term health service costs as well as the organizational strategies that are most effective for institutionalizing prevention approaches within worksite organizational practice and within a managed care organization.

CONCLUSION

As these examples of the Wellness Outreach at Work model make clear, proactive wellness programs that focus attention on health can engage the interest and participation of a sizable portion of the work force. Because of the clear relation of alcohol consumption levels to several CVD risks, cardiovascular wellness programs are a natural route for engaging employees in individualized alcohol education and prevention. As the EAP study demonstrates, proactive outreach and ongoing follow up can be an effective way to engage problem drinkers in health behavior change.

General wellness screening provides an effective point of entrée to most of the work force, because many worksites find that 70% or more of their employees have one or more health risks. Assessment of alcohol consumption can be a nonstigmatizing part of the health assessments, and alcohol education can become part of feedback given at the end of the screening session. Systematic, proactive follow up can be implemented thereafter, using computerized data management systems that keep track of when employees should be seen. Computerized records also should include detailed and confidential information about individual workers, their health risks, and their readiness to address those risks. With such organizational and record-keeping assistance, program staff can see employees regularly and adapt their interactions to each employee. When this approach is followed, significant changes occur: 50% to 60% of employees with an identified health risk will make efforts to change health behaviors that affect that risk. Changing alcohol consumption levels thus becomes part of general health improvement efforts. The method effectively alters the health behaviors of the work force as a whole, in part by helping to create new, health-oriented cultural norms.

MOVING BEYOND DRUG TESTING

The three program examples presented in this chapter show how the Wellness Outreach at Work model can affect alcohol behavior at many levels of alcohol consumption.

Advantages of the Wellness Outreach at Work Model

Although the approach is labor intensive, and therefore costlier than the common strategy of relying on mandatory drug testing to prevent substance abuse within the working population, the Wellness Outreach at Work model offers several advantages over drug testing. It provides a superior way to assess alcohol consumption in the work force and to intervene *before* health problems or job performance problems add to production costs or problems in labor relations. Unions often argue that behavior off the job cannot be regulated by employers, so long as job performance is not affected. Unions and workers themselves, however, value interventions with employees that help improve health as long as information about employees is confidential and cannot be used punitively against them. Moreover, some worksites that have strong unions actively resist the imposition of mandatory drug testing. In such settings, the Wellness Outreach model clearly is a practical way to proceed with concerns about substance abuse prevention. Its focus on general wellness gets the active cooperation of unions and the work force as well as management. Its confidentiality rules and focus on individual health issues quickly lead to levels of honest disclosure that a mandatory testing policy cannot generate. Even where mandatory drug testing programs are an enforced company policy, worksites must constantly deal with efforts to subvert them. In contrast, Wellness Outreach clients actively cooperate with the health goals that become mutually established through trust relationships with counselors. Biometric measurements of blood pressure and other processes affected by alcohol consumption confirm the accuracy of voluntary self-reports by employees to their wellness counselors.

The strongest advantage of using a broad focus on wellness comes from its impact beyond simply identifying problematic employees or the prevention of overt substance abuse. The general health of the work force improves, which in turn results in a reduction in health care costs over time. Successful programs begin to affect the culture of work, thereby reducing absenteeism, improving morale and productivity, and developing a culture of mutual support for health improvement. The result is a subtle and positive change in the atmosphere at work.

Wellness Outreach programs and mandatory drug testing do not have to be mutually exclusive, of course, but if both are used at a worksite, they have to be administered totally independent of one another. Otherwise, the confidentiality necessary for trust relations that underlie real behavior change will be impossible, and employees will not trust the wellness program.

Institutionalization of the Model

Government and foundation grants often fund demonstration programs, but successful innovations then have to be adopted more permanently and incorporated into budgets. To further institutionalization efforts at the local level, local wellness-coordinating committees can keep key decision makers at all levels informed of what is being accomplished and help create a sense of ownership of the program. The strongly positive feedback that begins to flow from program participants builds considerable pressure to continue the programs. In large corporations that frequently rotate plant management, a local wellness committee can help orient each new manager to the advantages of the program and help create additional support with each shift in top leadership. Other pressures, however, work against institutionalization of successful innovations.

Sometimes company rules about year-end bonuses for management penalize managers whose budget expands. Those practices build areas of resistance to incorporating new programs, no matter how successful. Conversely, introduction of a demonstration project that produces better results than the existing program can be seen as a threat to those who have a vested interest in the existing programs. They may work actively to ensure that their own programs are not subject to unfavorable comparisons with the innovation. Their efforts can threaten the new project's survival.

Faced with these realities of the organization of work, many analysts advise innovating only with the active endorsement and support of top management. The Wellness Outreach at Work program undertook major programs in two large corporations at the invitation of top management and had management's active support. In both cases, the demonstration projects were highly successful, and in one they became introduced in eighty worksites as part of company policy. Over a 15-year period, however, neither corporation's program survived. In one case, a complete turnover of top health management occurred at both the union and management level just before decisions to expand the program nationwide were to be made. As a result, the demonstration projects got pushed aside. In the other case, implementation became nationwide and was quite successful for the first few years. Once again, however, turnover in top management and the relegation of contracts to vendors who did not fully implement the protocols and who ceased to produce the striking results seen earlier led to abandonment of the earlier initiative.

It clearly is important to have the backing of top management, whenever possible, and to cultivate and educate any changes in leadership about what a successful program is accomplishing. In addition, it is important to develop ownership of programs at both the corporate and the local level and to discover ways to help guarantee that the quality of outcome will remain high through shifts in leadership or program vendors. It also is important to have regularly presented, well-documented evidence of changes in the health and health behaviors of the work force. Such information needs to be shared with local and corporate leadership regularly in a venue that gets their attention. Publication of results in peer-reviewed journals also focuses attention on successful innovations and helps build company pride in a job they are doing well. Such publications also can gain the interest of innovative managers in other companies. Finally, documentation of the savings that accrue over time because of a successful program becomes an important factor in decision making about the program's future.

None of these approaches guarantees the continuity of successful innovations over time—but some programs do survive and do well. One midsized company has used the Wellness Outreach approach for 20 years. When the company was bought out in a corporate merger, the remaining management, the union, and rank-and-file employees lobbied hard with the new owners to retain the program. Their enthusiasm, along with the hard evidence of reduced health care costs, better health status, lower absenteeism, and high morale, was persuasive. The program continued under new management.

In summary, the Wellness Outreach approach to health promotion and substance abuse prevention has many advantages. Although no one formula guarantees its successful institutionalization, its ability to attract the active, enthusiastic support of key employees at all levels of an organization increases its chances of affecting the work force over time.

REFERENCES

Allsop, S., Sannders, B., & Philips, M. (2000). Process of relapse in severely dependent male problem drinkers. *Addiction, 95*, 95–106.

Anton, R. F., Mook, P. H., Waid, L. R., Malcolm, R. J., & Dias, J. K. (1999). Naltrexone and cognitive behavior therapy for the treatment of outpatient alcoholics: Results of a placebo-controlled trial. *American Journal of Psychiatry, 156*, 1758–1764.

Association for Worksite Health Promotion. (1998). *Recommended guidelines for worksite health promotion programs*. Chicago: Author.

Basset, B., & Levental, J. Y. (2000). Utiliza de psychotherepres breves de groupe chez l'alcoldependent. Etude protant ser 390 patients [Using brief psychotherapy with residential groups who are alcohol-dependent: A study of 390 patients]. *Alcolgie, 21*, 57–64.

Center for AIDS Prevention Studies. (1996). Can theory help in AIDS prevention? [Fact sheet]. HIV Prevention: Looking Back, Looking Ahead Project, University of California.

Erfurt, J. C., Foote, A., Brock, B., & Heirich, M. A. (1995). *The Wellness Outreach at Work Program: A step-by-step guide* (NIH Publication No. 95-3043). Bethesda, MD: National Heart, Lung, and Blood Institute.

Erfurt, J. C., Foote, A., & Heirich, M. A. (1991a). Worksite wellness programs: Incremental comparison of screening and referral alone, health education, follow-up counseling, and plant organization. *American Journal of Health Promotion, 5*, 22–26.

Erfurt, J. C., Foote, A., & Heirich, M. A. (1991b). The cost-effectiveness of worksite wellness programs for hypertension control, weight loss, and smoking cessation. *Journal of Occupational Medicine, 33*, 962–970.

Erfurt, J. C., Foote, A., Heirich, M. A., & Gregg, W. (1990). Improving participation in worksite wellness programs: Comparing health education classes, a menu approach, and follow-up counseling. *American Journal of Health Promotion, 4,* 270–278.

Foote, A., & Erfurt, J. C. (1984). Cost effectiveness of worksite blood pressure control programs. *Journal of Occupational Medicine, 26,* 11283–11286.

Foote, A., & Erfurt, J. C. (1991). The benefit-to-cost ratio of worksite blood pressure control programs. *JAMA, 265,* 1283–1286.

Foote, A., Googins, B., Moriarity, M., Sandanato, C., Nadolski, J., & Jefferson, C. (1994). Implementing long-term EAP follow-up with clients and family members to prevent relapse. *Journal of Primary Prevention, 15,* 173–191.

Foster, J. H., Marshall, E. J., Hooper, R. L., & Peter, T. J. (2000). Measurement of quality of life in alcohol-dependent subjects by cancer symptoms checklist. *Alcohol: An International Biomedical Journal, 20,* 105–110.

Greenfield, S. F., Haffort, M. R., Vagga, L. M., Meaz, L. F., Costello, M. E., & Weiss, R. P. (2000). Relationship of self-efficacy expectancies to relapse among alcohol-dependent men and women: A prospective study. *Journal of Studies on Alcohol, 65,* 345–351.

Heirich, M. A., & Sieck, C. J. (2000). Worksite cardiovascular wellness programs as a route to substance abuse prevention. *Journal of Occupational Environmental Medicine, 42,* 47–56.

Kelly, R. B., Zyzanski, S. J., & Alemagno, S. A. (1991). Prediction of motivation and behavior change following health promotion: Role of health beliefs, social support, and self-efficacy. *Social Science and Medicine, 32,* 311–320.

National Committee for Quality Assurance/Health Plan Employer Data and Information Set. (1999). *The quality compass.* Washington, DC Author.

Pelletier, K. R. (1997). Clinical and cost outcomes of multifactorial, cardiovascular risk management interventions in worksites: A comprehensive review and analysis. *Journal of Occupational Environmental Medicine, 39,* 1154–1169.

Prochaska, J. O., DiClemente, C. C., & Norcross, J. C. (1992). In search of how people change. *American Psychologist, 47,* 1102–1114.

Root, L., & Sieck, C. (1998). *Impact of followup counseling on EAP recidivism.* Worker Health Program, Institute of Labor and Indsustrial Relations, University of Michigan. [Unpublished manuscript.]

Rosenstock, I. M., Strecher, V. J., & Becker, M. H. (1994). The health belief model and HIV risk behavior change. In R. J. DiClemente (Ed.), *Preventing AIDS: Theories and methods of behavioral interventions.* New York: Plenum Press.

Tempesta, E., Janir, L., Bignenmimi, A., Cliabac, S., & Pogieter, A. (2000). Acamprosate and relapse prevention in treatment of alcohol-dependencies: A placebo-controlled study. *Alcohol and Alcoholism, 35,* 202–209.

5

TEAM AND INFORMATIONAL TRAININGS FOR WORKPLACE SUBSTANCE ABUSE PREVENTION

WAYNE E. K. LEHMAN, G. SHAWN REYNOLDS, AND JOEL B. BENNETT

This chapter describes the evaluation of a team-oriented training for workplace substance abuse prevention. Traditionally, workplace substance abuse prevention has relied on a didactic approach that provides employees with information on substance abuse policy (e.g., drug-testing procedures and disciplinary approaches) and, when available, the employee assistance program (EAP). In contrast, the team-oriented training described here uses a psychosocial approach that emphasizes team responsibility for alcohol and other drug (AOD) use, including the reduction of tolerance and enabling; team communication; and the benefits of getting help for problems (as opposed to getting caught). The approach is based on established theoretical constructs and was designed to be interactive and participatory in nature. This chapter also describes a model of workplace psychosocial risks to help identify situations in which team-oriented training may be of greatest use.

Increasing evidence that psychosocial or group-level training is needed in some workplaces led to the development of the team-oriented approach. National surveys estimate that 1 in 10 employees report problems

Preparation of this chapter was supported by National Institute on Drug Abuse grant DA04390 (Wayne E. K. Lehman, Principal Investigator).

with AOD use (Substance Abuse and Mental Health Services Administration [SAMHSA], 1996; 1999), and as many as 1 in 3 coworkers report being affected by such use (Institute for a Drug-Free Workplace, 1997; Lehman, Farabee, & Bennett, 1998). Job problems that stem from substance abuse are often framed in terms of individual costs: absenteeism, accidents, poor performance, and turnover (Lehman & Simpson, 1992; Normand, Lempert, & O'Brien, 1994). Coworkers, however, experience collateral problems, such as picking up the slack and lowered morale (Bennett & Lehman, 1998; Roman & Blum, 1995), suggesting that a social–ecological approach to prevention has value.

This chapter briefly summarizes the development and context of the team-oriented training. Bennett, Lehman, and Reynolds (2000) provided a detailed description of this program, and the beginning of this chapter is patterned after that description. Next, the chapter describes an evaluation study in which the team-oriented training was implemented in two different municipal work forces and compared with an informational training and a no-training control group. The evaluation model used random assignment of work groups to the three training conditions; measures were collected pretraining, posttraining, and at 6-month follow up.

THE SOCIAL CONTEXT OF PREVENTION

Coworkers can have a negative or positive influence on employees with AOD problems. Coworkers may pick up the slack, actively enable use (Roman, Blum, & Martin, 1992), or increase alcohol availability at work (Ames & Grube, 1999). They also may facilitate the employee's efforts to get help (George & Tucker, 1996). The influence of coworkers suggests that intragroup relations can be a useful target for prevention efforts.

Recent changes in workplace organization and policies also are relevant for workplace prevention (Sauter & Hurrell, 1999). First, downsizing or restructuring in many organizations can place additional shared responsibility in the hands of workers (e.g., empowerment programming). Although supervisors traditionally have been trained to refer employees to get help for problems (Boone, 1995; Sonnenstuhl, 1990), interdependent work, team-oriented decision making, and decentralization may increase the need for informal sanctions that encourage problem coworkers to seek help (cf. Anderson, Chiricos, & Waldo, 1977). Coworkers may be motivated to encourage a troubled employee to seek help when the loss or firing of their colleague results in an increased workload (Hood & Duphorne, 1995). Increased surveillance in teams also may cause stress. Workers may have less time alone, face ambiguities associated with decentralization, and share increased responsibility for coworker behavior (Bennett & Lehman, 1999b).

Second, AOD testing has become common (Bahls, 1998). Although testing increases privacy concerns (Gillom, 1994; Hubbart, 1998; Sujak, Villanova, & Daly, 1995), most employees tend to favor testing when jobs involve safety risks or contact with the public (Murphy, Thornton, & Prue, 1991; Tepper, 1994) or when employees have been previously exposed to coworker use (Bennett & Lehman, 1997a). Sanctions associated with testing positive for drugs, such as job loss, may motivate employees to seek help for problems and avoid serious penalties if caught through a positive drug test.

Attention to contextual factors, such as coworker reactions to AOD use, teamwork, and policy attitudes, should enhance the relevance and effectiveness of current workplace policies. In many organizations, substance abuse education ignores contextual elements and instead focuses primarily on individual workers (Cook, Back, & Trudeau, 1996; Irwin, 1990). Core elements typically include a written policy, supervisor training, employee education, EAP availability, and identification of illegal drug users (e.g., Working Partners, 1998; Wright & Wright, 1993). In light of concerns about the increased relevance of the social context of prevention, we developed and implemented a team-oriented substance abuse prevention program for the workplace. Components of the program were derived from theoretical concerns and previous empirical work on workplace substance abuse.

Empirical Basis of Prevention Model

Figure 5.1 illustrates a general model of psychosocial factors, employee AOD use, and organizational reactions. Psychosocial factors include workplace environment, group processes, and perceptions and attitudes of employees toward AOD-using coworkers and policy. As shown at the top of Figure 5.1, problem AOD use leads to the need for policy. This policy is then influenced at multiple levels: the organization, group, and individual. At each level are specific risk and protective factors. For example, the organizational level of influence includes the workplace environment. *Risk factors* include safety-related occupations and drinking climate, and *protective factors* include social integration and organizational wellness. Risk factors at the group level include neutralizing deviance (i.e., employees denying or minimizing deviant behaviors of their coworkers); teamwork or work group cohesion constitutes a protective factor. At the individual level, exposure to coworker use and tolerant attitudes toward use are important risk factors, whereas support of policy is a protective factor. Because the team training was derived from this risk–protective factor model, we hypothesize that it may be most effective for work groups experiencing relatively more risk factors than protective factors.

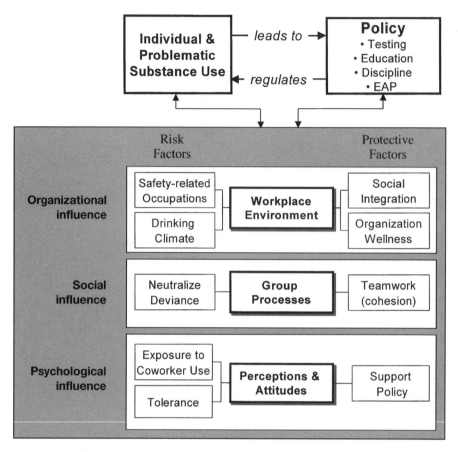

Figure 5.1. Workplace influences on employee substance use and exposure to coworker substance use.

Workplace Environment

Research on work environment can be framed in terms of two risk factors and two protective factors (see Figure 5.1). Risks include occupational subcultures that develop around safety and a work climate that may support the use of alcohol (i.e., drinking climate). Social integration and organizational wellness are protective factors.

A variety of studies have reported higher levels of AOD use among employees in occupations involving safety risk (e.g., machinery use, toxic chemicals), mobility (truck driving), and shift work (Ames & Grube, 1999; Lehman, Farabee, Holcom, & Simpson, 1995; Lund, Preusser, Blomberg, & Williams, 1991; Macdonald, Wells, & Wild, 1999; Trinkoff & Storr, 1998). Safety characteristics also combine with work culture to affect susceptibility to problem drinking. Occupational subcultures also can form (Fillmore, 1990; Sonnenstuhl, 1996) whereby employees either bend rules or view certain behaviors as normal rather than deviant. Examples include drinking on the job for assembly workers (Ames & Janes, 1990) and illicit prescription drug use among pharmacists (Dabney & Hollinger, 1999).

Job characteristics such as low job latitude and autonomy and repetitive or stressful work correlate with problem drinking (Greenberg & Grunberg, 1995; Seeman, Seeman, & Budros, 1988). Drinking climates develop in some work environments in which employees drink together to cope with stressful job situations, show solidarity with coworkers, or engage in joint leisure (Ames & Janes, 1990; Cosper, 1979). Such drinking climates include social drinking as well as attitudinal support for drinking (Beattie, Longabaugh, & Fava, 1992; Bennett & Lehman, 1998; Seeman & Anderson, 1983). Drinking climates may evolve throughout an organization or be limited to isolated work groups. Bennett and Lehman (1999a) noted that employees were more susceptible to negative consequences from exposure to coworker drinking when drinking climates were strong.

Two sets of protective factors include social integration and organizational wellness. Social integration includes workplace social support, job involvement, and the absence of alienation or estrangement at work. Integration appears to help employees cope with job-related problems in ways other than through alcohol. For example, the perceived presence of supportive coworkers or supervisors is negatively correlated with escapist or job stress reasons for drinking (Fennell, Rodin, & Kantor, 1981) and positively related to abstinence for employees admitted to outpatient treatment (Beattie et al., 1992). Alternatively, problem drinking may be a way of coping in jobs perceived as alienating (Greenberg & Grunberg, 1995; Parker & Farmer, 1990).

Organizational health or wellness (e.g., Guthrie & Olian, 1990; Rosen, 1991; Quick, 1999) is defined as a work culture that supports healthy lifestyles. Healthy work cultures emphasize employee involvement, family-friendly policies that promote work–life balance, peer support, and positive flow of communication. Bennett and Lehman (1997b), using a climate measure of organizational wellness, found that high levels of wellness were associated with low levels of AOD use and enabling of coworkers and with favorable attitudes toward substance use policy.

Group Processes

Figure 5.1 shows group processes to include neutralizing deviance as a risk factor and teamwork or group cohesion as a protective factor. *Neutralizing deviance* refers to processes whereby group members justify, rationalize, support, or tolerate deviant behaviors of coworkers (Robinson & Kraatz, 1998). Coworkers and supervisors sometimes enable problem employees either by actively covering for them or by ignoring problems. When employees work in teams, they are subject to the behavioral risks of problem workers (Yandrick, 1996).

Teamwork or group cohesion, however, provides an important protective factor. Research suggests that teamwork is associated with a decreased likelihood of alcohol problems or drinking climates (Beattie et al., 1992; Bennett & Lehman, 1998; Delaney & Ames, 1995; Fillmore, 1990; Greenberg & Grunberg, 1995). This benefit may result from social norms that promote and support task-related behavior among coworkers—norms that run counter to the support of deviant behavior. In cohesive groups, problems are typically addressed rather than avoided, leading to greater compliance with rules and less support for deviant behavior.

Perceptions and Attitudes

Risk factors at the individual level (i.e., perceptions and attitudes) include exposure to coworker AOD use and tolerant attitudes toward coworker use. Protective factors include support of company policy regarding AOD use. Employees who perceive AOD use among their coworkers report higher job stress and withdrawal (Bennett & Lehman, 1998), lower faith in management (Lehman et al., 1998), and less teamwork (Bennett & Lehman, 1999a) than do employees who are not aware of coworker AOD use.

Tolerant attitudes toward coworkers who are AOD users also reflect risk factors for substance abuse. Lehman (1994) classified employees into one of three groups according to their level of tolerance for AOD-using coworkers (i.e., low, medium, or high) and compared the groups on a profile of variables (e.g., personal background and job factors). The profile of variables that best described highly tolerant employees showed them to be young men with high levels of deviance (e.g., arrest records, peers with deviance, and risk-taking behaviors) who also worked in safety-sensitive jobs. The demographic profile of highly tolerant attitudes closely matches one that describes marijuana users (Lehman, 1995). Lehman, Olson, and Rosenbaum (1996) found that when compared with six personal background factors (e.g., religious attendance, arrest history, and depression) and job risk to estimate AOD use, tolerance was the best predictor of recent illicit drug use, and after arrest history, the best predictor for use at work.

Employees' attitudinal support of substance abuse policy may provide an additional protective factor from problematic AOD use. Bennett and Lehman (1997a) found that employees exposed to coworker drinking were more willing to endorse testing and discipline. In contrast, AOD users showed less support for testing (especially random) and more support for education. Interestingly, employees with a recent history of drunkenness or problem drinking disfavored both education and discipline. Employees appear to focus on different policy messages as a function of their own circumstances.

TEAM-ORIENTED PREVENTION TRAINING

To increase awareness of substance abuse as a group problem, a team-oriented training program was developed in accordance with the conceptual model described above. The training also sought to decrease tolerance and enabling of problem behaviors, enhance group responsiveness to problems, improve attitudes toward policy, and increase help seeking and peer referral to the EAP or other resources. The major objectives of our worksite prevention training program were to examine and address the role that work group culture and social dynamics play in enabling AOD use and how use by any member of the work group can negatively affect every member. Essentially, the training addresses five areas of workplace culture associated with AOD use: occupational subcultures, drinking climates, tolerance and enabling, group cohesion, and the social context of policy. In addition, the program uses principles associated with organizational downsizing and reengineering (e.g., team learning).

Several factors were considered in developing the training. First, the training was designed to be interactive and participatory. Activities such as group discussions and role playing help increase the relevance of the training and aid in comprehension and retention. Second, the construct of *transfer of training* was addressed. It is not enough for training to be effective in changing knowledge, attitudes, or behaviors among trainees if those changes are not then carried forth into the actual work environment. The effects of training may not transfer outside the training room for a variety of reasons, including lack of relevance to the work situation and barriers to transfer from the organization and supervisors. A third factor was the development of skills that work groups would find useful in dealing with a variety of problem situations. Skills addressed in the team training included communication skills, stress management, and problem solving.

Prevention programs in the workplace need to be strategically placed, relevant, and efficient. One way to ensure efficiency is to target areas of an organization that have high risk for problems, rather than apply a blanket approach for all employees, who may not always benefit from an intensive program. Because of its interactive nature, the team-oriented training requires longer training sessions and more involvement from trainees than standard information-based programs to be effective. Although skills are taught that are relevant for just about any work group in dealing with problem situations, the training emphasizes AOD use and work group cultures that enable and tolerate problem behaviors. This approach may not be relevant for work groups that do not function as integrated teams and are at low risk for developing unhealthy cultures. Participants from such groups may view the team-oriented training as overly intrusive and irrelevant to their work situation. Theoretically speaking, for maximum effectiveness and efficiency, the team-oriented training should target work groups that function as teams.

Team-Oriented Training Content

The team-oriented awareness training is an 8-hour program administered in two 4-hour sessions, 2 weeks apart (although shorter versions have been used). Six to 8 weeks prior to training delivery, we conduct interviews with EAP representatives and key personnel in human resources (e.g., employee relations and training directors), obtain copies of all relevant documents (e.g., policies, previous training material, and EAP promotional materials), and engage a sample of employees in different focus groups. Interviews and focus groups help identify issues that require addressing in training and help customize training in several ways; for example, we create a true–false policy quiz and design other questions to be used in a board game (see below). The training is suitable for 9 to 15 employees to allow for group discussion. This section summarizes the full training and focus groups.

Focus Groups

Previous studies suggest that focus groups may allay any resistance employees have to the idea of substance abuse prevention (Towers, Kishchuk, Sylvestre, Peters, & Bourgault, 1993). Such groups, even though they occur prior to training, are part of the intervention. Managers select a representative sample of employees to attend focus groups. The groups pilot training materials, attempt to enhance employee involvement, build rapport between researchers and employees, and help trainers understand the work climate.

Component 1: Relevance

Following a warm-up activity, we introduce a distinction between *standard training* (i.e., that focused on individual workers as separately vulnerable to problems) and *team-oriented training* (i.e., that focused on work groups and the issues they face—work climate, productivity, and job stress). Through short lectures, discussions, and various exercises, employees explore how the training might be helpful to them. We review and discuss principles of prevention (e.g., stress management). Small groups fill out an incomplete sentence task about community, teamwork, and perceived substance abuse at three societal levels: country, state, and local community and workplace. Using a questionnaire, employees receive feedback about cohesion in their group (a key protective factor, or strength) and exposure to problem workers (a key risk factor).

Component 2: Team Ownership of Policy

Employees complete and receive feedback on a policy quiz. A short lecture describes three aspects of policy: (a) recognizing the problem, (b) getting help (e.g., through the EAP), and (c) getting caught (i.e., testing and discipline). In small groups, employees complete a 22 matrix on which they list costs and benefits of "getting help" versus "getting caught." Employees are then divided into small groups and play a board game ("Risks and Strengths"), in the course of which each group has to work together to choose answers to multiple-choice or true-false questions. Questions refer back to the lecture, to policy, and to general knowledge about AOD use. Correct responses earn the team a "strength' (a green poker chip); incorrect responses earn a "risk" (red chip). Participants can reduce risks by going to "getting-help" spaces. The team with the most strengths wins, and every winning team member is given a $5 gift certificate.

Component 3: Understanding Stress

Employees self-assess their coping style and are then shown a video in which male coworkers choose to deal with stress either by going out for drinks or by playing basketball (cf. "The Stress Connection"; Cook et al., 1996). We next compare healthy and unhealthy coping and describe how stress and drug use are related. Using a flip-chart activity, employees identify stressors, how stressors keep work from being done or done well, and methods for coping.

Component 4: Understanding Tolerance

Employees complete a survey asking how much they would tolerate six different types of scenarios involving problems (e.g., a coworker repeatedly comes late to work or a coworker uses cocaine on weekends). They are then placed in small groups and asked to reach consensus on the same set of scenarios. The ensuing discussion is used to highlight how tolerance can occur at the group level and can be a risk factor for groups. The topic of drinking climate is discussed.

Component 5: Support and Encourage Help

A short lecture and activity reviews the positive and negative aspects of grapevine communication (i.e., rumors and gossip). Handouts describe effective listening tips and guidelines for approaching employees who have a problem. We present a NUDGE (i.e., notice–understand–decide–use guidelines–encourage) model and teach how to "roll with resistance" when trying to encourage a colleague to get help. Groups of three to four employees review case studies for role-play activities. One worker acts the part of the employee with an AOD problem, another "nudges" him or her to get help, and the third observes. This component also reviews EAP confidentiality. Policies commonly encourage self-referral to the EAP, indicating that employees cannot be disciplined for voluntarily using the EAP; by taking steps to resolve problems, employees reduce chances of future disciplinary action. By thorough review of this policy, the training seeks to alleviate fears that jobs may be in jeopardy if employees seek treatment.

Homework and Transfer Enhancement

At the end of Session 1, employees are given an optional "Taking it Back to Work" assignment. They choose to either bring back a magazine or newspaper article related to any topic discussed in training (e.g., substance abuse, stress, community, or policies) or to discuss with others any issue reviewed in training. These homework assignments are brought back in the second training session and used as a springboard for discussion before activities on understanding stress and tolerance, and encouraging help are presented.

AN INFORMATIONAL APPROACH TO PREVENTION

To fully evaluate the impact of the team-oriented training model, we contrasted it with two other training conditions. First, we wanted to know whether employees who were exposed to the team-oriented training fared better than employees who received no training at all. Thus, a no-training control condition was implemented in which work teams completed pretest, posttest, and follow-up surveys but did not attend any training. Many workplaces offer some form of prevention training, usually in the form of providing information in a didactic manner. This type of training often focuses on identifying individual AOD users and providing either referral and treatment or discipline. Training then, often includes information about substance abuse; company substance abuse policy, including discipline; and how to seek help from the EAP. The work groups assigned to the control conditions in the current study had already received some of this standard (often rudimentary) information.

We not only wanted to know whether the team-oriented training was more effective than no training, we also wanted to know how it compared with an advanced informational approach that did not address team or work culture issues. We developed an informational approach that consisted of two 2-hour sessions offered about 2 weeks apart. This approach differed in both format and length from the team-oriented training. Although we were concerned about comparing two training protocols that differed in length, to remain somewhat faithful to an informational model, we could not stretch the sessions enough to approach the same length as the interactive, team-oriented approach without including filler material that would waste employee time. Still, the advanced informational training provided significantly more information about policy and EAP services than was available in the standard format.

The information model was derived directly from human resource orientation practices in the current worksites. In the first session, employees received 2 hours of information about employee substance abuse and their workplace policy. The training included a video about the negative effects of different substances (e.g., alcohol, marijuana, and cocaine), a thorough review of different sections of their policy (e.g., testing and disciplinary procedures), and a participatory quiz. In the second session, employees received 2 hours of information about their EAP, including a video with follow-up discussion; a brief, game-oriented quiz; and a review of all EAP services. Supervisors attended the same informational training sessions as other employees.

PROXIMAL AND DISTAL TRAINING OUTCOME DOMAINS

The ultimate, or distal, goals of substance abuse prevention training are to reduce employee AOD use, reduce harm from AOD use and, ultimately, increase safety and productivity and reduce costs. To accomplish those goals, immediate, or proximal, goals are established, which should then lead to the distal goals listed above. For example, the team-oriented training is designed to create a more positive and responsible work group climate. This climate, in turn, should generate an increase in help seeking, buffer the negative effects of stress, and encourage development of positive group goals. Thus, group climate is an important proximal training outcome, whereas help seeking and reduction of AOD use is a long-term, or distal, goal. For the purposes of the present evaluation, group climate includes group cohesion, group care, peer helping, privacy regulation, and faith in management.

A second domain of interest is stress and problem solving. The team training emphasizes positive methods of coping with stress and increasing problem-solving skills. To the extent that the training is successful in improving those areas, stress-related drinking should decrease.

A major emphasis in the informational training is teaching about policy and the EAP. Thus, more positive attitudes toward the policy and the EAP and increased knowledge of both are a desired outcome of training. Although the team training spends much less time providing information in those areas, it teaches use of policy as a tool for improving the work group, emphasizes getting help for problems, and encourages problem coworkers to get help through the EAP.

Another focus of the team training is the group culture that enables and sometimes encourages AOD use. Team members often tolerate use among coworkers and enable use by looking the other way or picking up the slack, or a climate can exist that encourages drinking among team members. The team training uses exercises to reduce tolerance, reduce drinking as a way of coping, and encourage positive ways of group bonding. Thus, it is expected that drinking climates, tolerance, and stigma will be reduced and informal sanctions will increase if training is successful.

Finally, the theoretical model guiding the training suggests that problem drinking in the work group will diminish as the group climate becomes more supportive, group problem solving helps reduce negative reactions to stress, attitudes toward policy and the EAP become more positive, and drinking climates and tolerance diminish. The focus of this chapter, however, is to establish the effects of training on proximal outcomes, or mediators, of the relationship between training and problem drinking.

The current study attempted to examine the relative effectiveness on proximal outcomes of the team and informational training in two samples of municipal employees that were selected on the basis of previous reports of risk. That is, in one sample, EAP and previous survey data suggested that some of the departments within the city work force had higher levels of AOD use as well as the possible presence of a social climate that supported AOD use among coworkers. In terms of the model developed earlier (see Figure 5.1), one of the samples in the current analysis (City 2) appeared to have a higher level of organizational risk than did the other sample (City 1). Thus, we did not expect results to be similar across the two samples. Rather, we wished to explore whether the team-oriented approach might prove to be more effective when psychosocial risks are more prevalent and, perhaps, most salient.

METHODS

Study Sites

The samples were derived from two municipal work forces (excluding uniformed police and fire personnel) in the southwestern United States. City 1 (population 110,000) had approximately 400 employees; City 2 (population 480,000) had about 3,000 employees. Both cities reviewed their policies in employee orientation, and the EAP provided additional training. Until a year before the study, City 1 had had a local EAP in the form of a single gatekeeper, who provided some training. The city then contracted with a managed behavioral health care organization (MBHO), which offered services through a toll-free number. The EAP in City 2 was a single individual, employed for more than 6 years, who had conducted many 2-hour workshops for supervisors. Most employees in both cities had had additional policy training. Both cities had a well-developed policy with procedures for drug testing (i.e., applicant, suspicion, random, and postaccident), disclosure of information, and disciplinary and EAP referral procedures. Health plans included treatment for chemical dependency.

Participants

City 1

A total of 370 full-time employees from all city departments participated in the initial survey. Most were men (64%) between ages 31 and 40 (33%) or older (49%), were White (68%) and married (69%), and had at least some college (36%) or a college degree (24%). Many employees (52%) had worked for the city for more than 5 years, and many held jobs that involved some form of safety risk (e.g., 49% drove vehicles or worked with machinery or toxic chemicals). To obtain an estimate of the frequency of group interaction, we asked each employee how many hours in a typical workday he or she interacted with coworkers to get work done as a group. Responses showed 81% spending at least 1 hour, 70% spending at least 3 to 4 hours, and a full third (34%) spending 7 to 8 hours interacting with coworkers.

City 2

A total of 587 employees from three city departments completed the initial survey. Three at-risk departments—Parks and Recreation, Transportation, and Water—were chosen on the basis of previous surveys with the work force and information from the EAP that indicated higher than normal AOD problems. Most participants were men (83%) between ages 31 and 40 (35%) or older (49%), were married (64%), and had at least some college (35%) or a college degree (20%). City 2 was racially more diverse than City 1: The sample was 51% White, 27% African American, and 18% Hispanic/Mexican American. Many employees (57%) had worked for the city for more than 5 years. Compared with City 1, more employees in the City 2 sample held jobs that involved some form of safety risk (e.g., 68% drove vehicles or worked with machinery or toxic chemicals). When asked how many hours in a typical workday he or she interacted with coworkers to get work done as a group, 82% of the sample reported spending at least 1 hour, 53% reported spending at least 3 to 4 hours, and 25% reported spending 7 to 8 hours interacting with coworkers.

Experimental Design

Work groups were identified in each participating city department and were randomly assigned to one of three training conditions: (a) team-oriented training, (b) informational training, and (c) no-training control group. Each of the training conditions consisted of two training sessions that took place about 2 weeks apart. Approximately five separate sessions for each training condition were scheduled. Although all members of a work group attended the same type of training, they were scheduled into different sessions. This approach allowed each session to be composed of members from a variety of work groups, which facilitated greater diversity of experience and opinion in each session. It also prevented an entire work group from being away from the job at the same time. Training classes consisted of from 3 to 19 employees in City 1 ($M = 7.1$; $SD = 3.7$) and 3 to 22 employees in City 2 ($M = 9.7$; $SD = 4.8$).

Trained research staff administered questionnaires (entitled "Employee Health and Performance in the Workplace") to employee groups during working hours on city property in three phases: 2 to 4 weeks prior to training (pretest), 2 to 4 weeks following training (posttest), and 6 months following the posttest. All responses were anonymous, no names were collected, and no individual data were given to city officials. Participation was voluntary: Staff used informed consent procedures, and employees could choose to withdraw their participation at any time during the survey or training. To help keep track of individual data across phases, we randomly assigned employees an identification number and ID card to which only they had access. As an incentive to keep this card (and increase the amount of useful data), ID numbers were entered into a raffle system, and employees earned chances to win gift certificates each time they participated in a session.

Measures

The measures used in the current study are listed in Table 5.1. They are organized into five different domains: group perceptions (work group climate), stress and coping, policy (knowledge and attitudes), drinking norms, and EAP (knowledge and attitudes). The domains were chosen because they reflect areas that are addressed in either the team or informational training or are considered proximal or distal outcomes of the trainings. The dependent measures were collected 2 to 4 weeks after training and again about 6 months following training. All the measures asked on the posttraining survey were repeated in the 6-month follow-up survey, which included additional measures that were not in the posttraining survey. The number of participants in each of the two cities for each measurement period is presented in Table 5.2.

TABLE 5.1
Description of Outcome Variables

Variable	No. of Items	Sample Items
Group Perceptions		
Group cohesion	5	The people in my work group trust each other and cooperate to get the job done. People in my work group work together as a team for group objectives and goals.[a]
Group care	4	People in my work group are thoughtful and considerate of each other.[a]
Peer helping	3	If a coworker had a problem at home that was interfering with his/her ability to do the job, how likely would you be to say something to the employee? To say something to your supervisor?[b]
Privacy regulation	4	Employees respect each others' privacy when it comes to personal problems.[a]
Faith in management	3	I feel quite sure that supervisors in my department will always try to treat me fairly.[a]
Stress and Coping		
Group stress	4	The stress level in my work group is greater than the stress level of most other work groups.[a]
Personal stress	5	I am always under heavy pressure in my job.[a] I feel stress as a result of my job.[a]
Problem solving	4	If a fellow worker was having problems that interfered with work, someone in my group would find a way to help that employee deal with the problem.[a]
Risk	6	How much are you currently at risk of lost productivity and/or safety problems in your work setting because of improper handling of machinery or toxic chemicals? Coworker misuse or abuse of alcohol or drugs? Coworker hostility? (1 = no risk, 2 = a little risk, 3 = some risk, 4 = a lot of risk, 5 = great risk).
Coping	6	In the face of stress and difficulties on the job, how often do you and your coworkers take breaks during the workday together? Provide support and encouragement to each other? Plan together to solve the problem through some course of action?[c]
Work–family	4	On the job I have so much work to do that it takes away from my personal interests. After work, I come home too tired to do some of the things I'd like to do.[a]
Express concern	5	In the past 6 months, how often have you expressed any of the following to your coworkers or supervisor? ■ Concern that we are overstressed as a work group.[c] ■ Concern that they have an alcohol or drug problem.[c]

Table continues

TABLE 5.1 (*Continued*)

Variable	No. of Items	Sample Items
Policy		
Policy attitudes	5	I support the purpose and goals of the substance abuse policy. The policy is effective in reducing substance abuse (both alcohol and drug) by employees.[a]
Policy knowledge	10–20	True or false: Treatment for chemical dependency is not included under the medical plan (City 1 = false). True or false: Any employee can be tested at any time for alcohol while employed by the city (City 1 = false). True or false: Self-referral to the employee assistance program (EAP) for a problem with drugs does not count as a "violation" of the policy (City 2 = true). True or false: Any employee who fails an alcohol test will be evaluated by the EAP (City 2 = true).
Drinking Attitudes and Norms		
Drinking climate	5	How often is the talk at work about drinking or activities involving drinking? How often do any of your coworkers like to drink after work as a way of socializing together?[c]
Informal sanctions	4	If their own work was affected by a fellow employee who had a drinking or drug problem, how likely would your coworkers be to ignore the problem? Try to encourage the coworker to stop drinking or using or get help?[b]
Stigma	4	My coworkers would think less of me if they thought that I had a drinking problem.[a]
Tolerance	4 vignettes followed by 3 items each	A fellow worker smokes marijuana on a recreational basis, usually just on weekends. Much of his/her job involves talking on the telephone. While you see this person often during the work day, you rarely work together on the same tasks. I consider this behavior to be acceptable.[a] I would try to cover for this person.[a] I would report this person to a superior.[a]
Consequences	6	Based on your personal experience, how often has alcohol or drug use among your coworkers caused you to have to do more than your fair share of the work? Caused morale problems in your work group? Caused poor-quality work?[c]
Exposure to alcohol	4	In the past 6 months, how often was there someone at your job who drank alcohol either while at work or just before going to work?[d]

TABLE 5.1 (*Continued*)

Variable	No. of Items	Sample Items
Policy (cont.)		
Exposure to drugs	4	In the past 6 months, about how often were you aware of a coworker "under the influence" or "high" on illegally used drugs?[d]
EAP		
EAP confidentiality	2	If an employee called the EAP for help with a problem, how likely is it that the employee's supervisor would find out?[b]
EAP orientation	2	If you had a drug or alcohol problem, how likely would you be to go to the EAP for help?[b]
Contact the EAP	1	If you needed to contact the EAP, how would you do it? (Multiple choice: 0 = wrong answer, 1 = correct answer.)
EAP information	1	How much information do you feel that you have about the EAP? (1 = I do not know anything about it, 2 = I know that an EAP is available but nothing more, 3 = I know a little, 4 = I know a lot, 5 = I am very knowledgeable about the EAP.)
EAP efficacy	1	If an employee contacts the EAP for help with an alcohol or drug problem, how likely is it that the EAP could help the employee with the problem?[b]

[a] Response set: 1= strongly disagree, 2 = disagree, 3 = in between, 4 = agree, 5 = strongly agree.
[b] Response set: 1= very unlikely, 2 = unlikely, 3 = in between, 4 = likely, 5 = very likely.
[c] Response set: 1 = never, 2 = rarely, 3 = sometimes, 4 = often, 5 = almost always.
[d] Response set: 1 = never, 2 = once or twice, 3 = 3 or more times.

Attrition Analysis

We compared employees who completed the posttest with employees who did not complete the posttest. In City 1, employees who completed the posttest were more likely to know how to contact the EAP than those who did not complete the posttest. In addition, employees who dropped out of the team training condition reported less caring among coworkers in the group than did employees who completed the posttest, whereas dropouts from the control condition reported more group care than stayers did. Dropouts from the team and informational conditions reported less faith in management than did the stayers in those conditions, whereas dropouts from the control condition reported greater faith in management than did the stayers.

City 1 employees in all conditions who dropped out between pretest and 6-month follow up reported lower perceived risk, lower willingness to use the EAP, less knowledge of the EAP, higher group cohesiveness, and greater knowledge of policy than did the employees who completed the

TABLE 5.2
Number of Participants in Cities 1 and 2

	Condition			
	Team	Informational	Control	Total
City 1				
Pretraining	141	109	120	370
Posttraining	112	82	95	289
6-month follow up	78	60	59	197
City 2				
Pretraining	201	192	194	587
Posttraining	142	137	140	419
6-month follow up	119	96	102	317

follow-up questionnaire. Employees who dropped out of the team training reported lower group care than stayers did, whereas dropouts from the information and control conditions reported higher group care than stayers. Dropouts from the information condition reported less risk from lost productivity or safety issues than stayers, yet there were no differences between dropouts and stayers in the team or control conditions.

In City 2, employees from the team condition who did not complete the posttest reported less peer helping than did team-trained employees who completed the posttest, whereas dropouts and stayers in the other conditions reported similar peer helping. Similar to City 1, dropouts from the team training in City 2 reported lower group care than their counterparts who completed the posttest, whereas group care ratings did not differ between dropouts and stayers from the information and control conditions. Also, posttest dropouts from the team condition reported greater risk than stayers, whereas dropouts from the information and control groups reported less risk than stayers in those conditions.

City 2 employees who completed the pretest but did not complete the 6-month follow up across all conditions reported higher levels of personal stress, greater consequences resulting from coworker substance abuse, lower faith in management, less favorable attitudes toward policy and the EAP, and less knowledge of the EAP than did the employees who completed the pretest and the follow-up questionnaire. Dropouts from the team condition reported less privacy regulation than did study completers, whereas dropouts and completers did not differ on this variable in either the information or control conditions. Dropouts in the informational training condition reported higher levels of work-to-family spillover stress than did the information stayers, whereas dropouts from the team and the control conditions reported slightly less work-family spillover than did stayers.

The attrition analysis suggested that employees who dropped out of the study before the 6-month follow up might have had a less favorable orientation toward the EAP and substance abuse policy. Employees who dropped out before the posttest, however, were no less oriented toward policy than those employees who stayed until the posttest, and City 1 employees who dropped out before the follow up had more knowledge of their policy than stayers did. One noticeable pattern of the between-condition differences in attrition might have implications for the interpretations of the findings. Employees who dropped out of the team training condition reported less than favorable group care and other group perceptions (e.g., peer helping) than employees who completed all phases of the study. It is possible that the team training was only attractive to employees who already felt mutual and reciprocal care and responsibility for the co-workers within their work groups. This pattern of findings might limit the effectiveness of the team training within the group perceptions domain. This limitation is important because the team training was designed to influence workers' sense of teamwork and group care. Attrition may have restricted the team training from reaching the employees (with unfavorable attitudes) who could have benefited the most from the training.

Analytic Procedures

The effects of training were observed by comparing survey responses of trained and control employees at pretest with those at posttest and at 6-month follow up. Change scores were computed by subtracting pretest scores from posttest or follow-up scores.

Work groups, rather than individual employees, were assigned to the three training conditions to ensure that all the employees within a given work group received the same type of training. Because employees from the same work group all attended the same type of training and were more likely to interact and talk about the training with coworkers in their own work group, it was thought that their reactions to training would be more similar to their coworkers than to members of other work groups. Thus, observations of coworkers within the same work group were likely to be correlated.

Estimating training effects with traditional ordinary least squares (OLS) procedures requires that the random errors of the estimates be independent of one another, or uncorrelated. Because observations of coworkers within the same work group are likely to be correlated, OLS statistical methods are inappropriate because standard errors of means and effects will be underestimated, and therefore, the risk of Type I errors will be inflated (Burstein, 1980).

To better estimate the effect of training, the unique effect of group membership needs to be separated from the effect of training. Hierarchical linear modeling (HLM; Bryk & Raudenbush, 1992) efficiently estimates both effects (i.e., training and group membership) by constructing separate models for each level. Both models contain an estimate of random error uniquely associated with the unit of analysis of each model. That is, the individual-level model contains an estimate of the error associated with individual differences, and the group-level model contains an estimate of the error associated with group differences. Standard errors are better estimated with HLM because the variability of random effects is considered.

Because the dependent and independent variables in the current study exist on separate levels, HLM procedures were used to estimate the effects of training. We first present means on the set of dependent variables for baseline versus posttraining and baseline versus 6-month follow up for each of the three training conditions. Change scores were tested as being significantly different from zero by computing t tests.

Analysis of differential change between conditions was based on HLM. A two-level model of change scores was estimated: an employee-level model, in which change scores were allowed to vary around the work group's mean change score, and a group-level model, in which the estimate of the group's mean change from the employee-level model was predicted with variables representing contrasts between the training conditions (i.e., condition contrasts). Fixed training effect coefficients were estimated and are presented in the next section. The condition contrasts indicate the differences in change scores between each pairwise comparison of the three training conditions (team vs. control, informational vs. control, and team vs. informational). The coefficients (γ) were tested to be different from zero with t tests, and the standard errors were estimated with HLM.

RESULTS

Sample Differences

Table 5.3 shows comparisons on measures of personal alcohol use, exposure to coworker use, perceived risks and need for training, and safety characteristics and risk of jobs for the samples from City 1 and 2. Recall that City 1 included all city departments (excluding uniformed fire and police), whereas City 2 included three departments selected according to previous evidence that they had high risk for substance abuse problems. In all comparisons, City 2 showed higher risk than City 1. For example, City 2 participants were almost twice as likely to report getting drunk at least weekly and also were more likely to use alcohol and to work with a hangover (although differences were not large). City 2 participants were much more likely to report exposure to coworker AOD use, to report coworkers being high from alcohol at work, and to report awareness of coworkers being high on drugs at work.

City 2 participants also were more likely to perceive their work group

TABLE 5.3
Sample Comparisons on Risk

	City 1 (Low-Risk Sample) (%)	City 2 (High-Risk Sample) (%)
Personal Use		
Alcohol use (several days per week or more)	13.9	16.3
Drunkenness (5+ drinks in a row/weekly or more)	6.0	11.3
Work with hangover	7.1	9.7
Exposure to Coworker Use		
Drinking at or just before work	4.3	12.5
Alcohol high at work	6.7	19.8
Illicit drugs high at work	5.0	13.7
Observed signs of alcohol use (e.g., smelled alcohol)	11.4	23.9
Observed signs of marijuana use (e.g., smell or cigarette butts)	3.1	8.2
Perceived Risks and Need for Training		
Group is at risk because coworker is failing to get help for personal problems.	19.6	28.5
We would benefit from substance abuse training.	19.4	30.1
Safety-Sensitive Job (work at 3+ hours daily)		
Heavy machinery	20.9	30.6
Drive truck or vehicle	36.3	46.2
Work near or with toxic chemicals	11.9	25.3
Light machinery	23.5	39.7
Work by self or out in field	34.3	64.6
Work in job requiring drug testing	59.9	81.2

as at risk because of failure of coworkers to get help for problems and were more likely to report a need for substance abuse training (see Table 5.2). City 2 participants were more likely to work in safety-sensitive jobs in terms of working with heavy machinery, driving vehicles or working with or near toxic chemicals. Almost two-thirds worked by themselves out in the field, and 81% worked in jobs requiring drug testing. Together, the comparisons highlight the differences between the two samples and validate the high-risk nature of the selected departments from City 2.

Immediate Training Effects

Immediate training effects are presented in Table 5.4 for City 1 and Table 5.5 for City 2. We first examined whether significant changes occurred between pretest and posttest within each of the training conditions across the five variable domains. Pretest and posttest means are displayed in the left half of both tables. In City 1, no significant changes were found for any of the three training conditions for group perceptions or stress and coping; policy knowledge increased for the team training and informational

TABLE 5.4
Mean Responses at Pretest and Posttest, by Training Condition, and Training Effect Estimates for City 1

	Team (T) (N = 93)		Informational (I) (N = 74)		Control (C) (N = 90)		Level-2 γ Coefficients for Training Condition Contrasts		
	Pretest	Posttest	Pretest	Posttest	Pretest	Posttest	T vs. C	I vs. C	T vs. I
Group Perceptions									
Group cohesion	3.79	3.73	3.42	3.41	3.42	3.45	-.09	-.04	-.04
Group care	3.84	3.83	3.50	3.55	3.39	3.36	-.03	.03	-.07
Peer helping	3.05	3.15	3.02	3.14	3.03	3.15	-.06	-.01	-.05
Privacy regulation	3.30	3.40	3.05	3.07	3.10	3.06	.15	.06	.09
Faith in management	3.86	3.80	3.56	3.55	3.32	3.37	-.21	-.16	-.04
Stress and Coping									
Group stress	2.56	2.63	3.00	3.09	2.87	2.98	.04	.06	-.02
Personal stress	2.60	2.70	2.91	2.89	2.82	2.90	.03	-.05	.08
Problem solving	3.48	3.50	3.24	3.38	3.26	3.28	-.06	.09	-.15
Risk	1.50	1.52	1.90	1.99	1.75	1.80	.04	.09	-.05
Coping	3.25	3.29	3.18	3.27	3.04	3.06	.03	.09	-.06
Policy									
Policy attitudes	3.61	3.67	3.52	3.62	3.49	3.50	.06	.10	-.04
Policy knowledge	0.70	0.78***	0.67	0.76***	0.68	0.67	.09***	.10***	-.01
Drinking Attitudes and Norms									
Drinking climate	1.60	1.53	1.96	1.88	1.76	1.72	-.09	-.09	.00
Informal sanctions	3.02	2.97	2.85	2.96	3.01	2.85**	.14	.24*	-.10
Stigma	2.55	2.58	2.77	2.52***	2.68	2.65	.12	-.19	.31**
Tolerance	1.87	1.94	2.02	1.89*	1.89	1.96	-.02	-.19*	.17*
EAP									
EAP confidentiality	3.24	3.53**	3.37	3.51	3.30	3.38	.16	.05	.11
EAP orientation	3.73	3.74	3.39	3.70*	3.54	3.70	-.19	.12	-.30
Contact the EAP	1.16	1.60***	1.20	1.66***	1.17	1.21	.35***	.39***	-.04
EAP information	2.89	3.31***	2.48	3.61***	2.75	2.69	.43*	1.17***	-.74***
EAP efficacy	3.82	4.08**	3.49	4.03***	3.58	3.81*	.01	.30	-.29

*p < .05; **p < .01; ***p < .001.

TABLE 5.5
Mean Responses at Pretest and Posttest, by Training Condition, and Training Effect Estimates for City 2

	Team (T) (N = 129)		Informational (I) (N = 136)		Control (C) (N = 120)		Level 2 γ Coefficients for Training Condition Contrasts		
	Pretest	Posttest	Pretest	Posttest	Pretest	Posttest	T vs. C	I vs. C	T vs. I
Group Perceptions									
Group cohesion	3.62	3.41***	3.46	3.44	3.41	3.31	−.08	.09	−.17
Group care	3.74	3.63*	3.42	3.46	3.50	3.40	.00	.13	−.13
Peer helping	3.13	3.31	2.76	3.05***	2.98	3.15*	−.04	.09	−.13
Privacy regulation	3.18	3.15	3.02	3.03	3.08	3.01	.03	.08	−.05
Faith in management	3.51	3.37**	3.19	3.21**	3.27	3.17	−.06	.13	−.19
Stress and Coping									
Group stress	2.77	2.86	2.80	2.94*	2.89	2.97	−.03	.06	−.09
Personal stress	2.51	2.62*	2.54	2.70**	2.73	2.88**	−.06	.02	−.08
Problem solving	3.43	3.39	3.24	3.20	3.22	3.21	−.05	−.05	.00
Risk	2.07	2.14	2.19	2.32	1.97	2.15*	−.18	−.07	−.11
Coping	3.48	3.36*	3.32	3.22	3.37	3.23**	.04	.03	.01
Policy									
Policy attitudes	3.37	3.41	3.42	3.49	3.47	3.48	.01	.04	−.03
Policy knowledge	0.60	0.61	0.57	0.59	0.60	0.56*	.06*	.07***	−.01
Drinking Attitudes and Norms									
Drinking climate	1.83	1.78	1.81	1.75	1.61	1.57	−.03	−.06	.03
Informal sanctions	2.77	2.94***	2.76	2.82	2.87	2.92	.17*	.06	.11
Stigma	2.73	2.60	2.60	2.62	2.71	2.63	.01	.09	−.08
Tolerance	2.20	2.07**	2.15	2.08	2.13	2.04*	−.06	.04	−.10
EAP									
EAP confidentiality	2.97	2.92	2.80	3.02*	2.84	2.83	−.02	.23	−.25
EAP orientation	3.40	3.48	3.24	3.49**	3.34	3.20	.21	.41**	−.20
Contact the EAP	1.58	1.77***	1.63	1.70	1.63	1.73*	.09	−.03	.12
EAP information	3.05	3.40***	2.79	3.53***	2.98	3.03	.30*	.67***	−.36*
EAP efficacy	3.59	3.82*	3.68	3.98**	3.67	3.81	.06	.19	−.13

*$p < .05$; **$p < .01$; ***$p < .001$.

conditions, and stigma decreased for the informational condition. Drinking climate decreased for the control condition but did not change significantly for the team or informational training groups.

The most consistent changes were in the EAP domain. For the team condition, EAP confidentiality, contacting the EAP, EAP information, and EAP efficacy significantly increased. Similarly, EAP orientation, information, efficacy, and contacting the EAP increased for the informational condition. EAP efficacy was the only EAP variable to increase in the control condition.

The last three columns of Tables 5.3 and 5.4 provide results of contrasts that compared pretest and posttest measures across the different conditions. Changes differed between training groups for some policy, drinking norms, and EAP variables in City 1. For example, with policy knowledge, a significant difference was found between the insignificant change in the control group (pretest M = .68; posttest M = .67) and the increased knowledge among team-trained work groups (pretest M = .70; posttest M = .78); γ (T vs. C) = .09; $p < .001$. The informational condition also showed greater change in policy knowledge than did the control group, γ (I vs. C) = .10; $p < .001$. The informational condition showed a greater increase in informal sanctions and a larger decrease in tolerance than did the control group. In addition, the informational training groups showed greater decreases in stigma and tolerance than did the team training groups. The team and informational conditions also showed greater increases in contacting the EAP and EAP information than did the control group. The increase in EAP information was greater for the informational condition than for the team condition.

Results were mixed in City 2. Significant pretest–posttest changes were seen in group perceptions and stress and coping domains, although those changes did not differ across the three training conditions. For the team training groups, group cohesion, group care and faith in management decreased from pretest to posttest. It is not clear why decreases occurred in those areas, although the team groups scored higher on the measures at pretest than did the other conditions and were essentially equivalent to the other conditions at posttest. Team-trained groups also increased in personal stress and decreased in coping. Informational groups showed increases in peer helping, faith in management, and group and personal stress. Control groups showed increases in peer helping, personal stress, and risk, and decreases in coping.

Like City 1, the HLM results for City 2 showed differential change across training conditions for variables in the policy, drinking norms, and EAP domains (see Table 5.4). For drinking norms, team-trained groups showed greater increases in informal sanctions than the groups receiving informational training. Team and informational groups showed relatively greater increases on policy knowledge than did the control group (which showed decreases in knowledge). Groups receiving informational training showed greater increases in EAP orientation and EAP information than did the control group and greater increases in EAP information than the team-trained groups. Team-trained groups also showed greater increases in EAP information than did the control group.

Long-Term Training Effects

Table 5.6 presents the long-term training effects for City 1, as determined by the changes from pretest to 6-month follow up. For the team-training condition, a significant decrease occurred in faith in management; group and personal stress, as well as expressing concern, increased. The team-training condition also showed significant increases in tolerance, policy knowledge, contacting the EAP, and EAP information and a decrease in drinking climate. The groups receiving informational training showed significant increases in policy knowledge, contacting the EAP, EAP information, and EAP efficacy. The control group showed decreases in coping and exposure to drinking and drug use and an increase in contacting the EAP.

No differences were found between the training conditions in the 6-month changes in any of the variables from the group perceptions, stress and coping, and drinking norms domains in City 1. Both the team and the informational groups, however, showed greater increases in policy knowledge than did the control group. The groups receiving informational training also showed greater change than did the control group on contacting the EAP and EAP information and greater change than the team-trained groups on EAP information.

The 6-month results for City 2 are presented in Table 5.7. In the group perceptions and stress and coping domains, team-trained groups showed significant decreases in group care, coping, and work family stress and increases in group care. From pretest to 6-month follow up, groups receiving informational training showed a decrease in faith in management and coping, and the control group showed a decrease in coping. No differences were found between training conditions, however, for any of the group perceptions or stress domains.

Change at 6 months was more evident in the policy, drinking attitudes and norms, and EAP domains. Team-trained groups and the control group showed small decreases in policy knowledge, and the control group showed a decrease in policy attitudes. The decrease in policy attitudes was significantly different from the small increase in policy attitudes for the team condition.

Perhaps the most important changes were found in the drinking attitudes and drinking norms domain. Team-trained groups showed decreases in drinking climates, stigma, tolerance, and exposure to drinking and an

TABLE 5.6
Mean Responses at Pretest and 6-Month Follow Up, by Training Condition, and Training Effect Estimates for City 1

	Team (T) (N = 62)		Informational (I) (N = 65)		Control (C) (N = 69)		Level 2 γ Coefficients for Training Condition Contrasts		
	Pretest	Follow Up	Pretest	Follow Up	Pretest	Follow Up	T vs. C	I vs. C	T vs. I
Group Perceptions									
Group cohesion	3.80	3.59	3.31	3.25	3.41	3.37	−.20	.10	−.30
Group care	3.89	3.79	3.36	3.41	3.45	3.37	.03	.18	−.15
Peer helping	3.14	3.22	3.10	3.15	3.14	3.07	.17	.07	.10
Privacy regulation	3.28	3.27	2.98	3.07	3.14	3.04	.09	.26	−.16
Faith in management	3.90	3.67**	3.46	3.44	3.42	3.47	−.31	.09	−.40
Stress and Coping									
Group stress	2.58	2.86**	3.04	3.19	2.91	2.95	.21	.01	.20
Personal stress	2.68	2.96**	3.04	3.10	2.83	2.97	.13	−.10	.24
Problem solving	3.50	3.37	3.16	3.20	3.25	3.31	−.23	.00	−.23
Risk	1.53	1.53	2.00	2.02	1.72	1.65	.05	.07	−.02
Coping	3.18	3.08	3.06	3.05	3.06	2.83**	.09	.25	−.16
Express concern	2.20	2.40*	2.39	2.43	2.31	2.25	.21	.11	.10

Policy									
Policy attitudes	3.72	3.72	3.48	3.58	3.51	3.50	−.01	.13	−.14
Policy knowledge	0.69	0.76**	0.66	0.74***	0.67	0.68	.06*	.07*	−.01
Drinking Norms									
Drinking climate	1.52	1.40*	1.89	1.81	1.79	1.62	−.08	−.06	−.02
Informal sanctions	3.08	2.98	2.85	2.89	3.04	3.00	−.04	.12	−.16
Stigma	2.50	2.61	2.75	2.67	2.74	2.81	−.02	−.22	−.20
Tolerance	1.80	2.05***	2.00	2.12	1.92	2.05	.11	−.03	.14
Felt consequences	1.20	1.24	1.44	1.44	1.38	1.28	.14	.07	.07
Exposure to drinking	1.07	1.05	1.14	1.12	1.10	1.05**	.03	.05	−.02
Exposure to drug use	1.04	1.00	1.03	1.07	1.05	1.02*	−.01	.07	−.08
EAP									
EAP confidentiality	3.28	3.57	3.33	3.52	3.32	3.40	.22	.19	.03
EAP orientation	3.91	3.82	3.44	3.63	3.51	3.48	−.06	.17	−.24
Contact the EAP	1.19	1.56***	1.18	1.57***	1.11	1.22*	.21	.27*	−.06
EAP information	3.05	3.37*	2.62	3.53***	2.84	2.68	.39	1.16***	−.76***
EAP efficacy	3.98	3.91	3.56	3.92*	3.59	3.46	.02	.39	−.37

*p < .05; **p < .01; ***p < .001.

TABLE 5.7
Mean Responses at Pretest and 6-Month Follow Up, by Training Condition, and Training Effect Estimates for City 2

	Team (T) (N = 102)		Informational (I) (N = 114)		Control (C) (N = 82)		Level 2 γ Coefficients for Training Condition Contrasts		
	Pretest	Follow Up	Pretest	Follow Up	Pretest	Follow Up	T vs. C	I vs. C	T vs. I
Group Perceptions									
Group cohesion	3.59	3.56	3.46	3.42	3.47	3.30	.07	.04	.03
Group care	3.75	3.53**	3.44	3.41	3.59	3.53	−.25	−.04	−.21
Peer helping	3.13	3.47***	2.76	2.89	2.93	3.07	.27	.11	.16
Privacy regulation	3.32	3.22	3.07	3.02	3.06	2.83	.06	.17	−.11
Faith in manage-ment	3.57	3.47	3.29	3.13*	3.38	3.26	−.07	−.08	.01
Stress and Coping									
Group stress	2.78	2.70	2.75	2.71	2.80	2.96	−.20	−.24	.04
Personal stress	2.47	2.56	2.44	2.53	2.62	2.78	−.09	−.06	−.03
Problem solving	3.47	3.47	3.22	3.24	3.27	3.25	.04	.09	−.05
Risk	1.97	1.90	2.09	1.98	1.83	1.91	−.15	−.17	.02
Coping	3.46	3.30**	3.29	3.11**	3.38	3.20*	−.10	−.10	.00
Work–family	2.54	2.39*	2.39	2.34	2.85	2.73	−.06	.05	−.11
Express concern	2.51	2.46	2.37	2.36	2.62	2.50	.00	.06	−.06

Policy									
Policy attitudes	3.44	3.50	3.48	3.46	3.61	3.43*	.24*	.15	.09
Policy knowledge	0.60	0.56*	0.58	0.55	0.60	0.53**	.03	.02	.01
Drinking Attitudes and Norms									
Drinking climate	1.88	1.64***	1.76	1.62**	1.58	1.44**	−.08	.03	−.11
Informal sanctions	2.79	3.03***	2.78	2.67*	2.84	2.92	−.23*	−.11	−.35***
Stigma	2.75	2.44**	2.53	2.43	2.62	2.72	−.33*	−.08	−.25
Tolerance	2.18	2.05**	2.14	2.19	2.11	2.10	−.12	.05	−.16
Felt consequences	1.45	1.42	1.47	1.37	1.33	1.28	.15	.03	.12
Exposure to drinking	1.24	1.13*	1.16	1.12	1.23	1.12*	.02	.09	−.07
Exposure to drug use	1.12	1.07	1.11	1.06*	1.11	1.03**	.02	.03	−.01
EAP									
EAP confidentiality	3.05	3.25	2.77	3.07**	3.03	3.21	−.04	.14	−.18
EAP orientation	3.51	3.36	3.31	3.13	3.33	3.09*	.23	.17	.06
Contact the EAP	1.58	1.68	1.64	1.67	1.71	1.67	.11	.00	.11
EAP information	3.14	3.50**	2.83	3.43***	3.15	3.27	.24	.43*	.19
EAP efficacy	3.75	3.88	3.72	3.61	3.71	3.67	.23	−.02	.25

*$p < .05$; **$p < .01$; ***$p < .001$.

increase in informal sanctions. Groups receiving informational training showed decreases in drinking climate, informal sanctions, and exposure to drug use, and the control group showed decreases in drinking climate, and exposure to drinking and to drug use. HLM results indicated that the increase in informal sanctions was greater for the team condition than for the control condition ($\gamma = .23$) and was greater for the team condition than for the informational condition ($\gamma = -.35$). The drop in stigma for the team-training condition also differed significantly from that of the control condition ($\gamma = -.33$).

Finally, the team and informational conditions showed significant increases in EAP information, and the informational condition showed a significant increase in EAP confidentiality. The control condition showed a decrease in EAP orientation. The change in EAP information was greater for the informational condition than for the control condition.

DISCUSSION

Results from the current set of analyses suggest that both the team and informational approaches resulted in significant and relatively long-lasting improvements in knowledge about workplace substance abuse policy and the EAP. Because the informational training required less time from employees than the team training did (4 vs. 8 hours), the results suggest that the informational training may be sufficient for obtaining these increases in knowledge. We emphasize that increases in knowledge about how to contact the EAP were substantial, especially for City 1, which had an external EAP managed by a behavioral health care organization. In contrast, City 2 had a long-standing internal EAP; although many employees knew how to contact the EAP at pretest (about 60%), the team training produced a short-term improvement in this area.

Aside from the increase in knowledge about policy and EAP, results on other outcome measures appeared to be somewhat inconsistent across the two samples. It is possible to account for those inconsistencies, however, by looking at preexisting differences between the samples (see Table 5.2). City 1 had a smaller work force than City 2, and all city departments (except for uniformed firefighters and police officers) were included in the training. In contrast, City 2 was much larger, and we restricted the training to include three large departments that had previously been identified as having the highest risk for AOD abuse among all city departments. The three departments tended to be predominately male, much of the work involved machinery or toxic chemicals, and participants had relatively fewer office-type jobs. In addition, participants in City 2 reported higher levels of risk in terms of personal drinking, exposure to coworker AOD use, and coworkers' failing to get help for problems. Perhaps as a result of those risk factors, City 2 participants also were more likely to recognize a need for AOD training.

When we consider that City 2 had a relatively high level of risk, a number of positive results from the training are somewhat encouraging. Several of the results occurred in the area of drinking norms. First, team-trained employees reported that their coworkers had a greater willingness to take action when a fellow employee had a drinking or drug problem (i.e., increased informal sanctions). This improvement persisted from 2 weeks posttest to the 6-month follow up; a decrease in informal sanctions for the informational group was actually found at follow up, suggesting less group responsiveness to substance abuse. Second, only the team-trained employees showed decreased tolerance at both posttest and follow up. Third, at follow up, team-trained employees also showed less stigma, reduced exposure to coworker alcohol use, and a reduction in drinking climate. Although some of the latter changes also were seen among informational and control group, a trend for improvement was found among most of the drinking norms measures in the team condition. In addition, increases in peer helping suggested that team-trained employees were more willing to speak to a troubled coworker at follow up.

In contrast to City 2, positive changes in drinking norm–related measures were seen in the informational condition in City 1. At posttest, City 1 employees in the informational condition showed improvements on two of the drinking–norm related measures: stigma and tolerance. This finding suggests that employees in this sample who received information about substance abuse and policy reduced their stigmatization of substance abuse while decreasing their tolerance of users. Although stigma remained below baseline levels at follow up, tolerance levels increased after 6 months for both the informational group (not significant) and the team group (significant). Again, the results contrast with City 2, where team-trained employees decreased their level of tolerance.

The various results seen from this initial study offer mixed support for both the team and informational approaches and suggest that some combination of both approaches may be most beneficial. All positive results were seen on proximal variables or risk domains. The team approach may work better for groups or departments that have higher levels of substance abuse and related psychosocial risks, and the benefits of the team approach may take some time to manifest. In groups in which risk is low, it may be sufficient for training to present information on AOD use, policy, and the EAP, as in the informational training. In such groups, in which a developed drinking climate may not exist and enabling behavior may be low, extensive training on changing work group climate may not be an efficient use of training resources or employee time.

Although the team training appeared to be more effective in the high-risk sample (City 2) than in the low-risk sample (City 1), further research needs to be conducted at the group level to determine whether high-risk and low-risk groups within the same work force react differently to the two training approaches. Such analyses should further determine whether the different results are a function of work group risk or some other factor in which the two samples differed.

Limitations

The foregoing summary of results should be considered in the light of several limitations. First, many of the positive results were found with samples that had remained in the study over a 6-month period. It is possible that those workers were already highly motivated to reap benefits from training and therefore self-selected into the follow-up study. Second, despite random assignment of work groups into different conditions, employees showed initial group differences that could have contributed to results. It is also possible that the 6-month follow-up period was too short to detect significant culture changes in the groups.

Strengths

Despite the limitations just cited, the current analysis also contains several strengths worth considering. First, we innovate on other studies in this volume that have applied health promotion approaches to workplace AOD use prevention by combining health promotion with team building. This integration has relevance for the increasing number of organizations that are adopting team strategies. Second, the current study is among the first to use an experimental approach that examines the impact of training on work climate factors relevant to substance abuse. This innovation is important because many conceptual models highlight the role of work culture as a moderator of employee substance abuse (Ames & Janes, 1990; Cook et al., 1996; Trice & Sonnenstuhl, 1990; Walsh, Rudd, Biener, & Mangione, 1993). Third, the study was partly based on theory of work culture (e.g., Trice & Sonnenstuhl, 1990) and used quantitative methods to explore two types of prevention models, one targeting socialization and work climate and the other oriented toward information processing or cognition. This distinction has parallels with previous theoretical thought in social psychology (e.g., normative vs. informational influence; Deutsch & Gerard, 1955; affective- vs. cognitive-growth theories of social behavior; McGuire, 1991). Theoretical linkage is useful because program evaluation and prevention research are often atheoretical (Shadish, Cook, & Leviton, 1995). Fourth, previous qualitative studies describe the importance of perceptions of confidentiality, stigma, and problem avoidance in employee help-seeking and EAP utilization (e.g., Sonnenstuhl, 1990). Measures of work climate were specifically derived to capture the processes of help-seeking and EAP utilization and findings with them were consistent with hypotheses. Finally, we used a multilevel approach (i.e., HLM) that took into account correlations among members of the same work groups to contrast the three training conditions.

REFERENCES

Ames, G. M., & Grube, J. (1999). Alcohol availability and workplace drinking: Mixed method analyses. *Journal of Studies on Alcohol, 60,* 383–393.

Ames, G. M., & Janes, C. (1990). Drinking, social networks, and the workplace: Results of an environmentally focused study. In P. M. Roman (Ed.), *Alcohol problem intervention in the workplace: Employee assistance programs and strategic alternatives* (pp. 95–111). New York: Quorum Books.

Anderson, L. S., Chiricos, T. G., & Waldo, G. P. (1977). Formal and informal sanctions: A comparison of deterrent effects. *Social Problems, 25,* 103–114.

Bahls, J. E. (1998). Drugs in the workplace. *HR Magazine, 43,* 80–87.

Beattie, M. C., Longabaugh, R., & Fava, J. (1992). Assessment of alcohol-related workplace activities: Development and testing of "Your Workplace." *Journal of Studies on Alcohol, 53,* 469–475.

Bennett, J. B., & Lehman, W. E. K. (1997a). Employee views of organizational wellness and the EAP: Influence on substance use, drinking climates, and policy attitudes. *Employee Assistance Quarterly, 13*(1), 55–72.

Bennett, J. B., & Lehman, W. E. K. (1997b). From dual policy to dual attitudes: The social construction of substance use policy. *Review of Public Personnel Administration, 17,* 58–83.

Bennett, J. B., & Lehman, W. E. K. (1998). Workplace drinking climate, stress, and problem indicators: Assessing the influence of team work (group cohesion). *Journal of Studies on Alcohol, 59,* 608–618.

Bennett, J. B., & Lehman, W. E. K. (1999a). Employee exposure to co-worker substance use and negative consequences: The moderating effects of work group membership. *Journal of Health and Social Behavior, 40,* 307–322.

Bennett, J. B., & Lehman, W. E. K. (1999b). The relationship between problem co-workers and quality work practices: A case study of exposure to sex, drugs, violence, and stress. *Work and Stress, 13,* 299–311.

Bennett, J. B., Lehman, W. E. K., & Reynolds, G. S. (2000). Team awareness for workplace substance abuse prevention: The empirical and conceptual development of a training program. *Prevention Science, 1,* 157–171.

Boone, C. (1995). The effectiveness of EAP supervisory training. *Employee Assistance Quarterly, 11,* 17–27.

Bryk, A. S., & Raudenbush, S. W. (1992). *Hierarchical linear models: Applications and data analysis methods.* Newbury Park, CA: Sage.

Burstein, L. (1980). The analysis of multi-level data in educational research and evaluation. *Review of Research in Education, 8,* 158–233.

Cook, R. F., Back, A., & Trudeau, J. (1996). Substance abuse prevention in the workplace: Recent findings and an expanded conceptual model. *Journal of Primary Prevention, 16,* 319–339.

Cosper, R. (1979). Drinking as conformity: A critique of sociological literature on occupational differences in drinking. *Journal of Studies on Alcohol, 40,* 868–891.

Dabney, D., & Hollinger, R. C. (1999). Illicit prescription drug use among pharmacists: Evidence of a paradox of familiarity. *Work and Occupations, 26,* 77–106.

Delaney, W. P., & Ames, G. (1995). Work team attitudes, drinking norms, and workplace drinking. *Journal of Drug Issues, 25,* 275–290.

Deutsch, M., & Gerard, H. B. (1955). A study of normative and informational social influence upon individual judgment. *Journal of Abnormal and Social Psychology, 51,* 629–636.

Fennell, M. L., Rodin, M. B., & Kantor, G. K. (1981). Problems in the work setting, drinking, and reasons for drinking. *Social Forces, 60,* 114–132.

Fillmore, K. M. (1990). Occupational drinking subcultures: An exploratory epidemiological study. In P. M. Roman (Ed.), *Alcohol problem intervention in the workplace: Employee assistance programs and strategic alternatives.* New York: Quorum Books.

George, A. A., & Tucker, J. A. (1996). Help-seeking for alcohol-related problems: Social contexts surrounding entry into alcoholism treatment or Alcoholics Anonymous. *Journal of Studies on Alcohol, 57,* 449–457.

Gillom, J. (1994). *Surveillance, privacy, and the law: Employee drug testing and the politics of social control.* Ann Arbor: University of Michigan Press.

Greenberg, E. S., & Grunberg, L. (1995). Work alienation and problem alcohol behavior. *Journal of Health and Social Behavior, 36,* 83–102.

Guthrie, J. P., & Olian, J. D. (1990). Using psychological constructs to improve health and safety: The HRM niche. *Research in Personnel and Human Resource Management, 8,* 141–201.

Hood, J. C., & Duphorne, P. L. (1995). To report or not to report: Nurses' attitudes toward reporting co-workers suspected of substance abuse. *Journal of Drug Issues, 25,* 313–340.

Hubbart, W. S. (1998). *The new battle of workplace privacy: Safe practices to minimize conflict, confusion, and litigation.* New York: American Management Association.

Institute for a Drug-Free Workplace. (1997). *What American employees think about drug abuse (A Gallup Study).* Retrieved April 26, 2002, from http://www.drugfreeworkplace.org/survey

Irwin, D. D. (1990). *Deviance in the workplace: Case studies of drug testing in large organizations.* San Francisco, CA: Mellen Research University Press.

Lehman, W. E. K. (1994, May). *Antecedents and consequences of employee drug use within organizations.* Paper presented at Alcohol, Tobacco, and Other Drug Problems in the Workplace: Incentives for Prevention, San Diego, CA.

Lehman, W. E. K. (1995, July). *Marijuana and performance*. Paper presented at the National Conference on Marijuana Use: Prevention, Treatment, and Research, Crystal City, VA.

Lehman, W. E. K., Farabee, D., & Bennett, J. B. (1998). Perceptions and correlates of co-worker substance use. *Employee Assistance Quarterly, 13*(4), 1–22.

Lehman, W. E. K., Farabee, D. J., Holcom, M. L., & Simpson, D. D. (1995). Prediction of substance use in the workplace: Unique contributions of personal background and work environment variables. *Journal of Drug Issues, 25*, 253–274.

Lehman, W. E. K., Olson, K. E., & Rosenbaum, A. L. (1996). *Job risk and employee substance use: The influence of personal background and work environment factors*. Paper presented at the annual convention of the Society of Industrial/Organizational Psychology, San Diego, CA.

Lehman, W. E. K., & Simpson, D. D. (1992). Employee substance use and on-the-job behaviors. *Journal of Applied Psychology, 77*, 309–321.

Lund, A. K., Preusser, D. F., Blomberg, R., & Williams, A. F. (1991). Drug use by tractor trailer drivers. In S. W. Gust & J. M. Walsh (Eds.), *Drugs in the workplace: Research and evaluation data* (pp. 47–69). Rockville, MD: U.S. Department of Health and Human Services.

Macdonald, S., Wells, S., & Wild, T. C. (1999). Occupational risk factors associated with alcohol and drug problems. *American Journal of Drug and Alcohol Abuse, 25*, 351–369.

McGuire, W. J. (1991). Using guiding-idea theories of the person to develop educational campaigns against drug abuse and other health-threatening behavior. *Health Education Research, 6*, 173–184.

Murphy, K. R., Thornton, G. C., III, & Prue, K. (1991). Influence of job characteristics on the acceptability of employee drug testing. *Journal of Applied Psychology, 76*, 447–453.

Normand, J., Lempert, R. O., & O'Brien, C. P. (1994). *Under the influence? Drugs and the American work force*. Washington, DC: National Academy Press.

Parker, D. A., & Farmer, G. C. (1990). Employed adults at risk for diminished self-control over alcohol use: The alienated, the burned out, and the unchallenged. In P. M. Roman (Ed.), *Alcohol problem intervention in the workplace: Employee assistance programs and strategic alternatives* (pp. 27–44). New York: Quorum Books.

Quick, J. C. (1999). Occupational health psychology: The convergence of health and clinical psychology with public health and preventive medicine in an organizational context. *Professional Psychology, 30*, 123–128.

Robinson, S. L., & Kraatz, M. S. (1998). Constructing the reality of normative behavior: The use of neutralization strategies by organizational deviants. In R. W. Griffin & A. O'Leary-Kelly (Eds.), *Monographs in organizational behavior and industrial relations: Vol. 23. Dysfunctional behavior in organizations: Violent and deviant behavior* (pp. 203–220). Stamford, CT: JAI Press.

Roman, P. M., & Blum, T. C. (1995). Alcohol: A review of the impact of worksite interventions on health and behavioral outcomes. *American Journal of Health Promotion, 11,* 136–149.

Roman, P. M., Blum, T. C., & Martin, J. K. (1992). "Enabling" of male problem drinkers in work groups. *British Journal of Addiction, 87,* 275–289.

Rosen, R. H. (1991). *The healthy company: Eight strategies to develop people, productivity, and profits.* Los Angeles, CA: Jeremy P. Tarcher.

Sauter, S. L., & Hurrell, J. J., Jr. (1999). Occupational health psychology: Origins, content, and direction. *Professional Psychology: Research and Practice, 30,* 117–122.

Seeman, M., & Anderson, C. S. (1983). Alienation and alcohol: The role of work, mastery, and community in drinking behavior. *American Sociological Review, 48,* 60–77.

Seeman, M., Seeman, A. Z., & Budros, A. (1988). Powerlessness, work, and community: A longitudinal study of alienation and alcohol use. *Journal of Health and Social Behavior, 29,* 185–198.

Shadish, W. R., Cook, T. D., & Leviton, L. C. (1995). *Foundations of program evaluation: Theories of practice.* Thousand Oaks, CA: Sage.

Sonnenstuhl, W. (1990). Help-seeking and helping processes within the workplace: Assisting alcoholic and other troubled employees. In P. M. Roman (Ed.), *Alcohol problem intervention in the workplace: Employee assistance programs and strategic alternatives* (pp. 237–259). New York: Quorum Books.

Sonnenstuhl, W. J. (1996). *Working sober: The transformation of an occupational drinking culture.* Ithaca, NY: ILR Press/Cornell University Press.

Substance Abuse and Mental Health Services Administration. (1996). *Drug use among U.S. workers: Prevalence and trends by occupation and industry categories* (DHHS Publication No. SMA 96-3089). Washington, DC: U.S. Government Printing Office.

Substance Abuse and Mental Health Services Administration. (1999). *Worker drug use and workplace policies and programs: Results from the National Household Survey on Drug Abuse.* Retrieved April 26, 2002, from http://www.samhsa.gov/oas/nhsda/a-ll/toc.htm

Sujak, D. A., Villanova, P., & Daly, J. P. (1995). The effects of drug-testing program characteristics on applicants' attitudes toward potential employment. *Journal of Psychology, 129,* 401–416.

Tepper, B. J. (1994). Investigation of general and program-specific attitudes toward corporate drug-testing policies. *Journal of Applied Psychology, 79,* 392–401.

Towers, A. M., Kishchuk, N., Sylvestre, M., Peters, C., & Bourgault, C. (1993). A qualitative investigation of organizational issues in an alcohol awareness program for blue-collar workers. *American Journal of Health Promotion, 9,* 56–63.

Trice, H. M., & Sonnenstuhl, W. J. (1990). On the construction of drinking norms in work organizations. *Journal of Studies on Alcohol, 51,* 201–220.

Trinkoff, A. M., & Storr, C. L. (1998). Work schedule characteristics and substance use in nurses. *American Journal of Industrial Medicine, 34,* 266–271.

Walsh, D. C., Rudd, R. E., Biener, L., & Mangione, T. (1993). Researching and preventing alcohol problems at work: Toward an integrative model. *American Journal of Health Promotion, 7,* 289–295.

Working Partners for an Alcohol and Drug Free Workplace. (1998). *Establishing workplace substance abuse programs.* Retrieved April 26, 2002, from http://www.dol.gov/asp /programs/drugs/workingpartners/Screen5.htm

Wright, R. S., & Wright, D. G. (1993). *Creating and maintaining a drug-free workforce.* New York: McGraw-Hill.

Yandrick, R. M. (1996). *Behavioral risk management: How to avoid preventable losses from mental health problems in the workplace.* San Francisco, CA: Jossey-Bass.

6

LAY AND SCIENTIFIC PERSPECTIVES ON HARM PREVENTION: ENABLING THEORY AND PROGRAM INNOVATION

MARTIN SHAIN AND HELEN SUURVALI

This chapter is an account of an attempt to apply social scientific knowledge to the solution of a serious practical problem in a Canadian forest products company. The problem was, and continues to be, injuries that are sustained by workers on and off the job, particularly injuries that are believed or known to be related to alcohol and other drug (AOD) use. The story is ongoing and has some twists and turns that are perhaps not unusual in the world of industry. It is worth telling because it may offer insights to social scientists who aim to reduce workplace injuries through addressing an important factor that contributes to injury-causing accidents, namely, substance abuse.

The authors are indebted to Jim Stimson, director of the Employee and Family Assistance Programs at Weyerhaeuser Canada Ltd., and to Neil Menard, first vice president of the International Wood and Allied Workers of Canada, for their permission to tell the story of the project described in this chapter. We also thank Neal Berger for his ongoing efforts to refine the concept of enabling described here and Jacquie Brandt for her valiant fieldwork in conducting the surveys and developing the programs. Thanks also to Nancy Lee for her diligent coordination of all the work that goes into making a project like this successful.

More than anything, the story is a reminder that the workplace itself is a source of theory about the causes and prevention of substance abuse. Those theories may lead to solutions that are potentially superior to those that could be contrived by either external consultants or workplace actors operating exclusively from their own frames of reference. This chapter, however, focuses less on any solution or on program effectiveness and more on the processes underlying the story; that is, the narrative of the transactions that took place between the consultant and the workplace actors. Unlike the other chapters in this volume, the focus here is on understanding the dynamics of the relationship between the workplace and external consultants in health promotion and substance abuse prevention.

BACKGROUND

The forest products industry remains one of the most dangerous in North America and claimed 35 lives in 1999 in Canada alone (N. Menard, personal communication, Month, Day, Year). This figure, of course, is the tip of a large iceberg comprising many more instances of serious injuries and an even larger number of unreported minor and near-miss incidents. These fatalities, injuries, and incidents occur despite the many well-implemented occupational health and safety policies and programs aimed at prevention.

Within the particular forest products company that is the subject of this chapter, well-informed staff within the Employee Family Assistance Program (EFAP) and Occupational Health and Safety (OHS) departments had, by the mid-1990s, identified substance abuse as a significant contributor to injuries. That understanding led to the development and implementation of various educational programs within the framework of the EFAP. The programs were aimed at improving employee awareness of the link between substance abuse and injuries. In spite of those efforts, management and union remained concerned about the adequacy of the measures. The EFAP manager therefore contacted the first author to help redefine the problem and develop novel solutions to it. At the time of this invitation, the company had set up a time-limited task force across two of its divisions (sawmill and logging operations) consisting of EFAP and OHS staff and committee members, together with management and union representatives. This task force was the focus of the research consultant's activities: He concentrated on applying his research-based knowledge about factors involved in the genesis of occupational disease and injury to the problem at hand and on relating that knowledge in some manner to the knowledge of the company's staff. This attempt to reconcile general and local knowledge can also be seen as a meeting—sometimes a clash—between scientific and lay perspectives (Furnham, 1988).

The task force itself initially tended to see substance abuse as a problem arising more from personal origins than from structural or institutional origins. Clearly, such a difference is far from trivial: To bridge the gap, some conceptual frame of reference for communication—and, indeed, for studying the process—is required.

In this project, the conceptual framework for describing the communication between the parties is *diffusion of innovations* theory (Orlandi, 1986; Rogers, 1995; Rogers & Shoemaker, 1971). Taken at its broadest, this theory proposes that the acceptance and use of a new product, service, or idea by its intended users depends on a variety of factors related to perceptions of its intrinsic nature and of its compatibility with user characteristics and needs. A common concern is the fit between new ideas and a specific workplace. Diffusion of innovations theory focuses on more than simple acceptance or rejection scenarios; rather, it is concerned with ways in which ideas are adapted and modified to accommodate the needs of consumers. It postulates that new ideas are more likely to be adopted—or adapted—if consumers perceive them as being easy to understand, low in risk, high in benefit, and flexible. In contrast, the goal of "knowledge transfer" or "technology transfer" is to inculcate a target audience with information or perspectives that are considered fixed. In the context of knowledge or technology transfer, adaptation of new ideas would be considered a failure to communicate. Exhibit 6.1 provides further commentary on differences between technology transfer and the diffusion of innovations model in the field of prevention.

This approach may seem cavalier; after all, truth is truth, and the prospect of its being adapted or modified to suit the needs of consumers may appear cynical in the extreme. Indeed, the exercise does raise serious epistemological questions concerning truth and objectivity. Truth, however, is a distant destination, and the perspectives of social science and of the workplace are little more than milestones on the journey toward it. In other words, even the combined perspectives of social science and the workplace are but partial visions of truth, reality, and the whole picture.

Another way of expressing this relativistic view of truth is to describe scientific knowledge as "general" and specific workplace knowledge as "local," or "lay." Although the two do not amount to a whole, at least together they provide two perspectives on a phenomenon that is probably extremely complex and whose parts—if it has distinct parts—are constantly in motion and changing shape.

Diffusion of innovations theory is a useful framework for conceptualizing and delivering an account or story about the natural history of ideas as efforts are made to communicate them. As such, it lends itself well to narrative methods of explication. Qualitative methods are gaining in popularity as it becomes evident that quantitative approaches frequently raise questions of causality, even when they are theory driven. Storytelling, by

TECHNOLOGY TRANSFER

The phrase *technology transfer* indicates that (a) evidence that a given technology works has been found through experimental or clinical trials and (b) that procedures have been established to effectively transfer that technology into new settings. The emphasis is on developing a potent and widely applicable technology (see Schinke & Orlandi, 1997).

The assumptions of the technology transfer approach can be seen in recent guidelines and standards for prevention programming. For example, Holder and colleagues (1999) distinguish five phases of alcohol prevention research: foundational research, developmental studies, efficacy studies, effectiveness studies, and diffusion studies. This volume emphasizes developmental studies, which test the likely effectiveness of a program, and efficacy studies, or rigorous tests of a program under optimal conditions. Holder's model suggests that the ultimate test lies in diffusion studies, which examine the robustness of an intervention across a wide variety of settings.

DIFFUSION OF INNOVATIONS

This chapter makes a core distinction between scientific and local, or lay, knowledge. It suggests that effective prevention requires a series of interactions between these two knowledge sources. As this chapter shows, the lines between scientific and lay blur quickly within the context of transactions between the two.

This distinction is only one of many conceptual tools in diffusion of innovations theory. Rogers' (1995) seminal text includes many other ideas that can be applied to the current case study. For example, he describes the decision to adopt innovations as a process occurring in five stages (i.e., knowledge, persuasion, decision, implementation, confirmation) but highlights the process of reinvention, whereby an innovation is changed or modified by a user in the process of its adoption. Rogers identifies many other characteristics of the diffusion process: rate of adoption, adoption types (e.g., early adopters vs. laggards), diffusion networks, system norms, and types of diffusion consequences (e.g., desirable vs. undesirable). In the case study described in this chapter, the authors point to enabling theory as an innovation that emerged to help explain the cause and maintenance of substance abuse in the workplace. Although it is not clear whether having this enabling theory will help prevent substance abuse, the point is that it represents an opportunity to implement an approach that employees are more likely to own and diffuse than an approach that was simply transferred from an external source.

definition, focuses on process, an understanding of which is necessary in order to understand how ideas become changed or adapted, rather than simply adopted or rejected. Ideally, such a story would be "polyphonic"— in other words, told by many voices (see a helpful review of narrative methods by Barry & Elmes, 1997). For example, it would have been most authentic if the actual discourse of the actors involved in this project had been recorded at critical moments, transcribed, and then analyzed. This approach, however, still would have required the narrators of the story to make executive editorial decisions as to text inclusion, exclusion, ascription of meaning (i.e., interpretation), and so forth. Consequently, this chapter is a fairly conventional narrative told from the perspective of participant observers who have made conscious efforts to reflect the reciprocities of influence that occur when two worldviews come into contact with one another over a long period of time.

This project has unfolded over a number of years and in two major phases, the second of which is still under way. The process is best described as an ongoing dialectic between the company, its union, and the consultant. This dialectic is carried out through various means, including face-to-face meetings; conference calls; exchange of documents and action research.

PHASE 1: BRIDGING SCIENTIFIC AND LAY PERSPECTIVES

The first phase began late in 1995 with four initial steps, whereby the consultant interacted with a working group of management, union, EFAP, and OHS representatives. Within this initial period, the consultant presented a general social science view of the problem. The first phase ended an initial commitment from the participating divisions to develop a more circumscribed educational and training package for employees.

Steps 1–3

The first three steps in Phase 1 took place in fairly rapid succession.

- Step 1 (December 1995): The first meeting of the EFAP/OHS task force took place, during which the ongoing tragedy of fatalities was identified as the impetus for EFAP/OHS collaboration. At this time, the belief was that "personal difficulties," including substance abuse, might be behind some of the accident statistics. Different members of the task force had different levels of belief concerning the role of substance abuse in injury causation.[1] The need for external consultation was identified.
- Step 2 (January 1996): A steering committee comprising representatives from management, union, the EFAP, and OHS in two divisions was identified and activated.

---

[1]On reviewing the draft of this chapter, some readers from among those intimately involved in the process described here noted what they felt was a bias against the "disease" theory of substance abuse. The authors intend no such bias; they consider substance abuse to be a classification for a variety of disorders involving physical and psychological dependence that are often accompanied by ailments that might be considered diseases. We note our perspective to draw attention to the ongoing difficulties of maintaining open and honest communication even when all the concerned parties believe they have made themselves clear!

- Step 3 (March 1996): The consultant met with the steering committee (later to be called the working group) to assist in conceptualizing the project and its evaluation.

Step 4 (April 1996)

Following discussions at the March meeting, the consultant prepared an internally distributed document called *Getting the EFAP/OHS Model on Track: Notes for the Working Group.* This document proposed that the working group try to define a common knowledge base that could be "owned" by all constituents. This knowledge base would pertain to perceptions and beliefs about the causes of occupational injuries and diseases. The document suggested that a survey of employees and their families be carried out to determine the extent to which the work force in the two divisions shared a common knowledge base.

The document included a synopsis of literature reviews that the consultant had conducted. The reviews concerned factors identified by research studies as contributing to the success of EFAP- and OHS-type programs. The document emphasized that in both cases, success (according to the research literature) was partly attributable to strong organizational leadership that supported EFAP and OHS goals. At this point, the consultant proposed a model, described below, to start the process of defining a common knowledge base.

In part, the model was intended as a challenge for the working group: The goal was for them to either endorse, modify, or refute it by importing their lay knowledge. The final "mental model" then could be used to generate a series of key messages that could be communicated to all employees concerning the working group's best advice on occupational injury and illness causation.

THE SCIENTIFIC PERSPECTIVE

During the course of the project, the consultant tried to communicate the importance of psychosocial hazards in occupational injury and illness causation. *Psychosocial hazards* were defined by the consultants as threats to health and safety emanating from the nature and quality of human transactions in the workplace. The nature and quality of those transactions are related to the type of work involved (e.g., producing automobiles, felling trees, mining gold, or providing financial services) and arise from, in large measure, the formal and informal organization of work. Influences from outside the workplace include individual predisposition, socialization, and community norms or standards. Transactions may be characterized by various degrees of harmony or conflict, pressure, demands, mutual trust and regard, cooperative or supportive behavior, fairness, and consensuality. At a deeper level, transactions can be described according to power and status relations between workplace actors in the framework of a division of labor, which itself varies along a continuum of consensuality from free and informed participation to duress and coercion (Kemper, 1981, 1991; Kemper & Collins, 1990). Transactions, in turn, may lead to various degrees of stress and strain, which may then contribute (if sustained for long enough and at a high enough level of intensity) to a variety of health-threatening practices, adverse health outcomes, and injuries. Adverse outcomes almost certainly will contribute to lost productivity and inefficiency.

Individuals and organizations may respond to adverse outcomes in a variety of ways. Some responses may serve to abate the harmful conditions of work driving the outcomes; others may exacerbate such conditions. The extent to which such responses abate or exacerbate the harmfulness of working conditions depends on a number of factors, many of which revolve around the degree to which employers are willing to confront stress-generating transactions at their source. The process just sketched is summarized in Figure 6.1. Within the model depicted in Figure 6.1, a subset of particularly noxious psychosocial hazards has been identified: *high pressure* (i.e., having too much to do in too short a time over too long a period) combined with *low control* (not having enough influence over the means,

A. Type of work (relatively fixed, given), e.g.
- production of automobiles
- felling of trees
- mining of nickel
- provision of financial services

↓

B. Organization of work (constrained by type of work, but options, choices exist)

↓

C. Conditions of work (resulting from A and B)

↓

D. Individual and group responses to conditions of work

↓

E. Individual and organizational outcomes of responses to C and D

↓

F. Individual and organizational responses to outcomes, E

↓

G. Repeat cycle from B

Figure 6.1. Work, health, and injuries: A scientific paradigm.

manner, and method of one's daily work). *Social support* (i.e., the availability of at least one person who can be counted on in times of stress) is thought to moderate the impact of high pressure and low control. Those factors have been found to be associated with elevated levels of distress, which in turn contribute to a variety of adverse health outcomes, including drinking problems (see Figure 6.2).

Other conditions of work associated with drinking problems are *alienation* (i.e., a lack of personal involvement with or commitment to the organization's objectives or the lack of a sense of meaning with regard to work); *chronic ambiguity* (i.e., absence or inconsistency of rules, lack of clear job descriptions, cross-pressures); and *isolation* (i.e., lack of contact with

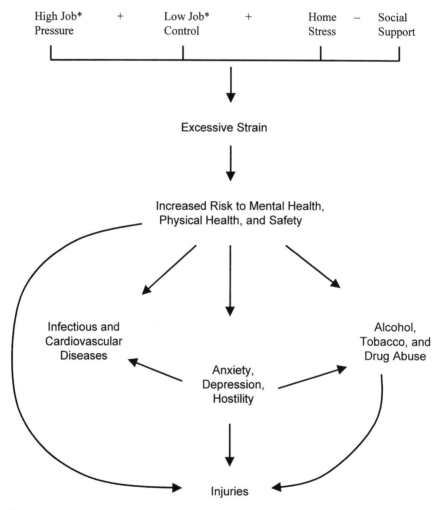

Figure 6.2. Key psychosocial hazards, health, and safety: Important connections. *See Karasek and Theorell (1990). This is often referred to as "Demand/Control Theory."

others or highly managed contact with others). In addition, the presence of drinking and drug-using subcultures (particularly if left alone by management), conflictful labor relations, lack of social controls discouraging alcohol use, and a low preventive or remedial response by management all are associated with workplace drinking (see Ames & Janes 1987, 1990, 1992; Greenberg & Grunberg, 1995; Parker & Brody, 1982; Seeman, Seeman, & Budros, 1988; Trice, 1992; Webb et al., 1994). Whether or to what extent psychosocial hazards result in drinking problems appears to depend on a variety of conditions, prominent among which are the subjective beliefs associated with alcohol use (Ames & Janes, 1987, 1990, 1992). To summarize, those beliefs hold that alcohol use

- is a normal and effective way of coping with negative emotions (e.g., depression, anxiety, disappointment, meaninglessness, anger, boredom, or demoralization);
- is a normal and effective way to enhance positive emotions (e.g., sense of belonging, bonding, identity with others, or sense of well-being);
- can be a symbol of defiance of authority;
- can be a symbol of distaste for or disgust with working conditions; and
- can be a symbol of doing well.

Although it is not necessary for all those beliefs to be present simultaneously for heavy drinking to emerge as a response to working conditions, it is not difficult to see how they can be related, particularly in the context of subcultures that may form both within and outside the workplace. For example, workers may use drinking as a symbol of unity and as a way of dealing with negative emotions.

This account of the relationships between psychosocial hazards, drinking, and injuries is simplified, because that is the way in which the consultant "told the story" of the social science relationships to the players in the worksite involved in this project. The simplification, however, comes largely from the consultant's interpretation of the social science literature. Such an interpretation is required because the literature is difficult to read and to summarize. It is fraught with paradoxes and contradictions. No effort will be made here to review the literature, but readers are invited to consider the references as a reasonable but not comprehensive list of the material available on this subject. The consultant chose to explain the paradoxes and contradictions in this literature by referring to Ames and Janes's (1992) theory concerning the role of subjective meanings associated with alcohol use in the workplace. This qualitative anthropological account provides a missing link that, in this writer's view, goes a long way toward explaining the difficulties encountered in the literature. Unfortunately, it seems that quantitative methods with highly sophisticated forms of analysis have outrun common sense in their attempts to portray the actualities of the relationships among psychosocial hazards, drinking, and injuries.

Step 5 (May 1996)

The response of the working group to the consultant's document was to produce its own report after a 2-day meeting. In the working group's document, *EFAP/OHS Pilot Project*, the working group presented its perspective on the causes and prevention of occupational injuries and illnesses. This perspective was couched in the form of key messages and assumptions that the working group felt were fundamental to success. This document is of great significance in the history of the project because it represents the first official attempt to define a common knowledge base. Following are the messages that the working group felt were fundamental to success and listed in its document (the original wording is retained):

- A safer, healthier workplace comes from both EFAP and OH&S efforts.
- A safe, productive workplace comes from healthy individuals, families and communities. They cannot be separated.
- Trust and honesty are the foundation to a healthy, safe workplace. Trust and honesty are necessary when discussing root causes of an accident.
- Different work cultures require different approaches or priorities.
- People can make healthier choices, the more informed they are. This will be key to minimizing/removing accidents from our lives (work, home, community).
- People do need support in dealing with issues. Healthy employees are the business of the workplace.
- We need to make some changes in the area of safety and occupational health. We have some serious gaps in current performance from where we need to be.
- We need to look out for each other (caring, but not enabling).
- There is a correlation between a workplace that experiences high anxiety and occupational disease and accidents.
- Low morale can result in poor mental health which can result in accidents.
- High control and participation results in better mental health. Participation is at the heart of mental and physical health.
- There should be no stigma attached to having or addressing personal problems.

The assumptions constitute an acknowledgment by all parties that occupational injuries and illnesses arise from both personal and organizational factors. At the end of the report, however, the working group emphasized personal factors in the key messages that should be reflected in educational resource materials for employees and their families. The consultant noted this shift and recommended to the working group that a separate set of messages focusing on organizational factors be crafted for managers and supervisors.

The phenomenon in which the working group advances toward and retreats from the inclusion of organizational factors in its mental model of occupational injury and illness causation is one that characterizes the entire project. Some explanation of this phenomenon in the context of diffusion of innovations theory is required at this point.

THE LAY PERSPECTIVE

By the usual standards of social science, the relationships between psychosocial hazards and drinking described above carry some weight. Although the relationships are stated in terms of probabilities and are characterized by conditionality, social scientists tend to be comfortable with them; one might wish and strive for greater specificity and greater parsimony, but at least one may place some weight on the data and not see it give way.

Lay people, in contrast, are inclined to see such information through a different lens, one that leaves them with a sense of vagueness and indeterminacy. Indeed, where the social scientist sees probability, the lay person often sees uncertainty, nonspecificity, and unpredictability. Consequently, getting the working group to take this information seriously was a challenge.

In terms of diffusion of innovations theory, cautious or suspicious reactions to social science (i.e., general) knowledge are obvious barriers to acting on it. Because the ideas described in the scientific story tend to be seen by lay audiences as complex, they also are considered to be of unknown value, potentially risky, and disruptive. The kind of language used in the social science story often has an intuitive appeal to lay people, but it is unfamiliar; unless it is colored with specific practical examples, it tends to be considered abstract and its implications difficult to discern.

In this instance, the working group was faced with the practical and serious problem of figuring out why personal injuries were increasing despite the best efforts of the firm to prevent them. Both management and union were familiar with the concept of organizationally generated stress and its allegedly corrosive impact on mental and physical health, as described in the consultant's scientific story. They were unfamiliar, however, with using that knowledge to plan corrective and preventive interventions and were inclined to think that stress is too vague and amorphous a notion to address. From a traditional health and safety perspective, indeed, stress is a difficult hazard to measure: It cannot be quantified in parts per million, for instance, as chemicals can be. Nevertheless, the parties were open to listening to the scientific perspective summarized in Figure 6.1. Their response, however, was to assert that if the story were true, it must be possible to validate it in the lay context. The "ifs, buts, and maybes" that permeated the social science account given in abstract and general terms should, if they corresponded to their concrete reality, translate into the texture and color of lay knowledge about the links between psychosocial hazards, stress, and adverse health and safety outcomes. In other words, a "lay language" should be able to give an account of the relationships that was simpler, more concrete, and more familiar than the language of social science. Where social science emphasized concept and theory, lay language would emphasize example and practice. Both accounts would reflect different perspectives on a common reality.

Step 6 (June–September 1996)

As a test of this theory, management and union, with the help of the consultant, undertook a study to gather lay knowledge about the links between psychosocial hazards, stress, poor health, and injuries. This task involved an interview survey of employees and their families conducted by members of the company's OHS-EFAP committees and program consultants long familiar with the organization.

Respondents were selected randomly to create a sample of 20% of the work force (approximately 100 employees from sawmill and logging operations and a corresponding number of family members). The authors analyzed the data, and the results were reported back to the project steering committee.

The core of the interviews revolved around employee and family beliefs, attitudes, and values regarding the links between organizational factors, personal factors, health, and safety. A surprisingly large majority subscribed to beliefs that correspond with the major elements of the scientific perspective of those links. Important differences of emphasis, however, which essentially assign different weights to elements of the scientific perspective, could be found in the lay accounts. Those differences are important from a local policy and program-planning point of view.

With regard to the relation of drinking to psychosocial hazards, the lay perspective surfaces elements that are present within the scientific perspective but are not given superordinate importance. First, employees and family members saw a vital connection between conflict, drinking, and injuries; second, employees felt that safety hazards were involved in work-

Figure 6.3. Lay theory of the conflict–drinking–injuries connection, as described by participants in the study.

ing with fellow employees who drink or use drugs. The conflict–drinking–injuries connection as described by participants in this study is portrayed in Figure 6.3.

In the lay theory, drinking and conflict are seen as having joint and independent effects on the probability of injuries occurring. Conflict, in this context, refers to disputes of all kinds involving employees. Two typical scenarios described were (a) a drinking episode at night followed by a domestic dispute in the morning, after which an employee leaves for work angry, tired, unsettled, and distracted, and (b) a midmorning dispute between a foreman and a sawmiller concerning overtime, followed by unusual lunchtime drinking on the part of the employee. Both scenarios are seen as raising the odds that an accident will occur because the normal safety-scanning practices of the vulnerable employee are disrupted through anger, tiredness, or preoccupation with other matters. Respondents also pointed to the impossibility of regarding work and home as independent spheres of activity. What happens in the one influences what happens in the other. Work invades home, and home invades work.

This lay perspective was found to be common among employees and their families except among those who had actually been injured in the past year or so. The injured group was distinguished by the fact that many of its members did not believe in a connection between stress, emotions, ill health, and injuries. The reasons for this phenomenon are still unclear and require future elucidation through qualitative methods. Two possibilities have been touted so far. One is that the subjective experience of the injured worker, as captured in interview recall, emphasizes factors in the work environment as he or she perceived them at the time of the accident: It was too dark, it was too slippery, there was too much time pressure, etc. In other words, the cause of the accident is attributed to immediate conditions at the time of the accident, regardless of what might have preceded it. Another possibility is that lack of awareness of psychosocial factors as contributors to ill health and injuries may be a risk factor for injuries in its own right. Conversely, an awareness of, say, stress as a risk factor for injuries may act as a protective factor against them. It will be important to further examine the phenomenology of this situation when resources become available.

One immediately clear aspect of the findings is that psychosocial hazards have come to be seen as an OHS issue as well as an employee assistance issue at the local level. The traditional domain of OHS is the abatement of physical hazards associated with unsafe places and things. It is now evident, in the worksite in question, that the abatement of psychosocial hazards associated with risky human transactions is also a legitimate part of the OHS domain, at least according to most of the employees and family members surveyed.

The traditional domain of EAFP has been the counseling of employees who have personal difficulties that may, sooner or later, impinge upon their job performance. The often unspoken assumption is that employees bring their problems to work with them. It is now evident, in the worksite in question, that psychosocial hazards at work increase the likelihood of personal problems (i.e., negative spillover from work to the personal sphere). Consequently, a proper role for employee assistance committees and service providers is to provide feedback to management on the nature of those hazards and to recommend methods for abating them.

The widening visions of OHS and EAFP in this regard suggest a collaboration between the two parties that could synergize OHS and employee assistance efforts. This possibility was perceived at the worksite in question even prior to the survey, as noted earlier. During this phase, however, the partnership between OHS and EAFP evolved as an ongoing institutional relationship, rather than as simply a project-related convenience. Strong evidence of the organization's commitment to this partnership during this period can be seen in its allocation of a senior vice president to oversee its implementation.

The acknowledgment that fellow workers who use alcohol or drugs are safety hazards was a second major issue to arise from the survey data. Family members were more likely than employees to identify this hazard, although it is arguable that their perceptions owe much to employee remarks and stories told in the domestic environment. An essential point here, again, is that people are seen as potentially unsafe, suggesting that a proper role for OHS is management of people, not just of places and things.

A specific lay theory that nonetheless has some scientific support emerges in this context: the theory of "enabling" (see Roman, Blum, and Martin, 1992, for an overview and preliminary test of this theory). This theory holds that substance abusers in the workplace could not keep their jobs, or at least could not avoid some sort of sanctions, were it not for the fact that they were supported, or enabled, in their deviant behavior by a number of significant others. Those others include coworkers, supervisors, union comrades and officials, family, friends, and even family doctors. For a variety of quite complicated reasons, these people often will cover up the deviant behavior of the substance abuser, thus perpetuating and extending the problem. Sometimes this covering behavior is overt and conscious; sometimes it is less so. This theory of enabling, as noted above, has some sociological validation (Roman et al., 1992) but it appears to have originated in certain types of clinical practice. Treatment approaches that focus or draw on the philosophy and practices of Alcoholics Anonymous tend to give special credence to the theory of enabling, although variants of it can be found in many clinical orientations, such as Transactional Analysis. It therefore was somewhat surprising to find specific reference to enabling theory in the interviews that were conducted with family members. It is quite likely, however, that a sample of the size that eventually was recruited for the local study would have included people who had been in treatment for substance abuse at some point. Another strong possibility is that the EFAP staff at the company in question had disseminated information about enabling to families with sufficient success that it "came back" to the interviewers.

Indeed, around this time it dawned on the consultant that *two* levels of diffusion of innovations were in play within the divisions party to this project. As ongoing diffusion of the idea that psychosocial hazards arising from the organization of work affect the development and maintenance of substance abuse was occurring, the EFAP and, increasingly, OHS took it upon themselves to diffuse the idea of enabling to employees, supervisors, and managers. Although it was difficult to discern at this stage of the project, it turned out later that the two ideas were linked in a significant manner, the one (enabling) in a sense paving the way for the other (psychosocial hazards).

During the same period in which the surveys were being conducted, baseline accident and illness data were collected from the two participating divisions to develop a statistical baseline against which the effectiveness of any further interventions could later be measured. The same purpose was assigned to the employee and family surveys. Employees reported absences due to injuries and illnesses at a rate that actually was higher than the official statistics showed.

Step 7 (November 1996–January 1997)

The working group reviewed the survey results with the consultant to determine implications for program planning. Again, the advance-retreat phenomenon could be observed as the working group wrestled with the role of organizational factors relative to personal factors in the precipitation of injuries and illnesses. In principle, the group acknowledged the importance of organizational factors in verbatim statements such as the following, which appeared in communications about the project to the entire company:

There are many factors which contribute to accidents and injuries, but the one area we know play [sic] a role which has not been dealt with adequately in workplace safety programs is the "human factor." Research has shown that psychosocial hazards (factors such as high job pressure, low job control, and personal challenges—including substance abuse—that result in someone being "dis-stressed") can lead to accidents, injuries and illness.

When employees are dealing with considerable stress at work or at home, they may respond by sleeping badly, over-medicating themselves, drinking too much, feeling depressed, anxious, nervous, angry or reckless. When any one of these is the case, the person is more likely to become momentarily, but dangerously distracted; make serious errors in judgement [sic]; put their [sic] bodies under stress, raising the potential for strains and sprains; and fail in otherwise normal activities involving hand–eye or foot–eye coordination.

In practice, however, the working group focused increasingly on personal factors associated with AOD use and abuse, and it developed and refined educational and training programs around the phenomenon of enabling.

Enabling theory is not really a theory about the causation of substance abuse; rather, it is a theory about how problem behavior can be maintained, supported, and even encouraged by the psychosocial system in which an employee works and lives. Because the psychosocial system includes the dynamics of the workplace and, therefore, its management and supervisory practices, enabling theory does reach past personal behavior into certain aspects of organizational culture and structure. Compared with the demand–control theory (see Figure 6.2) described earlier, enabling theory deals with organization of work issues in a more oblique fashion; it stops short of saying that the way work is managed plays a role in the precipitation of substance abuse problems. Nevertheless, enabling theory does bridge some of the distance between personal and organizational factors. Depending on who is using it, enabling theory can become a way into organizational issues. Over the course of the project described here, enabling has—from the consultant's perspective—evolved into a structural theory. The staff responsible for developing and implementing the educational and training materials for the antienabling strategy increasingly have shown a willingness to use an understanding of enabling behavior as a door into a deeper and broader engagement with supervisors and managers with regard to how they do their jobs.

In terms of diffusion of innovations theory, enabling is an intriguing conceptual bridge between scientific and lay accounts of how AOD use is generated and maintained within a work force. It accomplishes this task by allowing for the possibility of emphasizing either personal or organizational factors in the maintenance of substance abuse among employees.

Seen in a certain light, enabling is a Trojan Horse concept that allows structuralist thinking to invade the individualist camp. From yet another perspective, it is a blend of sociological and psychological "imaginations."

In short, enabling theory provides a two-way channel through which scientific and lay accounts of reality can inform each other. In so doing, the theory addresses two of the major barriers to diffusion of innovations, namely, risk and complexity. Risk is lowered in the eyes of managers because enabling theory allows for a period of acculturation during which they can move at their own pace, from seeing substance abuse as a purely personal problem to seeing it as a complex phenomenon in which their own behavior and that of significant others can play important roles. In other words, what lowers the riskiness of adopting the theory of enabling is the fact that one can calibrate or control the rate at which its various elements are incorporated into one's consciousness. One is not overwhelmed or made anxious by new knowledge that seems to have threatening implications.

With regard to complexity, enabling is again an interesting concept. First, it appears to be a fairly simple idea and therefore readily acceptable. Later, subtleties reveal themselves, but only when the student is ready to see and understand them. In this sense, enabling theory addresses two related incentives to adoption or adaptation of innovations, namely, flexibility and simplicity. An idea that can be used at different levels in different ways and incorporated at one's own pace is more flexible and attractive than one requiring total cognitive embrace from day one. Enabling is not a "take it or leave it" theory; rather, it is a "grow into it" theory that can be used to some advantage from the first day of exposure while gaining in usefulness as more of its aspects are appreciated and understood. So even though its simplicity may be somewhat deceptive, the basic idea is easy enough to grasp, even if all the hues and colors take a while to fill in.

Step 8 (September–October 1997)

By this time, the company again appeared to be in retreat from the idea that styles of management play a role in generating stress and substance abuse. The focus on enabling was entrenched, and commitments had been made by both management and union to develop a sophisticated educational and training package on the subject (i.e., the *Courage to Care* program; see Exhibit 6.2). The consultant made various proposals—solicited by the EFAP—aimed at creating more awareness about some of the other issues that had surfaced the previous year during the survey (e.g., the role of conflict in accident causation). The climate at the company had become antagonistic, or at least suspicious, toward such inquiries, probably as a result of factors such as adverse market conditions (creating economic stress), the approach of collective bargaining, and other imponderables.

EXHIBIT 6.2
A Description of the Courage to Care Program

The Courage to Care program is designed to increase knowledge and skills that will help those who are "near" substance abusers to (a) express care and concern; (b) be descriptive, but not judgmental; (c) offer specific help; and (d) set boundaries. Central to the knowledge required to acquire those skills is an understanding of enabling both as a modifiable individual behavior and as a modifiable function of workplace social systems. As the *Courage to Care Leaders' Guide* states, "Enabling is behavior that is intended to help the person in distress, but in fact perpetuates the problem. Enabling puts up a barrier between the distressed person and the consequences of his or her behavior" (p. 7). The program is directed at recognizing how and when enabling occurs and at teaching alternative and constructive behaviors. A thorough understanding of enabling develops a willingness and motivation on the part of trainees to develop and use the skills of "caring confrontation," which is familiar to some readers as "constructive confrontation." Caring or constructive confrontation refers to addressing problematic behavior in others in a manner designed to focus attention on what needs to change, without blame, and in the spirit of seeking solutions. However, it also involves the delineation of possible consequences for not attending to the legitimate concerns of others with regard to the resolution of problematic behavior. This knowledge and skill set provide the strongest alternative to drug testing as a means of preventing, containing, and managing substance abuse in the workplace. Indeed, it may be fair to say that the failure to courageously adopt the practice of caring or constructive confrontation has opened the door to workplace drug testing as a quick but ineffective fix.

The program consists of 15 hours of leader training and 3 hours for other employees. It is supported by an award-winning video called *Deadly Silence* (1998) and a small booklet, *Courage to Care* (Berger & Lee, 2000). The booklet provides a section on understanding enabling; provides examples of enabling responses and healthy alternatives; and sets forth specific guidelines for expressing care and concern, offering help, and setting boundaries.

Currently, *Courage to Care* is the subject of an evaluation designed to determine the extent to which the program reduces enabling behavior and increases caring confrontation and personal accountability. In addition, records are being kept of injuries and absences for employees who are exposed to the program and within worksites as a whole.

PHASE 2: ONGOING STUDY AND DEVELOPMENT

The second phase began in September 1998 and is ongoing.

Step 9 (September 1998)

For most of a year, the consultant had nothing to do with regard to this project until, at last, the EFAP signaled a development within the company that required a repositioning of the joint EFAP/OHS approach to injury prevention. The relatively new CEO required that all activities had to be supported by a convincing "business case." This requirement led to the consultant's preparation of a document on behalf of the EFAP outlining a corporate rationale for the "combined forces" approach to injury prevention. This document said, in part

> A business case for injury prevention through coordination of EFAP/ OHS efforts must include forceful claims not only for cost efficiency but also for ethical behavior as it relates to internal corporate governance and to external relations with the community. In other words, the modern corporate business case for injury prevention is not just about cost but also about ethics and stewardship. (Shain, 1999)

The EFAP/OHS partnership was identified in this context as a logical vehicle through which the values of efficiency, ethics, and stewardship could be expressed in the form of new and expanded programming.

Steps 10 and 11 (October 1998–August 1999)

During Step 10, which lasted from October 1998 to March 1999, the EFAP continued to elaborate its plans for expansion under a general mandate to collaborate whenever possible with OHS and with enhanced direct and regular accountability to a senior vice president (a new and important development). The plans included a proposal to conduct cyclical surveys within the workplace to monitor trends in key areas of concern.

During Step 11, which spanned the period from May to August 1999, a new owner acquired the company. This sort of development frequently upsets plans of the kind described so far, but not in this case. Much to everyone's surprise, the project actually gained impetus, and a decision was made to conduct regular monitoring studies in any division of the company that agreed to do them. The studies focus on stress, satisfaction, attitudes toward substance abuse (including, of course, enabling), and general health status. The surveys are conducted by interview on a random basis, much like those carried out in 1996 but with the important difference that they are to be repeated at intervals. The commitment to repeat signals a major development in the company's willingness and desire to measure results because the surveys are intended to show changes from one administration to the next. The changes can be related, at least anecdotally, to interventions such as EFAP initiatives in service delivery, education, and training. Although experimental trials are not planned at this time, the pretest–posttest analyses will provide useful material for planning purposes. The company appears to intend to cultivate a culture of evaluation with regard to all its main activities.

The surveys also provide an opportunity—soon to be exploited—to analyze relationships between general conditions of work (as captured by measures of stress and satisfaction) and the prevalence of enabling conditions. It will be important to determine whether high-stress and low-satisfaction work environments are likely to be typified by enabling or whether enabling makes no difference. Determining the relationship between high-stress and low-satisfaction environments and enabling conditions would have major implications for management training. In the grand scheme of things, such information will provide more substance for the ongoing tension between scientific and lay theory concerning the causation and maintenance of substance abuse in the workplace.

ENABLING THEORY AS CORE IDEA

The project described in this chapter illustrates the possibility of combining scientific and lay perspectives on the causes and prevention of substance abuse in the workplace to produce potentially more effective strategies. At this writing, it has yet to be shown that this joint perspective can achieve superior results in terms of injury prevention; however, the company has committed to evaluating the impact of comprehensive approaches incorporating attention to both organizational and personal factors in injury causation.

In terms of diffusion of innovations theory, the concept of enabling has shown itself to be an effective intellectual, emotional, and practical bridge between personal and organizational perspectives on substance abuse causation, maintenance, and prevention. Enabling theory reduces the risk of adoption to all involved (including managers and supervisors) by providing a flexible, relatively simple idea that can be accepted at various levels, depending on the intellectual and emotional receptivity of the individual. It appears, in fact, that the longevity of this project depends on the ability of enabling theory to shrink and expand according to the conditions of the host environment. During periods when things are going well for the company, enabling theory can expose its structural, organizational factors. When things are going not so well, enabling theory can allow the company to focus on personal factors. Although this shift may be counterproductive in some respects, it allows for the survival of the theory as part of the culture of the company—as such, it can live to serve another day.

Enabling theory and discourse present themselves in this context as a kind of common language in which otherwise differing worldviews can meet and inform one another. In terms of the kind of discourse or narrative analysis discussed by Barry and Elmes (1997), enabling theory allows for multiple stories (i.e., polyphony) within a single framework. It therefore serves the highly significant organizational function of facilitating communication among what might otherwise be quite isolated camps. Key people involved in this project on both management and union sides have consistently reported that enabling theory facilitates dialogue between the parties not only at a strategic level (e.g., planning and collective bargaining) but also on a day-to-day level. Because the EFAP and now, increasingly, OHS departments are seen as champions of the common language embedded in enabling theory, the programs are regarded even more favorably and are identified with organizational harmonization.

CONCLUSION: ON A NARRATIVE ORGANIZATIONAL APPROACH TO WORKPLACE PREVENTION[2]

A central, and often hidden, assumption of prevention research is that good research tells us whether and why a particular intervention or strategy worked. In contrast, this chapter focuses less on outcomes and more on the relationship between a consultant and an organization and the ways in which the organization conceptualized or contextualized the problem of workplace substance abuse. This focus highlights processes also found in each of the preceding chapters, even though the authors do not emphasize them. For example, Heirich and Seick (see chapter 4, this volume) modified their initial approach because of changes in the nature of work in their study site and because many employees originally assigned to a control group requested screenings. From the traditional research perspective, this change is considered a "contamination" of the experimental design. From the narrative approach, however, employee self-selection may represent a successful intervention.

A review of some of the literature on narrative in organizations may help clarify this approach. Morgan (1986) showed how metaphors help workers understand and manage organizational life. Across different times and places, organizations may be viewed (metaphorically) as machines, organisms, brains, cultures, political systems, and instruments of domination. The metaphors create a social reality that guides the behavior and norms of an organization. The cultural perspective suggests that the stories and meanings on which workers rely are "enacted" in their behavior. The story told in this chapter reveals ways in which certain divisions within forest products companies gradually shaped its cultural reaction to substance abuse.

Pentland (1999) concluded that organizational narrative does more than indicate features of the social world: It also "constitutes" that world. That is, actors construct their interactions with others in ways that are sensible to themselves and others. Pentland argues that people do not just tell stories, they also enact them, thus providing legitimacy and accountability for their actions (Pentland, 1999). Narratives are more than just sequence; they are ways for actors to make sense of and rationalize their

---

[2]Joel B. Bennett coauthored "Conclusion: On a Narrative Organizational Approach to Workplace Prevention."

actions, and they represent theories about processes that underlie organizational life. This chapter may be seen as an account of how organizational players developed a story that would best address the legitimacy and accountability of their response to substance abuse.

O'Connor (2000) pointed to the "embedded narrative" or particular texts that can be identified as reflecting the whole narrative of an organizational story. This chapter provides two instances in which the working group produced documents through which it communicated key messages about occupational safety and health (Step 5) and its view of the human factor in safety and health (Step 7). The documents are embedded narratives that reflect the larger narrative; namely, tension between loci of responsibility for substance abuse–related accidents.

At this writing, the company and union have agreed to avoid all forms of drug testing except, possibly, pre-employment. The agreement is predicated on the understanding that the EFAP–OHS partnership has the capacity and credibility to control and prevent substance abuse through the *Courage to Care program* and the measures described in this chapter. Even though the agreement represents a vote of confidence for alternatives to drug testing, a high level of scrutiny of the partners' actions and accomplishments will exist. Fortunately, the project is developed to the point at which evaluative mechanisms have been put in place to provide the kind of accountability that the company requires to defend its drug-testing policy to shareholders and the public. In fact, the ongoing, developmental, and innovative diffusion process—as documented in this chapter—has provided the firm foundation for this accountability.

O'Connor (2000) concluded that "the narrative form often leaves the moral of the story for the reader to decide" (p. 190). One question for the reader of this chapter is whether the company's agreement to avoid some forms of drug testing had anything to do with the process described here, or whether it resulted form other considerations altogether. Is it possible that the consultative approach presented in this chapter actually led to a greater focus on training and less emphasis on testing?

REFERENCES

Ames, G. M., & Janes, C. R. (1987). Heavy and problem drinking in an American blue-collar population: Implications for prevention. *Social Science and Medicine, 25,* 949–960.

Ames, G., & Janes, C. (1990). Drinking, social networks, and the workplace. In P. M. Roman (Ed.), *Alcohol problem intervention in the workplace: Employee assistance programs and strategic alternatives* (pp. 95–111). New York: Quorum Books.

Ames, G. M., & Janes, C. (1992). A cultural approach to conceptualizing alcohol and the workplace. *Alcohol Health and Research World, 16,* 112–119.

Barry, D., & Elmes, M. (1997). Strategy retold: Toward a narrative view of strategic discourse. *Academy of Management Review (Mississippi State), 22*(2), 429–452.

Berger, N., & Lee, N. (2000). *Courage to care: Stop enabling and build caring, effective relationships.* Vancouver, BC. Available from Centre for Workplace and Community Well-Being, EFAPs Department, Suite 503, 4190 Lougheed Highway, Burnaby, BC, Canada, V5C 6A8.

Furnham, A. F. (1988). *Lay theories: Everyday understanding of problems in the social sciences.* Oxford, UK: Pergamon Press.

Greenberg, E. S., & Grunberg, L. (1995). Work alienation and problem alcohol behavior. *Journal of Health and Social Behavior, 36,* 83–102.

Holder, H., Flay, B., Howard, J., Boyd, G., Voas, R., & Grossman, M. (1999). Phases of alcohol problem prevention research. *Alcoholism: Clinical and Experimental Research, 23*(1), 183–194.

Karasek, R., & Theorell, T. (1990). *Healthy work: Stress, productivity and the reconstruction of working life.* New York: Basic Books.

Kemper, T. D. (1981). Social constructionist and positivist approaches to the sociology of emotions. *American Journal of Sociology, 87*(2), 336–363.

Kemper, T. D. (1991). Predicting emotions from social relations. *Social Psychology Quarterly, 54*(4), 330–342.

Kemper, T. D., & Collins, R. (1990). Dimensions of microinteraction. *American Journal of Sociology, 96*(1), 36–68.

MacMillan Bloedel Limited, I.W.A. Canada & Worker's Compensation Board of British Columbia (Producers). (1998). *Deadly silence* [Videotape]. Available from: Centre for Workplace and Community Well-Being, EFAPs Department, Suite 503, 4190 Lougheed Highway, Burnaby, BC, Canada, V5C 6A8.

Morgan, G. (1986). *Images of organization.* Newbury Park, CA: Sage.

O'Connor, E. S. (2000). Plotting the organization: The embedded narrative as a construct for studying change. *Journal of Applied Behavioral Science, 36,* 174–192.

Orlandi, M. A. (1986). The diffusion and adoption of worksite health promotion innovations: An analysis of barriers. *Preventive Medicine, 15,* 522–536.

Parker, D. A., & Brody, J. A. (1982). Risk factors for alcoholism and alcohol problems among employed women and men. In *Occupational alcoholism: A review of research issues* (pp. 99–127). Rockville, MD: U.S. Department of Health and Human Services, NIAAA Research Monograph No. 8, U.S. Government Printing Office.

Pentland, B. T. (1999). Building process theory with narrative: From description to explanation. *Academy of Management Review, 24,* 711–724.

Rogers, E. M. (1995). *Diffusion of innovations* (4th ed.). New York: Free Press.

Rogers, E. M., & Shoemaker, F. F. (1971). *The diffusion of innovations: A cross-cultural approach.* New York: Free Press.

Roman, P. M., Blum, T. C., & Martin, J. K. (1992). "Enabling" of male problem drinkers in work groups. *British Journal of Addictions, 87,* 275–289.

Schinke, S. P., & Orlandi, M. A. (1997). Technology transfer. *Substance Use and Misuse, 32,* 1679–1684.

Seeman, M., Seeman, A. Z., & Budros, A. (1988). Powerlessness, work and community: A longitudinal study of alienation and alcohol use. *Journal of Health and Social Behavior, 29,* 185–198.

Shain, M. (1999). The role of the workplace in the production and containment of health costs: the case of stress-related disorders. *International Journal of Health Care Quality Assurance incorporating Leadership in Health Services, 12*(2), 1–7.

Trice, H. M. (1992). Work-related risk factors associated with alcohol abuse. *Alcohol Health and Research World, 16,* 106–111.

Webb, G. R., Redman, S., Hennrickus, D. J., Kelman, G. R., Gibberd, R. W., & Sanson-Fisher, R. W. (1994). The relationship between high risk and problem drinking and the occurrence of work injuries and related absences. *Journal of Studies on Alcohol, 55*(4), 434–446.

7

SYMBOLIC CRUSADES AND ORGANIZATIONAL ADOPTION OF SUBSTANCE ABUSE PREVENTION PROGRAMS

WILLIAM J. SONNENSTUHL

Alcohol and other drugs are Janus-faced symbols. On the one hand, they symbolize happiness, health, and escape from pain: the cocktail party, the glass of wine shared over a candlelit meal with a lover, the pills taken to fight illness, or the morphine taken by the dying hospice patient. On the other hand, they also symbolize sadness, illness, and destruction: the child killed by a drunken driver, the emergency wards populated by addicts who have overdosed, or the innocent bystander murdered in a shootout between rival drug gangs. Although alcohol and other drugs are Janus faced, the public face Americans most often see is the destructive one. Moral entrepreneurs such as Alcoholics Anonymous, the Institute for a Drug-Free Workplace, or the Center for Substance Abuse Prevention collect statistics and horror stories on the destructive capabilities of alcohol and other drugs and deploy them as armaments in their crusades to enlist Americans in their reform campaigns (Becker, 1963).

Since the colonial era, Americans have waged a number of crusades against the evils of alcohol. Sociologists refer to them as *symbolic crusades* because, in these temperance reform campaigns, the abuse of alcohol symbolizes the crusaders' anxiety about society's ills (Ben-Yehuda, 1990; Gusfield, 1963). This relationship is deeply rooted in American society, which values temperance in all things. Within this framework, intemperate drinking is seen as disrupting social life and irresponsible drinkers are viewed as "folk devils" whose selfish pursuit of alcohol must be controlled to resolve America's social problems.

Since the beginning of the 19th century, America has undergone five cycles of temperance reform (Blocker, 1989; see Figure 7.1). During each period, some groups, such as the Women's Christian Temperance Union and Mothers Against Drunk Drivers, have attributed America's social problems—from poverty to death on the highways—to the intemperate use of alcohol and sought to reform problem drinkers. These groups initially sought to persuade problem drinkers to change their behavior by teaching them to drink responsibly or abstain. When persuasion failed, the reformers pursued coercive techniques to force the drinkers to be socially responsible; their efforts included enacting legislation prohibiting the sales of alcoholic beverages and imprisoning sellers and users. Typically, each cycle of reform ended when Americans began to experience the coercive techniques as restraining their sense of freedom and started to advocate for loosening social controls. For instance, Prohibition came to an abrupt end when businessmen, who had lobbied for its passage, organized and pressed for its repeal (Kyvig, 1979).

The workplace has always been a focus of temperance reform (Lender & Martin, 1987; Staudenmeier, 1985). Consequently, America's symbolic crusades were much on my mind as I read and thought about my assignment to summarize and integrate the six chapters that make up *Beyond Drug Testing*. The Reagan administration's War on Drugs was foremost in my thoughts. Through its adroit use of horror stories about malformed crack babies and urban drug gangs invading respectable suburbia, the Reagan administration effectively scared the hell out of most Americans and established drug testing as an acceptable part of modern work life (Reinarman & Levine, 1995). Even though most Americans do not use illicit drugs and many feel embarrassed about urinating into a bottle under the watchful eye of an attendant, most people came to believe that urinalysis is an indignity to be endured to save our children and society from the ravages of drugs. The heyday of the War on Drugs is long gone, but its effects on the workplace linger.

REVIEW OF CHAPTERS

The chapters in this volume have been written against the background of the War on Drugs and its lingering effects on the workplace.

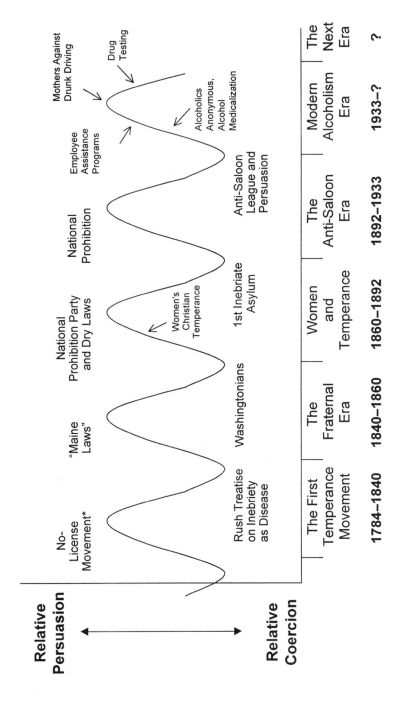

The First Temperance Movement	The Fraternal Era	Women and Temperance	The Anti-Saloon Era	Modern Alcoholism Era	The Next Era
1784–1840	**1840–1860**	**1860–1892**	**1892–1933**	**1933–?**	**?**

Figure 7.1. A brief history of symbolic crusades in temperance reform.

Note. * Listed social movements and landmarks serve to illustrate key characteristics during a phase of symbolic crusade. Adapted from Blocker (1989).

Whereas the War on Drugs whipped up public hysteria about drug abuse and advocated punishing those who would sell or use illicit drugs as an effective mechanism for preventing substance abuse, the authors in this volume write from a different perspective. First, all are social scientists, rather than moral entrepreneurs, and they eschew emotional arguments. Instead, they bring to their work the objectivity of conscientious social scientists. This perspective is evident in the wide range of research methods the authors use to further understanding of the preventive complements and alternatives to drug testing. Second, all the authors adopt a compassionate stance toward those who use alcohol and other drugs. In contrast to the punitive prescriptions advocated by Drug War advocates, the authors believe in the powers of persuasion, and they prescribe education as an effective strategy for reducing the incidence of alcohol and other drug (AOD) abuse. Third, all the authors are essentially writing about the prevention of alcohol problems rather than the prevention of illicit drug use. This distinction is important: Alcohol is a legal drug, in contrast to cocaine, heroin, or marijuana, which are illegal and the focus of most testing programs. The authors' alcohol focus, however, is as much strategic as it is pragmatic. Strategically, this focus highlights that alcohol is the most prevalent drug abused by workers. Pragmatically, it highlights that for social scientists, it may be easier to construct and evaluate alcohol-related workplace interventions than drug-related ones. For example, soliciting valid and reliable information from workers about their legal drug use may be easier than soliciting valid and reliable information about their illicit drug use.

The authors' contributions to understanding prevention alternatives to drug testing may be assessed in many ways. One strategy would be to focus on the methodological shortcomings. This concern is valid because, as a group, the studies rely on participants who were self-selected and may have been predisposed to changing their behavior. Thus, the experimental findings may be artificially inflated. In some of the studies, the number of participants is small; in others, controls are comparatively weak or lacking altogether. Such criticisms should not obscure the larger picture: As a group, the studies complement existing studies, which highlight the centrality of norms—shared rules or guidelines that prescribe the appropriate behavior in a given situation—in changing AOD use.

A growing body of research suggests that workplace drinking norms are a critical factor in predicting workers' drinking behavior (e.g., Ames, Grube, & Moore, 2000; Bacharach, Bamberger, & Sonnenstuhl, in press; Roman & Blum, 1998; Trice & Sonnenstuhl, 1990). The chapters in this volume build on that body of knowledge by highlighting a variety of interventions that workplaces can use to teach workers new drinking norms. The next section briefly reviews some of the findings in the chapters and their relationship to changing workplace norms.

The introductory chapter, by Joel Bennett, Shawn Reynolds, and Wayne Lehman, provides a thoughtful and comprehensive review of current workplace substance abuse research, arguing that it is time to move beyond drug testing to embrace other approaches. In particular, the authors draw our attention to the wide variation in occupational and organizational norms that affect workers' drinking behavior and illicit drug use. Simply put, some occupational groups, such as construction workers and bartenders, have workplace cultures supportive of heavy drinking and illicit drug use. Of special interest, however, is the authors' finding that occupations reporting heavy AOD use are also less likely to have an effective drug-testing program or access to an employee assistance program (EAP). This finding complements Trice and Beyer's (1982) study, which found that unions possessing cultures of heavy drinking are least likely to adopt job-based alcohol programs because local officers are unwilling to violate the group's drinking norms. Taken together, these findings highlight the potency of workplace norms and signaled that the groups most in need of substance abuse prevention and intervention programs may be the least likely to adopt them. Nevertheless, the authors' meta-analysis of prevention studies suggests that when prevention programs are adopted and implemented, they can have an appreciable impact on workers, increasing their sense of well-being and reducing their levels of stress and AOD abuse.

In chapter 2, David Snow, Suzanne Swan, and Leo Wilton provide evidence from two prevention studies that seek to modify workers' coping skills. The studies are crucial to our understanding of the relationship between drinking norms, stress, and drinking problems. Many interventionists have long believed that workplace cultures of heavy drinking support workers' use of alcohol and other drugs to escape from the physical and emotional strains of work. Within this context, stress reduction techniques and coping strategies are seen as alternative mechanisms for dealing with work strains. In both interventions, the authors focused on teaching workers how to cope with stressful work and family situations. Workers learned methods for eliminating or modifying sources of stress, for restructuring their thoughts about stressful situations, and for managing their stress levels. The authors' findings are encouraging: They report that workers improved their coping skills and reduced their alcohol consumption. Reduction in alcohol consumption also was observed among heavy drinkers who did not drop out of the study.

Royer Cook, Anita Back, James Trudeau, and Tracy McPherson provide evidence in chapter 3 that including lessons about AOD use in employee health promotion programs can be an effective mechanism for reducing substance abuse. More important, the authors' findings from their stress management program parallel the findings reported in chapter 2, even when the AOD lessons were not included in the intervention. Under both conditions, participants reported significant improvements in substance abuse attitudes and perceptions along with reductions in AOD use. More troubling, however, was the researchers' finding that when their interventions focused mainly on substance abuse, participants reacted negatively to the program.

In chapter 4, Max Heirich and Cynthia Sieck take yet another tack toward workplace education: a proactive substance abuse outreach and counseling strategy incorporated into a corporate cardiovascular wellness program. This study extends the pioneering EAP/wellness studies of Erfurt and Foote, who demonstrated the importance of intensive case finding and follow up to successful program outcomes (Erfurt, Foote, & Heirich, 1992). As the authors of this study note, a strong correlation exists between substance abuse and cardiovascular disease (CVD); the intervention takes advantage of that relationship by offering employees an opportunity for CVD screening. When employees volunteered for the screening, counselors also assessed workers' risk for alcohol abuse and counseled them about how to reduce their CVD risks and improve their health generally. Employees were assigned to either a class or individual counseling designed to reduce their cardiovascular risk. One surprise finding was that relatively few employees assigned to the classes followed through; most dropped out and sought individual counseling instead. The authors conclude that the employees who received individual counseling made significant gains in reducing their risk for alcohol abuse and CVD and attribute the gains to the counselors' proactive counseling and follow up.

Chapter 5, by Lehman, Reynolds, and Bennett, provides compelling evidence from a comparison of team and informational training and its impact on workers' knowledge about EAPs. This study is particularly relevant to our understanding of changing workplace norms because, through the team training, it focused on altering the organizational climate supportive of substance abuse. More specifically, the team training is built around five components that emphasize the relevance of the work group, its ownership of the substance abuse policy, the use of alcohol as a coping mechanism, and workers' role in providing help to coworkers experiencing substance abuse problems. Team training was compared with two other training conditions. Some employees completed the pretest, posttest, and follow-up surveys but received no training; other employees were given information about the organization's substance abuse policy and the processes for seeking assistance for substance abuse from the EAP. The researchers report mixed results for team and informational training and conclude that some combination of the two may be most beneficial for changing the drinking climate in most organizations. In addition, they conclude that the team approach may work better in occupations and organizations with high levels of substance abuse; however, they caution that the team approach takes some time to generate changes in drinking climate. Unfortunately, they report no evidence that the training had an impact on employees' use of alcohol.

In Chapter 6, Martin Shain and Helen Suurvali provide yet another approach to educating workers about the risks of substance abuse. In contrast to the other chapters in this volume, which describe experimental studies, Shain and Suurvali provide a narrative describing their efforts to change a Canadian company's drinking culture and reduce work-related injuries. The narrative emphasizes the consulting process and the difficulties of diffusing new programs in a work setting buffeted by management and labor disagreements and a turbulent organizational environment. Although the intervention has yet to be completed and evaluated, the authors provide valuable insight into the difficulties of working with organizations to change drinking norms. In their narrative, they highlight the difficulty posed by conflicting theories of the problem. Scientists are guided by scientific theories, and members of the work organization are guided by lay theories. Shain and Suurvali argue that "enabling theory" provides a bridge between the conflicting orientations and gives all the parties a common language. Most important, the researchers highlight that this common language has been an important mechanism for maintaining their engagement with the organization. During periods of low external threat to the organization, the enabling language has permitted them to work with management and labor to expose the structural and organizational factors that encourage drinking problems and lead to injuries. During periods of high external threat to the organization, the enabling language has permitted them to retain their consulting relationship and work with management and labor on personal factors that contribute to drinking problems and lead to injuries.

IMPLICATIONS

As noted earlier, the chapters in this volume build on our existing knowledge about the centrality of workplace drinking norms in our understanding of workers' drinking behavior. Each study demonstrates gains that may be made by mounting educational programs that directly and indirectly target drinking norms. Although one may criticize the researchers' methodologies and findings, the information certainly complements our existing knowledge about substance abuse. Within this context, one may justifiably ask why more companies are not adopting educational interventions targeted at changing drinking norms. After all, the weight of the evidence shows that substance abuse is costly to work organizations, and researchers have shown that they can reduce the risks associated with this costly behavior and reduce workers' AOD use. Businesses are supposed to be concerned about their bottom line, and the rational approach would be to adopt educational programs targeted at substance abuse.

The image of work organizations as rational actors is deeply embedded in American culture; however, this image is a myth (Meyer & Rowan, 1977; Powell & DiMaggio, 1991). Organizations seldom adopt new programs for purely rational reasons; more often than not, organizations adopt them ritualistically to demonstrate their legitimacy to the government, competitors, customers, and workers. For example, if hospitals were truly concerned about minimizing costs, they would fire all the doctors and replace them with practical nurses. Of course, hospitals do not do that because the government, the medical community, and patients would regard them as illegitimate. The hospitals would lose their accreditation, and patients would avoid them. Similarly, work organizations adopt human resource policies primarily to maintain their legitimacy (Sutton, Dobbin, Meyer, & Scott, 1994). Adopting affirmative action programs signal to the government, competitors, and employees that the organizations are conforming to expectations, are up-to-date, and are trustworthy. Organizations adopt EAPs and drug-screening programs for similar reasons. Today, every credible human resources department has an EAP because organizations now regard them as essential for maintaining their legitimacy (Blum & Roman, 1989). Similarly, organizations have not adopted screening programs because it is the rational thing to do; rather they have adopted them to demonstrate that they are not soft on drugs and are meeting their social obligations. This information is not an argument that organizations are unconcerned with the costs of EAPs or drug screening. Indeed, organizations, which are steeped in the myth of rational actors, use cost–benefit language to justify their decisions to adopt EAPs and drug screening and to maintain the appearance of rationality. Those analyses, however, are better understood as post hoc justifications of decisions made on other grounds (Trice & Beyer, 1984).

Today, EAPs and drug screening are institutionalized in American workplaces. The term "to institutionalize" has two different meanings, however (Tolbert & Zucker, 1996). In one instance, to institutionalize a program means to embed it into the organization's culture and structure. This process often occurs when a program is seen as being intimately linked to the organization's core mission. Thus, when a paper plant adopts a new paper-making technology, the plant will go to extraordinary lengths to make sure that everyone knows how to use it correctly. In this instance, the new technology and the plant's core mission are tightly coupled. A second meaning of "to institutionalize" is to adopt a program and implement it ritualistically, which is what often happens when organizations adopt programs to maintain their legitimacy and do not regard the adopted programs as being intimately linked to their core mission. Most human resource programs, including EAPs and drug-screening programs, are good examples of this kind of institutionalization.

A brief look at the evolution of EAPs should be sufficient to highlight the meaning of ritualistic implementation. EAPs are a natural outgrowth of earlier efforts to provide counseling to alcoholic and other troubled workers (Sonnenstuhl, 1986). In 1970, Congress, building on the labors of Alcoholics Anonymous and the National Council on Alcoholism, established the National Institute on Alcohol Abuse and Alcoholism (NIAAA), which promoted the idea that alcoholism was a treatable illness. To make alcoholism treatment a reality, NIAAA encouraged employers to adopt health insurance policies for alcoholism treatment and the private and public sectors to develop alcoholism treatment programs. In addition, NIAAA trained two cadres of occupational program consultants to promote EAPs to labor and management.

At this time, EAPs were defined as having two crucial components. The first was a training component, which would teach labor and management to identify suspected alcoholics and other troubled employees by using job performance standards and to use the "constructive confrontation" strategy to motivate them to change their behavior. Supervisors use the strategy to motivate employees to recognize that they have a problem and accept help from the EAP. Following the principles of industrial jurisprudence, supervisors identify problem employees according to the job performance standard and use progressive discipline to motivate them to correct their behavior. At each step of the disciplinary process, employees are encouraged to seek help from the EAP. If employees fail to improve their performance either on their own or with the help of the EAP, they are subject to discharge. The second component was a diagnostic component to evaluate employees' problems and refer them for treatment. The consultants encountered a great deal of resistance from labor and management to adopting and implementing the components. Employers primarily wanted the consultants to take the problem employees off their hands. Within this context, the consultants promoted the development of out-of-house EAPs. The framework of this simplified model meant that work organizations were not required to train supervisors and stewards to identify and motivate alcoholic and other troubled workers, and the constructive confrontation strategy atrophied. Instead, workers were encouraged to seek assistance on their own from the out-of-house provider, who would either treat them using short-term counseling or refer them to other help in the community.

Today, this form of employee assistance is the most prevalent model in work organizations (Hartwell et al., 1996; Hayghe, 1991). In some instances, the out-of-house provider model has been even more simplified. With the advent of managed care in the late 1980s, many managed care providers became EAPs because, as part of their cost containment service, they referred employees to alcohol and mental health treatment (Heck, 1999; Masi, 1998). In those cases, the concept of employee assistance was simplified to a phone call. Although each EAP model varies in the complexity of its implementation, they all permit work organizations to claim that they have an EAP, possess up-to-date human resource departments, and should be regarded as legitimate. Much the same argument could be made for drug testing, and it highlights why organizations pay so little heed to the shortcomings of screening programs described in chapter 1. Organizations are more concerned with maintaining their legitimacy than with implementing an effective drug-screening program; therefore, they turn a blind eye to studies questioning its efficacy.

Organizations will not immediately adopt prevention programs, no matter how compelling our research data, for yet another reason, which is rooted in my earlier discussion of symbolic crusades. Here it is useful to think of EAPs and drug testing as bookends marking the beginning and ending of a temperance reform cycle. Recall that in the beginning of a cycle, reformists seek to persuade alcoholics or addicts to change, and at the end of a cycle, they attempt to coerce them to change. EAPs were developed during a period when the government provided strong support for workers' rights and the American economy was expanding. Within this context, the original EAP model reflected the concern for protecting workers' rights by building on the concept of progressive discipline, which was intended to constructively persuade alcoholic and other troubled workers to seek help before they lost their job. In contrast, drug testing was adopted during a period when the government was becoming less supportive of workers' rights and the American economy was contracting. Within this context, crack came to symbolize everything that was wrong with American society and drug testing became accepted as the necessary price for keeping illicit drugs from further wreaking destruction on families, communities, and workplaces. Drug users, as well as alcoholics, were no longer tolerated. Instead of being progressively disciplined at work, they were often summarily discharged.

Today, the War on Drugs is past, and the last cycle of reform is complete. It is unclear whether another has begun or is about to begin soon. Indeed, the next cycle may be delayed by an expanding economy and a government less supportive of workers' rights. Within this context, none of us should be surprised to find that organizations continue to put their faith in their institutionalized EAPs and drug screening to solve their substance abuse worries. Why should companies rush to invest in new programs if the existing ones continue to provide them with legitimacy?

This conclusion may seem overly pessimistic; nevertheless, I believe that it is realistic and reflects the experiences of this volume's authors as they have sought to promote substance abuse prevention programs. Currently, it is a tough sell. Still, I am an optimist. I believe that if 200 years is a reliable guide to American society, another round of temperance reform will develop. Like the earlier cycles, it will begin with efforts to persuade substance abusers to change their behavior and will build on the work of a vanguard whose research and actions have demonstrated the value of persuading rather than coercing substance abusers to change their behavior. The authors of this volume are part of that vanguard, and their research and interventions are preparing the ground for that time.

REFERENCES

Ames, G. M., Grube, J. W., & Moore, R. S. (2000). Social control and workplace drinking norms: A comparison of two organizational cultures. *Journal of Studies on Alcohol, 61*, 203–219.

Bacharach, S., Bamberger, P., & Sonnenstuhl, W. (in press). Driven to drink: Managerial control, work-related risk factors, and employee drinking behavior. *Academy of Management Journal.*

Becker, H. (1963). *Outsiders.* New York: Free Press.

Ben-Yehuda, N. (1990). *The politics and morality of deviance: Moral panics, drug abuse, and reversed stigmatization.* Albany: SUNY Press.

Blocker, J. (1989). *American temperance movements: Cycles of reform.* Boston: Twayne.

Blum, T. C., & Roman, P. M. (1989). Employee assistance programs and human resource management. In K. Rowland & G. Ferris (Eds.), *Research in personnel and human resources management, 7,* 259–312.

Erfurt, J. C., Foote, A., & Heirich, M. (1992). Integrating employee assistance and wellness: Current and future core technologies of a megabrush program. *Journal of Employee Assistance Research, 1,* 1–31.

Gusfield, J. (1963). *Symbolic crusade: Status politics and the temperance movement.* Urbana: University of Illinois Press.

Hartwell, T. D., Steele, P., French, M. T., Potter, F. J., Rodman, N. F., & Zarkin, G. A. (1996). Aiding troubled employees: The prevalence, cost, and characteristics of employee assistance programs in the United States. *American Journal of Public Health, 86,* 804–808.

Hayghe, H. (1991). Anti-drug programs in the workplace: Are they here to stay? *Monthly Labor Review, 114,* 26–28.

Heck, P. W. (1999). The evolving role of EAPs in managed behavioral healthcare: A case study of Du Pont. In J. M. Oher (Ed.), *The employee assistance handbook* (pp. 291–304). New York: John Wiley & Sons.

Kyvig, D. (1979). *Repealing national prohibition.* Chicago: University of Chicago Press.

Lender, M. E., & Martin, J. K. (1987). *Drinking in America: A history.* New York: Free Press.

Masi, D. (1998). *The role of employee assistance programs in managed behavioral health-care*. Rockville, MD: Substance and Mental Health Services Administration, Center for Mental Health Services.

Meyer, J. W., & Rowan, B. (1977). Institutionalized organizations: Formal structure as myth and ceremony. *American Journal of Sociology, 83*, 340–363.

Powell, W. W., & DiMaggio, P. J. (Eds.). (1991). *The new institutionalism in organizational analysis*. Chicago: University of Chicago Press.

Reinarman, C., & Levine, H. G. (1995). The crack attack: America's latest drug scare. In J. Best (Ed.), *Images of issues: Typifying contemporary social problems* (2nd ed.). New York: Aldine de Gruyter.

Roman, P. M., & Blum, T. C. (1998). The prevention of behavioral disabilities from non-work sources: Employee assistance and related strategies. In T. Thomason, J. F. Burton, Jr., & D. E. Hyatt (Eds.), *New approaches to disability in the workplace* (pp. 85–120). Madison, WI: Industrial Relations Research Association.

Sonnenstuhl, W. (1986). *Inside an emotional health program: A field study of workplace assistance for troubled employees*. Ithaca, NY: ILR Press.

Staudenmeier, W. J., Jr. (1985). *Alcohol and the workplace: A study of social policy in a changing America*. Unpublished doctoral dissertation, Washington University, St. Louis.

Sutton, J., Dobbin, F., Meyer, J., & Scott, W. R. (1994). The legalization of the workplace. *American Journal of Sociology, 99*, 944–971.

Tolbert, P. S., & Zucker, L. G. (1996). The institutionalization of institutional theory. In S. Clegg, C. Hardy, & W. Nord (Eds.), *Handbook of organization studies* (pp. 175–190). London: Sage.

Trice, H. M., & Beyer, J. M. (1982). A study of union–management cooperation in a long-standing alcoholism program. *Contemporary Drug Problems, 11*, 295–317.

Trice, H. M., & Beyer, J. M. (1984). Employee assistance programs: Blending performance-oriented and humanitarian ideologies to assist emotionally disturbed employees. In J. R. Greenley (Ed.), *Research in community and mental health* (Vol. 4, pp. 245–297). Greenwich, CT: JAI Press.

Trice, H. M., & Sonnenstuhl, W. (1990). On the construction of drinking norms in work organizations. *Journal of Studies on Alcohol, 51*, 201–220.

8

CAUTIOUS OPTIMISM AND RECOMMENDATIONS: A CALL FOR MORE RESEARCH FROM APPLIED PSYCHOLOGY

JOEL B. BENNETT, G. SHAWN REYNOLDS, AND WAYNE E. K. LEHMAN

This chapter has two main goals. First, we hope to encourage researchers from different areas of social science and psychology to bring their knowledge and methods to bear on the problem of employee substance abuse, including improved ways of addressing barriers to program implementation. To that end, this chapter demonstrates that the preceding chapters of this book actually helped raise more questions than they answer. The field of psychology is well positioned to address those questions, and by so doing, psychologists can help sharpen researchers' practical knowledge of why certain programs work, which program elements may need enhancement, and when certain programs are directly indicated. Second, we summarize findings and make some recommendations about ways in which the specific programs described in chapters 2 through 6 might be adapted and evaluated in different work settings. Thus, this chapter attempts to come full circle to issues raised in the introduction to this volume. It is necessary not only to make the business case but also to provide employers with tips, guidelines, and strategies that will optimize the impact of programs.

The different chapter authors share a sense of optimism when looking to the future and to the possibility that proactive prevention education will become more common and reach workers who need such programs. As Sonnenstuhl argues in chapter 7, although programs may demonstrate the value of persuading rather than coercing employees, the prevailing cultural ethos is more significant than scientific evidence in shaping the prevalence of prevention programming. Other chapter authors have noted the lack of incentives for businesses, the exclusion of substance abuse prevention within the field of workplace health promotion, and the failure to effectively translate general scientific knowledge into ways that can be used in workplaces.

The road from strong evidence in the field of health promotion and prevention to actual changes in policy and program implementation is often rocky. Health policy and government spending places a much greater emphasis on medicine and disease management than on the field of prevention. McGinnis (2001) clearly explains this phenomenon: "Despite the fact that prevention was the major contributor to the health gains of the last century . . . most studies of health expenditures indicate that less than 5% are devoted to prevention" (p. 392). McGinnis lists 12 factors that account for the limited investment in prevention, despite evidence for success. They include the fact that the positive effects of prevention often are invisible compared with the vivid rescues in clinical medicine. Such effects also take time to emerge, and our present-minded culture, which has a blunted time horizon, tends to discount such benefits in favor of the quick intervention. Says McGinnis, "We are a people who appreciate the technological 'fix' to a problem—and the more novel or dramatic the fix, the more our attention is drawn" (p. 393).

Moreover, prevention often treats myriad preexisting factors rather than the visible manifestation of a disease. As a result, it is often difficult to understand that the intervention for a risk profile follows a different logic and probability of success than the intervention for a disease: "In a world in which our biomedical model—grouping causes and effects into neat, distinguishable biologic pathways—leads us to associate certainty of action with simplicity of task, prevention is inherently disadvantaged. In the fog of complexity, established opportunities are easily ignored" (McGinnis, 2001, p. 393).

We do not review these issues regarding the obstruction of prevention in order to make readers more cautious than optimistic. Rather, a straightforward discussion of practical issues is necessary to set realistic goals for business applications. We also hasten to build reader optimism by pointing out the existence of several research programs other than those showcased in this book. As this book goes to press, the Workplace Managed Care

(WMC) project, a division of the Center for Substance Abuse Prevention, is winding up a 4-year cross-site prevention study (see Bennett & Beaudin, 2000; Cook & Schlenger, in press).

The WMC study included more than 20 different worksites nationwide and provided interventions to more than 52,000 employees. A wide variety of interventions were represented across nine different researchers, including drug testing, health promotion, health risk assessments, parenting programs, peer counseling, specialized videos, interactive Web sites, and enhanced employee assistance program (EAP) services. Preliminary positive findings from this study are highlighted in Exhibit 8.1. The programs

EXHIBIT 8.1
Preliminary Findings From the Workplace Managed Care Project From the Center for Substance Abuse Prevention (CSAP)

The following findings are preliminary results of a workplace prevention cross-site study as posted on the Web site for the Third Knowledge Exchange Workshop, September 6 and 7, 2001, in Crystal City, Arlington, Virginia (http://www. health.org/promos/futurework/). This list does not represent final conclusions of the study. Interested readers should contact CSAP's Division of Workplace Programs or visit http://wmcare.samhsa.gov.

- Peer-based substance abuse prevention programs, in conjunction with random drug testing, avoided $750,000 per year in discipline costs and $26 million to $35 million per year in worker injury costs at a major transportation company; the return on investment was 30 or 40 to 1.
- Substance abuse prevention interventions delivered in a health promotion context decreased problem alcohol use.
- An interactive Web-based alcohol intervention decreased alcohol use in moderate and high-risk drinkers.
- Employees were more receptive to substance abuse prevention messages that were embedded in broad health promotion interventions (e.g., stress, nutrition, or cardiac care programs) than when presented as substance abuse programs.
- Randomized drug testing at a manufacturing company significantly decreased total medical care costs. Doubling the frequency of drug testing maximizes the benefit of drug testing.
- Alcohol and other drug (AOD) users detected by random drug testing had higher injury rates than other workers.
- AOD use on the job increases injury risk for women and youth more than for other workers. Because different workplace substance abuse prevention interventions work best for different employee groups, programs need to be tailored for high-risk workers.
- 73% of university-based managers and supervisors found Web-based supervisory training about AOD use "very useful."
- A primary care physician-based screening and referral protocol was effective at identifying problem employees and referring them to appropriate interventions and treatment.
- Proactive peer-to-peer or professional outreach increased the impact of workplace substance abuse prevention efforts.
- Cross-site analysis of survey data from four grantees suggested that interventions are reducing binge drinking.

and findings echo two major themes described in chapter 1. First, "moving beyond" drug testing should not be taken as a criticism; rather, testing should be considered as only one strategy that needs to be complemented with proactive educative programs. Second, because different programs may work in different settings and with different types of employees, it is important to move beyond a "one-size-fits-all" approach and pay attention to diversity of settings when planning and implementing programs.

A thorough understanding of these strategic issues will add to the success of any specific program as well as workplace prevention in general. Consider the range of programs evaluated in this book: Each will stand a greater chance of successful implementation when barriers are considered in the earliest stages of planning an intervention. The Substance Abuse and Mental Health Services Administration (SAMHSA, 1997) lists 10 guidelines for prevention programming, all of which require careful analysis of the target population, the multilevel nature of the systems they live in, and the barriers present within those systems.

In a review of intervention in the fields of youth violence, smoking, and HIV/AIDS, Reppucci, Woolard, and Fried (1999) concluded that programs that do not consider the surrounding community (i.e., that only focus on the individual) often fail (see Gutman & Clayton, 1999). Repucci et al. argue, as we do in this chapter, that scientific knowledge from psychology can and should be at the forefront in informing multilevel preventive interventions. We would like readers to consider how their own research interests apply to the problem of alcohol and other drug (AOD) abuse among employees.

THE CALL FOR MORE RESEARCH FROM APPLIED PSYCHOLOGY

This section suggests how the field of psychology might be applied to the study of workplace AOD abuse prevention. We encourage researchers from different areas of psychology to either bring knowledge from within their discipline to bear on AOD use in the workplace or to conduct new research on how the workplace can be an effective medium for the application of psychological principles to workplace AOD prevention.

Before listing the fields of application, we summarize the preceding chapters with the following five claims:

1. Employee AOD abuse remains a problem and creates significant costs for workplaces.
2. Although some evidence suggests that drug testing may be an effective deterrent, more research is needed to demonstrate that testing helps reduce substance abuse.

3. Drug testing alone is not sufficient to address workplace substance abuse because it generally does not attempt to deter alcohol use, does not eliminate underlying causes of substance abuse, and ignores social and contextual workplace factors.

4. Evidence is beginning to accumulate that prevention programs that go beyond standard employee educational sessions can be effective in reducing AOD use, as demonstrated in previous chapters and the preliminary meta-analysis in chapter 1.

5. Because organizational- and occupational-level factors (e.g., work climate) can influence employee AOD use, prevention programmers and evaluators should be aware of contextual influences when designing, implementing, and evaluating their interventions.

Organizational and occupational factors also can be viewed as elements within an organizational system or workplace "social ecology" (Stokols, 1992). That is, the system or organization—with its attendant occupational and climate features—has an identified problem (i.e., substance abuse) and has adapted one of several responses (e.g., drug testing, an EAP, or education) to that problem. We locate prevention within any given organization and hypothesize that educational and training programs can be effectively integrated into the social ecosystem of an organization. We propose that such training programs (as described in previous chapters) may be more easily integrated than drug testing, which is apt to be viewed as external to the social ecosystem (cf. *technological* subsystems; Kast & Rosenzweig, 1973). This systems view provides a framework for applying psychological models to the problem of workplace AOD prevention. We encourage psychologists to adapt this view and determine how their specific specialty within psychology may be applied to the problem of substance abuse, discover which factors enhance institutionalization of prevention as a more dominant response, and learn how to enhance program effectiveness.

To that end, the varied set of topics within the field of psychology awaits application to the goal of preventing workplace substance abuse. We review some of those topics below and note that knowledge about AOD problems in the workplace can benefit from basic research outside of work settings. In particular, researchers who work on college campuses and with student populations have the opportunity to conduct studies on prevention and use many of the psychological topic areas described below. The problem of alcohol use and binge drinking on campus (Wechsler, Davenport, Dowdall, Moeykens, & Castillo, 1994) provides an excellent opportunity for conducting undergraduate research studies that apply various topics in psychology. For example, risky drinking practices are shaped by social norms on college campuses (Perkins & Wechsler, 1996), and a number of studies show that brief interventions can be effective in reducing alcohol intake among college students (e.g., Borsari & Carey, 2000; Roberts, Neal, Kivlahan, Baer, & Marlatt, 2000). It is plausible that at least some of the psychosocial mechanisms underlying prevention of substance abuse on college campuses parallel the mechanisms that underlie workplace prevention. Again, we offer the following overview to encourage researchers to apply their own knowledge and interests.

Group Processes: Conformity and Social Influence

As described in chapter 5, research indicates the existence of workplace drinking climates or subcultures. Conformity pressures are one feature of those group cultures. Macdonald, Wells, and Wild (1999) used the following item in their survey of drinking subcultures: "Sometimes I feel that I might lose my friends if I don't drink alcohol with them." Employees with reported alcohol problems scored significantly higher on this item (and other measures of social drinking with coworkers) than employees with no alcohol problem. In fact, of all measures used (i.e., social control, quality of work, job stress, and drinking subculture), drinking subculture appeared to best distinguish employees with and without alcohol problems.

Classic studies in social psychology indicate that groups can influence their members in a number of ways, including pressure to conform on the basis of information provided by group members (i.e., *informational* influence) or beliefs about whether other members of the group will accept or reject them (i.e., *normative* influence; Deutsch & Gerard, 1955). People also have been found to accept greater levels of risk when they are asked to reach a decision as a group than when they decide alone (i.e., "risky shift"; Stoner, 1961). Other research on diffusion of responsibility (Latané & Darley, 1970) and moral drift (Haney, Banks, & Zimbardo, 1973) suggests that, as a function of being a group member, individuals will ignore their personal values to the point of either harming others or ignoring those in distress.

Insight into group dynamics might help strategize prevention programs to address group factors shaping employee AOD use. Research with adolescents and college students has established relationships between group pressures to conformity and AOD use. Much of this research, which assessed self-reported motives for use, pointed to conformity as a reason for drinking or marijuana use (e.g., MacLean & Lecci, 2000; Simons, Correia, & Carey, 2000). Other studies solicited responses to scenarios of AOD consumption by their peers (Bearden, Rose, & Teel, 1994; Rose, Bearden,

& Teel, 1992). Senchak, Leonard, and Greene (1998) also found that student alcohol consumption was influenced by social context, after controlling for individual differences.

Psychologists could use these research methods with employee samples to identify mechanisms of social influence that could either reduce group pressures toward heavy drinking or increase such pressures to moderation. For example, would exposing groups to increased information about the hazards of drinking from coworkers (i.e., informational pressures) be effective? Or are normative pressures more powerful? What factors in the work setting help diffuse responsibility when a coworker comes to work under the influence, such that all coworkers "look the other way?" Do coworkers take more risks and drink more heavily with each other than when alone? Also, because people vary in their conformity motives for drinking or drug use, will prevention programs that focus on group norms (see *Team Awareness*, chapter 5) be more effective for those with high conformity needs? Conversely, will an intervention model that appears to address institutional and occupational norms (e.g., the *Courage to Care* program described in chapter 6) be more effective? Answers to those questions can enhance our ability to strategize prevention programming at the group level.

Clinical and Counseling Psychology (Work Dysfunction)

Any program that provides employees with information on how to get help should point employees toward help-givers who know how to deal with substance abuse. In this regard, the field of clinical and counseling psychology can identify effective methods for risk identification and early intervention in AOD dependence. Case studies describe work dysfunctions involving AOD dependence (e.g., Rosecan, 1993; Schaef & Fassel, 1988; Schuster, 1993), and several models exist for conducting counseling or brief interventions with employees at work (e.g., Bruhnsen, 1999; Feltham, 1997; Lowman, 1993). O'Hair (1998) described an EAP strategy for talking with troubled employees and motivating them to get into treatment. The "Employee Assistance Treatment Planner" (Oher, Conti, & Jongsma, 1998) also provided specific guidelines for chemical dependence that could be used in early intervention with employees. The case studies and brief intervention models and guidelines provide a basis for a systematic application of counseling psychology to workplace prevention.

Comerford (1999) argued that substance abuse and vocational dysfunction share a common cause: low self-efficacy (e.g., self-destructive beliefs, alienation, and pessimism). He suggested that vocational counseling targeting positive self-efficacy and self-esteem may offer a prevention or early intervention strategy. Some evidence, however, suggests that training in clinical and counseling psychology tends to underemphasize vocational or career counseling (see Heppner, O'Brien, Hinkelman, & Flores, 1996) and that counselors deemphasize vocational concerns among current clients (cf. "vocational overshadowing"; Spengler, Blustein, & Strohmer, 1990). Because patients complaining of mental symptoms do not usually divulge information about their AOD use (Rosenthal & Westreich, 1999), it is possible that counselors fail to recognize substance dependence early on (if at all) in the counseling process.

Despite these drawbacks, we are encouraged by Comerford's (1999) self-efficacy model and recent evidence demonstrating the effectiveness of brief interventions for AOD problems (Zweben & Fleming, 1999). The health promotion models developed by Cook and colleagues (see chapter 3) may complement such efforts, given Cook et al.'s finding that employees improved their levels of self-efficacy with regard to exercise. Clearly, the opportunity exists for counseling psychology to adapt self-efficacy interventions into work settings. Moreover, research is needed to demonstrate the effectiveness of this approach within the venue of vocational counseling. For example, could workplace programs that enhance career planning and development or job enhancement also have the effect of reducing drinking or drug use? Would it be possible to effectively integrate messages about health promotion and AOD prevention in vocational counseling?

Other findings raise interesting questions for researchers in clinical psychology. For example, does increased self-efficacy in one life area (e.g., exercise, as described in chapter 3) or improved stress coping (see chapter 2) have spillover or rippling effects in other areas of mental health? Is it possible that improvements in cardiovascular health that stem from workplace counseling (see chapter 4) have additional mental health benefits? Because research links cardiovascular disease with various psychosocial risks (e.g., depression, anxiety, and social isolation; see Hemingway & Marmot, 1999; Rozanski, Blumenthal, & Kaplan, 1999), is it possible that the outreach health promotion model can have added benefits in reducing those psychosocial risks?

Prosocial Behavior: Help Giving and Help Seeking

Some key goals of prevention programming are to provide referral information or direct help to workers or to encourage and enable workers to get help before problems reach a level of significant risk. In that regard, research on altruism and help-seeking and -giving behavior may be useful, especially in training supervisors and peers who could encourage or nudge troubled coworkers to get help. Bayer and Gerstein (1988) developed a "bystander-equity model of supervisory helping behavior," which suggests that various characteristics of the employee, supervisor, and problem situation interact to affect a supervisor's level of affective arousal, anxiety, or concern; perceptions about the costs of helping; and eventual helping response. The model predicts, for example, that as their arousal increases, supervisors will be more apt to seek relief by helping an employee. Supervisors, however, are often less aware than immediate coworkers are of troubled employees; those coworkers, as members of a group, might say or think, "Why should I be the one to intervene?" (i.e., diffusion of responsibility; Latané & Darley, 1970).

Batson's (1998) review of the helping literature also provides some insights that could be applied to enhance supervisory and employee willingness to encourage a coworker to seek help as well as increase employees' chances of self-referring or seeking help on their own. For example, evidence suggests that people are more likely to help as a function of social learning (e.g., received rewards for helping), tension reduction, and social norms of reciprocity and social responsibility. Batson also suggests that people will not seek help because it might be seen as an admission of lack of competence or some other valued aspect of the self. Indeed, Sonnenstuhl (1990) suggests that alcohol is a highly stigmatized problem and that

> employees may not be predisposed to talking about their problems because they are not knowledgeable about mental health problems and have never learned to talk about them or because they are knowledgeable about them and believe that if others discover that they may have such difficulties, they will be stigmatized. . . . [Moreover], troubled employees, in order to preserve their sense of self, generally do not seek advice from others and become the targets of unsolicited comments when their disruptive behavior exceeds the tolerance levels of others. (pp. 244–246)

Sonnenstuhl pointed out that help-seeking and helping processes exist within the social context of the work setting. That context includes social norms and social learning processes (as described by Batson, 1998) along with variable awareness of resources for help (e.g., EAP), disciplinary policy, drug testing, and supervisors who may or may not offer constructive comments. Research is needed to show how much those factors contribute to employee's decisions to seek help and to coworkers' decisions to offer encouragement. A growing body of literature on attitudes associated with seeking help for psychological problems in general (Komiya, Good, & Sherrod, 2000), and alcohol problems specifically (Rather, 1991), may be helpful here.

Stigma

Perhaps the greatest barrier to seeking help for psychological problems is stigma. Employees may believe that either the problem—or seeking help to deal with the problem—will devalue their character as being immoral or out of control. Little quantitative evidence demonstrates that people avoid substance abuse treatment to avoid being stigmatized; however, in one qualitative study, treatment clients most frequently cited the stigma of addiction as the reason for not coming to treatment earlier (Copeland, 1997). Nevertheless, ample research demonstrates an inverse relationship between endorsing negative attitudes toward psychiatric disorders and willingness to seek mental health treatment (e.g., Link, 1987; Pugh, Ackerman, McColgan, & de Mesquita, 1994). More important, stigma can have a lasting effect on dual-diagnosed patients even after treatment (Link et al., 1997).

Classical sociological discussions of stigma describe a blemish of character or a spoiled identity (Goffman, 1963). Theoretically, awareness that one's blemished identity could be evaluated negatively by others influences people to avoid conforming to other people's negative stereotypes. People cope with stigma by using a number of self-presentational strategies, including concealing certain attributes of the self (Goffman, 1963). Contemporary definitions of stigma include beliefs about other people's potential evaluations *and* the context as important components of the stigma construct. Research suggests that stigma probably affects substance abusers by creating stressful, stereotype-threatening predicaments (Steele, 1992; Steele & Aronson, 1995). People cope with such predicaments by learning to avoid them (Brown, 1998), initiating self-esteem maintenance (Crocker & Major, 1994), and activating mental control processes (Smart & Wegner, 1999).

Any program with the goal of increasing the use of the EAP or other help sources must consider the concept of stigma and attitudinal factors that might ameliorate stigma. The program could itself create the threatening predicament discussed by Steele and Aronson (1995): Employees who are asked to attend AOD prevention training might refrain just from fear of being considered a *potential* substance abuser. In this instance, substance abuse prevention trainings might be framed as wellness or health trainings to increase participation (as described in chapters 2, 3, 4, & 5). Research with college students suggests that stigma is negatively associated with beliefs in both the disease and the social learning models of alcoholism (Rather, 1991) and with emotional openness (Komiya et al., 2000). Prevention training might include discussions about models of alcoholism, encourage openness, and include particularly interesting and relevant content to pique the attention of the most potentially stigmatized employees. Content or delivery that allows trainees to compartmentalize the information into that which is relevant to "them" ("*those* problem substance abusers") and that which is relevant to "us" ("*we* would never have *such* a problem") will be ineffective, especially when there is a tendency to stigmatize AOD problems in a particular workplace context.

PRELIMINARY FINDINGS AND RECOMMENDATIONS FOR THE WORKPLACE

This section lists several preliminary findings about workplace prevention of AOD abuse that are based on the research presented in this volume. The findings also may be interpreted as recommendations for employers, human resource personnel, and others who might design or implement programs. In crafting the list of findings, we emphasize that research is still in the early stages, and although conclusions are based on positive results, the studies in this volume have several limitations that should be considered. Workplace preventive interventions have been shown to have some measurable impact on AOD use, although the work to date only represents the beginning stages of what needs to be studied. We highly encourage longitudinal research involving extensive examination and comparisons of interventions across diverse settings and populations.

The summary of findings shown in Table 8.1 is organized into four areas: (a) findings related to effectiveness, (b) program implementation and strategy issues, (c) participation and retention, and (d) radiating and collateral effects. We briefly discuss each area below, paying particular attention to how the limitations of current studies make some of the conclusions tentative. Regardless of those limitations, we believe that it is worth paying attention to the 18 listed recommendations because they will help optimize the impact of programs on preventing substance abuse.

Issues Related to Effectiveness

The best indicator of program effectiveness is demonstration of statistically superior effects of an intervention group compared with a control group in a well-controlled, randomized, experimental study. Several of the studies reported in this book included experimental controls. Items 1–6 in the table are based on those studies. The studies have several concerns that limit the strength of the conclusions, including problems with attrition, reliance on self-reports, and low statistical power. In addition, all studies were conducted by researchers who were themselves involved in designing —and sometimes implementing—the actual intervention, leaving room for experimenter bias to influence study results. Nevertheless, we believe that the six recommendations represent wise strategies for those who wish to assess whether a program is effective.

Program Implementation and Strategy Issues

Items 7–11 in the table represent general positive outcomes involving programmatic content. We assume that programs work—keeping in mind the limitations mentioned above—because of something about the specific

TABLE 8.1
Findings/Preliminary Conclusions and Recommendations Regarding Evidence-Based Workplace Substance Abuse Prevention Program

Findings and Preliminary Conclusions	Recommendations
Issues Related to Effectiveness	
1. The positive effects of workplace programs on actual reductions in substance abuse (or the loss of initial effects) may not appear until several months after the program.	Avoid drawing conclusions about program impact without assessing long-term effects of interventions (perhaps until at least 6 months following program delivery).
2. Workplace characteristics may influence the degree to which particular interventions are effective.	Avoid making generalized statements about program effectiveness and remember that programs may work in some but not all work environments. Keep in mind that programs may require adaptation to the specific needs of individual work settings (including work groups and departments as well as different business units within a single organization).
3. Workplace prevention programs may have a stronger positive effect on alcohol reduction among subgroups of heavy alcohol users.	Whenever possible, make additional efforts to recruit and retain employees suspected of problem drinking. Maintain willingness to remain in the program.
4. Workplace prevention programs may have a stronger positive effect on employees in occupational groups known to have higher levels of safety risks.	Provide training programs to employees who (based on research) are identified to be "at risk." These groups include young men, employees in safety-sensitive jobs, and work units or businesses in safety-sensitive occupations. (See Figure 1.1)
5. Together, all studies provide more information about reducing substance abuse than about keeping those at risk from developing problems over time.	When evaluating the positive impact of a program, assess whether employees with no symptoms at pretest also remain problem-free at posttest and follow up.
6. Most workplace prevention programs primarily emphasize person-centered approaches and do not address organizational or system factors related to substance abuse.	Whenever possible, attempt to implement programs aimed at modifying individual- *and* organizational-level risk and protective factors.
Program Implementation and Strategy Issues	
7. Substance abuse prevention materials can be inserted into workplace health promotion offerings without diluting the impact of such programs.	Whenever possible, workplace health promotion programs on any topic (e.g., diet, exercise, and cardiovascular disease [CVD] risk) should link to information on substance abuse.

TABLE 8.1 (*Continued*)

Findings and Preliminary Conclusions	Recommendations
8. Stress management programs can help reduce a variety of risk indicators for substance abuse, including stressors both within and outside the work environment.	Offer stress management programs that include messages about how alcohol and drug use are ineffective methods for dealing with stress.
9. Workplace cardiovascular risk screening and counseling is an effective way to gain access to the adult population for alcohol education and to reduce adult substance abuse.	Enhance programs that promote cardiovascular health (health risk screenings, health fairs) by including self-assessment measures for heavy or problem drinking and prescription drug abuse.
10. Providing enhanced psychosocial training (e.g., stress reduction, health promotion, communications) may not always be necessary for employees at lower risk. Such employees, however, benefit from didactic training that is enhanced beyond standard short informational programs. The best approach to substance abuse prevention may be a mixture of psychosocial and enhanced informational methods.	Always include some psychosocial and experiential components for general employee populations or for standard or didactic drug-free workplace programs that review policy and employee assistance programs (EAP). When possible, avoid the sole use of videos, overheads, and handouts.
11. Individual, one-on-one proactive counseling by health professionals with employees in cardiovascular health promotion can be effective in reducing risky levels of drinking.	In certain high-risk settings (see item 4 above), consider using health professionals to conduct one-on-one CVD screenings that include periodic follow up.
Participation and Retention Issues (also see items 3 and 16)	
12. When a workplace health promotion program focuses mainly on substance abuse, participants react negatively.	Avoid using health promotion programs that only focus on substance abuse prevention (e.g., only signs and symptoms).
13. It is possible to achieve high levels of participation (greater than 65%) in training programs that require multiple sessions.	Whenever possible, provide cash or gift incentives to participants for attendance and provide follow-up contact.

Table continues

TABLE 8.1 (*Continued*)

Findings and Preliminary Conclusions	Recommendations
Radiating and Collateral Effects	
14. Classroom training in peer referral skills and team awareness can have a positive impact on reducing social norms that enable drinking among coworkers.	When possible, include communication and peer referral skills in high-risk settings (see item 4) involving work teams or high level of coworker interaction.
15. Evidence suggests that employee-to-employee reinforcement (i.e., social marketing) of health behavior norms will develop as an outgrowth of the one-to-one outreach counseling by health professionals.	When evaluating the impact of health promotion or classroom training, include estimates of secondary or positive collateral effects that involve employee-to-employee marketing of programs.
16. Taken together, various education programs appear to either bypass or reduce concerns about stigma around seeking help for substance abuse.	Always include information about outside counseling supports, ways to access EAPs, and other avenues for getting help for substance abuse for employees as well as their dependents.
17. Evidence suggests that prevention programs can positively affect social systems, which enable or support problem drinkers (and potentially drug users).	Design programs to include messages to peers, coworkers, family members, and others who might enable, support, or minimize problem workers.
18. Linking messages about the negative effects of enabling (see items 14 and 17) with the psychosocial and safety risks of drinking effectively mobilize social support for prevention in the workplace and for facilitating diffusion of the program into an organization.	For any psychosocial or health promotion training, consider crafting messages that link the risks of enabling with safety and psychosocial hazards.

materials and exercises used in training. Unfortunately, because all interventions described in this volume used long-term, multicomponent strategies, it is difficult to pinpoint with any precision why programs worked. Three programs that used some aspect of stress management showed positive effects on substance abuse or related outcomes (see chapters 2, 3, and 5), a finding that speaks to the strength of recommendation 8. Taken together, we believe that the studies summarized in this volume have clear implementations for program strategy and hope that future studies follow the listed recommendations.

Participation and Retention Issues

Table 8.1 includes four findings that are relevant for increased retention (items 3, 12, 13, and 16). As discussed previously, stigma is perhaps the greatest barrier to getting employees to participate in AOD prevention programs, especially for those who might need the program the most. It helps to use a health promotion framework, provide worker incentives, suggest multiple resources for getting help, and target high-risk workers, perhaps through health screening (see chapter 4). Having listed those positive strategies, one must always keep in mind some realistic objectives in busy workplaces that cannot spare even an hour for employees to attend training. Thus, strong leadership and executive "buy in" is the essential and underlying strategy needed to support the recommendations described in the table.

Radiating and Collateral Effects

The introduction to this volume described programs in subsequent chapters as "humanistic, proactive, employee-centered, and interpersonal" (see p. 16). Items 14–18 in the table speak to the strength and promise of the interpersonal aspects of the training programs. Those interpersonal aspects ranged from one-on-one consultation in health outreach (see chapter 4) to widespread, committee-driven changes in policy (see chapter 6). The positive effects of those programs suggest that it is possible to influence the social context in which workers who drink heavily or use illicit drugs (or who are at risk for doing so) may come to see the benefits of ceasing or moderating their risky behaviors. The five recommendations may also be seen as a special subset of program implementation and strategy issues. As strategy, we recognize that the recommendations may have limited use for workers who spend most of their day working alone (e.g., truck drivers) or who are otherwise isolated.

CONCLUSION

Having made the above recommendations, we recognize that scientific knowledge often does not equate with program adoption and implementation. The seasoned reader of the workplace substance abuse literature will recognize that the highlighted recommendations are not too different from earlier suggestions regarding strategy in workplace programming (Backer, 1987; Beyer & Trice, 1978; Roman, 1990; Vicary, 1994a, 1994b).

Perhaps the only—and, we hope, significant—difference is the growing wealth of empirical evidence compiled in this book.

Indeed, this evidence may be the very difference necessary to advance the several goals implied throughout this book and in this chapter; namely, to spur on other researchers, increase government spending in the area of workplace AOD prevention, create additional buy in from employers and executives, increase the role of prevention programs within drug-testing agencies, stimulate inclusion of AOD programs in health promotion research, create federal and state policies that give businesses incentives for adopting prevention, and empower employees or others (e.g., civil libertarians) who resist drug testing as the sole avenue for dealing with the problem.

Barring any immediate or recognizable advancement toward those goals, we remind ourselves (and our readers) that a certain pleasure is to be gained by taking on the challenge of this work. One has to have a long time horizon and consider that, despite the odds, the eventual payoff may indeed be great.

> Sometimes right is its own reward. Part of the attraction of work in prevention is the nature and size of the challenge and the prospect of payoff to society. With the dichotomy between the strong evidence in support of the possible and the sizable forces pulling attention in different directions, there is a certain draw to the challenge. . . . Cultivating the interests of those willing to play to the challenge should serve prevention well. With proof in hand, the payoff will be better health for all. (McGinnis, 2001, p. 295)

At the very least, we believe this book will serve to validate and cultivate the interests of those "willing to play to the challenge." Moreover, we hope to have provided sufficient proof to warrant continued work to meet that challenge. It would seem that in the final analysis, individual workers and their dependents would stand to benefit most, but the costs of substance abuse extend far beyond individual workers and in many directions. Again, we assert our claim that it is time to invest in programs that are humanistic, proactive, employee-centered, and interpersonal. In the long run, the benefits of such an investment will far outweigh the costs.

REFERENCES

Backer, T. E. (1987). *Strategic planning for workplace drug abuse programs* (DHHS Pub.No. ADM 87-1538). Rockville, MD: U.S. Department of Health and Human Services.

Batson, C. D. (1998). Altruism and prosocial behavior. In D. T. Gilbert, S. T. Fiske, & G. Lindzey (Eds.), *The handbook of social psychology* (Vol. 2, pp. 282–316). Boston: McGraw-Hill.

Bayer, G. A., & Gerstein, L. H. (1988). An adaptation of a model of prosocial behavior to supervisor interventions with troubled employees. *Journal of Applied Social Psychology, 18*, 23–37.

Bearden, W. O., Rose, R. L., & Teel, J. E. (1994). Correlates of conformity in the consumption of illicit drugs and alcohol. *Journal of Business Research, 30*, 25–31.

Bennett, J. B., & Beaudin, C. (2000). Modeling research partnerships in prevention: A framework for collaboration in workplace substance abuse prevention. *Journal of Healthcare Quality, 22*, 24–30.

Beyer, J. M., & Trice, H. M. (1978). *Implementing change: Alcoholism policies in work organizations.* New York: Free Press.

Borsari, B., & Carey, K. B. (2000). Effects of a brief motivational intervention in college student drinkers. *Journal of Consulting and Clinical Psychology, 68*, 728–733.

Brown, L. M. (1998). Ethnic stigma as a contextual experience: A possible selves perspective. *Personality and Social Psychological Bulletin, 24*, 163–172.

Bruhnsen, K. D. (1999). Brief interventions and moderation approaches for preventing alcohol problems. In J. M. Oher (Ed.), *The employee assistance handbook* (pp. 221–246). New York: Wiley.

Comerford, A. W. (1999). Work dysfunction and addiction: Common roots. *Journal of Substance Abuse Treatment, 16*, 247–253.

Cook, R., & Schlenger, W. (in press). Prevention of substance abuse in the workplace: Review of research on the delivery of services. *Journal of Primary Prevention.*

Copeland, J. (1997). A qualitative study of barriers to formal treatment among women who self-managed change in addictive behaviours. *Journal of Substance Abuse Treatment, 14*, 183–190.

Crocker, J., & Major, B. (1994). Reactions to stigma: The moderating role of justification. In M. Zanna & J. M. Olson (Eds.), *The psychology of prejudice: The Ontario Symposium* (Vol. 7, pp. 289–314). Hillsdale, NJ: Erlbaum.

Deutsch, M., & Gerard, H. B. (1955). A study of normative and informational social influence upon individual judgment. *Journal of Abnormal and Social Psychology, 51*, 629–636.

Feltham, C. (1997). *The gains of listening: Perspectives on counseling at work.* Buckingham, England: Open University Press.

Goffman, E. (1963). *Stigma: Notes on the management of spoiled identity.* Englewood Cliffs, NJ: Prentice-Hall.

Gutman, M., & Clayton, R. (1999). Treatment and prevention of use and abuse of illegal drugs: Progress on interventions and future directions. *American Journal of Health Promotion, 14*, 92–97.

Haney, C., Banks C., & Zimbardo, P. (1973). Interpersonal dynamics in a simulated prison. *International Journal of Criminology and Penology, 1*, 69–97.

Hemingway, H., & Marmot, M. (1999). Psychosocial factors in the aetiology and prognosis of coronary heart disease: Systematic review of prospective cohort studies. *British Medicine Journal, 318,* 1460–1467.

Heppner, M. J., O'Brien, K. M., Hinkelman, J. M., & Flores, L. Y. (1996). Training counseling psychologists in career development: Are we our own worst enemies? *Counseling Psychologist, 40,* 303–315.

Kast, F. E., & Rosenzweig, J. E. (1973). *Contingency views of organization and management.* Chicago: Science Research Associates.

Komiya, N., Good, G. E., & Sherrod, N. B. (2000). Emotional openness as a predictor of college students' attitudes toward seeking psychological help. *Journal of Counseling Psychology, 47,* 138–143.

Latané, B., & Darley, J. M. (1970). *The unresponsive bystander: Why doesn't he help?* New York: Appleton-Century-Crofts.

Link, B. G. (1987). Understanding labeling effects in the area of mental disorders: An assessment of the effects of expectations of rejection. *American Sociological Review, 52,* 96–112.

Link, B. G., Struening, E. L., Rahav, M., & Phelan, J. C., & Nuttbrock, L. (1997). On stigma and its consequences: Evidence from a longitudinal study of men with dual diagnoses of mental illness and substance abuse. *Journal of Health and Social Behavior, 38,* 177–190.

Lowman, R. L. (1993). *Counseling and psychotherapy of work dysfunctions.* Washington, DC: American Psychological Association.

Macdonald, S., Wells, S., & Wild, T. C. (1999). Occupational risk factors associated with alcohol and drug problems. *American Journal of Drug and Alcohol Abuse, 25,* 351–369.

MacLean, M. G., & Lecci, L. (2000). A comparison of models of drinking motives in a university sample. *Psychology of Addictive Behaviors, 14,* 83–87.

McGinnis, J. M. (2001). Does proof matter? Why strong evidence sometimes yields weak action. *American Journal of Health Promotion, 15,* 391–396.

O'Hair, J. (1998). Employee assistance program strategy. In R. K. White & D. G. Wright (Eds.), *Addiction intervention: Strategies to motivate treatment seeking-behavior* (pp. 55–72). New York: Haworth Press.

Oher, J. M., Conti, D. J., & Jongsma, A. E. (1998). *The employee assistance treatment planner.* New York: Wiley.

Perkins, H. W., & Wechsler, H. (1996). Variation in perceived college drinking norms and its impact on alcohol abuse: A nationwide study. *Journal of Drug Issues, 26,* 961–974.

Pugh, R. L., Ackerman, B. J., McColgan, E. B., & de Mesquita, P. B. (1994). Attitudes of adolescents toward adolescent psychiatric treatment. *Journal of Child and Family Studies, 3,* 351–363.

Rather, B. C. (1991). Disease versus social-learning models of alcoholism in the prediction of alcohol problem recognition, help-seeking, and stigma. *Journal of Drug Education, 21,* 119–132.

Reppucci, N. D., Woolard, J. L., & Fried, C. S. (1999). Social, community, and preventive interventions. *Annual Review of Psychology, 50,* 387–418.

Roberts, L., Neal, D. J., Kivlahan, D. R., Baer, J. S., & Marlatt, G. A. (2000). Individual drinking changes following a brief intervention among college students: Clinical significance in an indicated preventive context. *Journal of Consulting and Clinical Psychology, 68,* 500–505.

Roman, P. M. (1990). *Alcohol problem intervention in the workplace: Employee assistance programs and strategic alternatives.* New York: Quorum Books.

Rose, R. L., Bearden, W. O., & Teel, J. E. (1992). An attributional analysis of resistance to group pressure regarding illicit drug and alcohol consumption by young people. *Journal of Consumer Research, 19,* 1–13.

Rosecan, J. S. (1993). Drug abuse and dependence. In J. P. Kahn (Ed.), *Mental health in the workplace: A practical psychiatric guide* (pp. 346–365). New York: Van Nostrand.

Rosenthal, R. N., & Westreich, L. (1999). Treatment of persons with dual diagnoses of substance use disorder and other psychological problems. In B. S. McCrady & E. E. Epstein (Eds.), *Addictions: A comprehensive guidebook* (pp. 439–476). New York: Oxford University Press.

Rozanski, A., Blumenthal, J. A., & Kaplan, J. (1999). Impact of psychological factors on the pathogenesis of cardiovascular disease and implications for therapy. *Circulation, 99,* 2192–2217.

Schaef, A. W., & Fassel, D. (1988). *The addictive organization.* New York: Harper & Row.

Schuster, C. L. (1993). Alcohol abuse and dependence. In J. P. Kahn (Ed.), *Mental health in the workplace: A practical psychiatric guide* (pp. 366–387). New York: Van Nostrand.

Senchak, M., Leonard, K. E., & Greene, B. W. (1998). Alcohol use among college students as a function of their typical social drinking context. *Psychology of Addictive Behaviors, 12,* 62–70.

Simons, J., Correia, C. J., & Carey, K. B. (2000). A comparison of motives for marijuana and alcohol use among experienced users. *Addictive Behaviors, 25,* 153–160.

Smart, L., & Wegner, D. M. (1999). Covering up what can't be seen: Concealable stigma and mental control. *Journal of Personality and Social Psychology, 77,* 474–486.

Sonnenstuhl, W. J. (1990). Help-seeking and helping processes within the workplace: Assisting alcoholic and other troubled employees. In P. M. Roman (Ed.), *Alcohol problem intervention in the workplace: Employee assistance programs and strategic alternatives* (pp. 237–259). New York: Quorum Books.

Spengler, P. M., Blustein, D. L., & Strohmer, D. C. (1990). Diagnostic and treatment overshadowing of vocational problems by personal problems. *Journal of Counseling Psychology, 37,* 372–381.

Steele, C. (1992, April). Race and the schooling of black Americans. *Atlantic Monthly, 269*(4), 68–78.

Steele, C., & Aronson, J. (1995). Stereotype threat and the intellectual test performance of African Americans. *Journal of Personality and Social Psychology,* 69, 797–811.

Stokols, D. (1992). Establishing and maintaining healthy environments: Toward a social ecology of health promotion. *American Psychologist, 47,* 6–22.

Stoner, J. A. F. (1961). *A comparison of individual and group decisions involving risk.* Unpublished Master's thesis, Massachusetts Institute of Technology, Cambridge.

Substance Abuse and Mental Health Services Administration. (1997). *Guidelines and Benchmarks for Prevention Programming: Implementation Guide.* DHHS Publication No. (SMA) 95-3033. Rockville, MD: U.S.

U.S. Department of Agriculture. (1992). *Food Guide Pyramid.* Home and Garden Bulletin No. 249. Washington, DC: US Government Printing Office.

Vicary, J. R. (1994a). Prevention strategies for the workplace. In *Alcohol, tobacco, and other drug problems in the workplace: Incentives for prevention* (pp. 70–73). San Diego: University of California.

Vicary, J. R. (1994b). Primary prevention and the workplace. *Journal of Primary Prevention, 15,* 99–104.

Wechsler, H., Davenport, A., Dowdall, G., Moeykens, B., & Castillo, S. (1994). Health and behavioral consequences of binge drinking in college: A national survey of students at 140 campuses. *Journal of the American Medical Association, 272,* 1672–1677.

Zweben, A., & Fleming, M. F. (1999). Brief interventions for alcohol and drug problems. In J. A. Tucker, D. M. Donovan, & G. A. Marlatt (Eds.), *Changing addictive behavior: Bridging clinical and public health strategies* (pp. 251–282). New York: Guilford Press.

INDEX

Computerized databases, 47
Computerized records, 160
Confidentiality, in Wellness Outreach at
    Work model, 139
Conflict, work-family, 62
Confrontation, caring or constructive, 16,
    220, 235
Connections program. *See* Make the Con-
    nection program
Constructive confrontation, 16, 220,
    235
Consultation with forest products com-
    pany. *See* Case study on consulta-
    tion with forest products com-
    pany
Cook, R. F., 105, 107
Coping, as outcome variable, 179
Coping-skills intervention, 17
    in workplace coping-skills intervention,
        84, 85
Coping strategies
    active, 59–60, 63–64, 84, 85
    adaptive, 64–65
    avoidance, 59, 63–64
        in workplace coping-skills interven-
            tion, 69, 72, 73, 74, 81, 84, 85
    cognitive, 69, 74
    in workplace coping-skills intervention,
        69, 74, 81, 231
Coping Strategies Inventory, 79
Corporate cultures, drinking embedded
    in, 99, 100
Cost(s) of alcohol and other drug use
    (substance abuse), 3, 6, 8, 31–32,
    47, 233, 242, 254
Counseling
    vs. disease model for health care
        delivery, 137
    in Wellness Outreach at Work study,
        145, 147, 150, 150–151, 155,
        156, 157, 158, 232
Courage to Care program, 19, 220, 224,
    245
Coworker drinking norms, as predictor of
    employee problem drinking, 39,
    40. *See also* Culture, workplace
    (worksite) or group; Norms
Cultural ethos
    and persuasive vs. coercive approach,
        20

and prevention programming, 240
    See also Norms
Culture, corporate, drinking embedded
    in, 99, 100
Culture, workplace (worksite) or group
    and AOD use, 168, 176, 231
    healthy, 169
    importance of, 38–40
    and individual behavior change, 139–
        140
    as moderator, 196
    in team-oriented prevention training,
        171, 196
    theory of, 196
    See also Group processes; Subculture
Customized strategy or program, 9–10, 40

Databases, computerized, 47
Deadly Silence (video), 220
Delayed effects, 47
Demand-control theory, 208–210, 218
Didactic approach to prevention, 165.
        See also Informational prevention
        training
Diffusion of innovations theory, 205, 206,
        213, 218, 222
Disease model for health care delivery,
    137
Disease theory of substance abuse, 207n
Downsizing, and workers' responsibilities,
    166
Drinking climate, 168
Drinking networks, 12
Drinking norms, workplace, 233
Drinking subcultures, 244
    as social support, 63
DrinkWise, 156–157
Drug-Free Workplace Act (1988), 3
Drug testing, 4, 166–167
    as business, 13–14
    vs. caring confrontation, 220
    as coercive approach, 19
    as combined with other programs, 15,
        242
    continuing costs in spite of, 3
    decrease in prevalence of, 34
    and economic cycle, 236
    empowering of resistance to, 254
    flaws in, 29, 243

Psychosocial hazards, 208–212, 213, 214–215, 216, 217, 218

Radiating and collateral effects, 252, 253
Reagan administration, and War on Drugs, 228
Records, computerized, 160
Reinvention, 206
Repeated-measures analysis of variance (ANOVA), 70, 70n, 79, 120, 121, 123
Rescreening
    in Wellness Outreach at Work program, 140, 141
    in cardiovascular wellness programs study, 147–148
    in managed care study, 159
Research
    and ANOVA, 70n
    phases of, 206
Research, future
    on AOD abuse, 239
    on AOD abuse prevention, 242–248
    on changes in stressor, social support, and coping variables, 90
Research in workplace AOD prevention training, meta-analytic review of, 42–49
Responding, in workplace coping-skills intervention, 67
Restructuring, and workers' responsibilities, 166
Risk, and enabling theory, 219
Risk factors, 58, 167, 168
    related to alcohol use, 59–60
        avoidance coping, 63–64
        work-family stressors, 61–62
        work stressors, 60–61
    in workplace environment, 168–169
    and perceptions or attitudes, 170
Role ambiguity, and heavy alcohol use, 61
Role conflict, of managers, 60
Role Quality Scale, 69
Role stress, in workplace coping-skills intervention, 75, 84, 85, 87

SAMHSA (Substance Abuse and Mental Health Services Administration), 34, 36, 242
SAY YES! program, 107–109, 111, 111–112
"Scare tactics" approach, vs. health promotion model, 105
School-based interventions, 41
School-based prevention messages, adult AOD use as undercutting, 4
Scientific perspective, 208–213, 233
Scientific study, of workplace AOD abuse prevention, 30
Screening
    for general wellness, 160
    in Wellness Outreach at Work model, 139, 140, 141, 223
        in cardiovascular wellness programs study, 145, 147, 149
        in EAP study, 142
        in managed-care study, 156
Secondary prevention of drug and alcohol abuse, through health promotion programs, 99
Selective preventive interventions, 41
Self-control, in social cognitive theory, 102
Self-efficacy, 245, 246
    in social cognitive theory, 102
Self-monitoring, in workplace coping-skills intervention, 68
Self-referral
    as ineffective strategy, 137
    as policy goal, 9
Self-reports, underreporting from, 128–129
Self-talk, in workplace coping-skills intervention, 67
Situation, in social cognitive theory, 102
Skills development, 171
"Sleeper" effect, 47
Smoking cessation programs, 20
Social cognitive theory, 101, 102
    and health promotion programs, 97, 98
    and workplace health promotion approach, 101, 129
Social context of prevention, 166–167
Social or cultural aspects, of employee drinking, 12
Social-ecological approach to prevention, 166

ABOUT THE EDITORS

Joel B. Bennett, PhD, is president of Organizational Wellness and Learning Systems, a consulting firm that delivers customized assessments and programs to help improve total organizational health. Dr. Bennett was a research scientist with the Institute of Behavioral Research at Texas Christian University from 1994 to 2002, where he helped design and evaluate the Team Awareness training. In addition to his work in substance abuse prevention, his research interests include the role of work culture in health promotion, training and development, spirituality and temporality in organizations, work–life integration, and alternative health promotion. He recently authored *Time and Intimacy: The New Science of Personal Relationships*. Dr. Bennett has served on the board of the Management, Spirituality, and Religion division of the Academy of Management and the Prevention Advisory Board for Magellan Behavioral Healthcare. He received the Commitment to People Award from the Council of Hotel and Restaurant Trainers in 2000. He has also reviewed for a variety of organizational, occupational health, and substance abuse journals.

Wayne E. K. Lehman, PhD, has been a research scientist with the Institute of Behavioral Research at Texas Christian University since 1989. Prior to that, he was with the Behavioral Research Program at Texas A&M University from 1982 to 1989. Dr. Lehman has been the principal investigator for the Workplace Project for the past 13 years. His research interests include employee substance use and its impact on organizational effectiveness, assessment of organizational substance use problems, and methodological issues in applied research. More recent research interests have involved organizational analysis of substance abuse treatment and issues regarding technology transfer in treatment organizations. Methodological specializations include design and implementation of large-scale survey studies, management of complex data systems, multivariate data analysis, structural equation modeling, and hierarchical linear modeling. Dr. Lehman has served as a member of several National Institutes of Health and National Institute on Drug Abuse (NIDA) study sections for grant review and a planning committee for NIDA's National Marijuana Conference in 1995. He was a member of the Committee on Drug Use in the Workplace for the National Academy of Science from 1991 to 1993 that produced the volume *Under the Influence? Drugs and the American Work Force*. He has consulted with national communications corporations, insurance companies, airlines, local police departments, adolescent prevention programs and state substance abuse agencies, and he has reviewed for a variety of organizational, occupational health, and substance abuse journals.